Hospitality Property Management

HOSPITALITY PROPERTY MANAGEMENT

Shikha Pratap

CENTRUM PRESS
NEW DELHI-110002 (INDIA)

CENTRUM PRESS
H.O.: 4360/4, Ansari Road, Daryaganj,
New Delhi-110002 (India)
Tel: 23278000, 23261597, 23255577, 23286875

B.O.: No. 1015, Ist Main Road, BSK IIIrd Stage,
IIIrd Phase, IIIrd Block, Bengaluru-560085 (INDIA)
Tel: 080-41723429

Email: centrumpress@gmail.com
Visit us at: www.centrumpress.com

Hospitality Property Management

First Edition, 2013

ISBN 978-93-81460-26-9

PRINTED IN INDIA

Printed at Balaji Offset, Delhi.

Contents

Preface

In the highly competitive hospitality industry, it is the intangibles that encourage guests to spend more, provide positive feedback and return to the property in the future. The most powerful of these intangibles is service. No amount of hiring, training or incentives can ensure top-notch service if employees don't have appropriate systems providing information at their fingertips. In addition, as properties incorporate more services and amenities, the need to integrate these functions becomes increasingly challenging – and important. In the hospitality industry a property management system also known as a PMS is a computerized system used to manage guest bookings, online reservations, point of sale, telephone and other amenities. Hotel property management systems may interface with central reservation systems and revenue or yield management systems, front office, back office and point of sale systems. There are many different types of property management systems available like OPERA and GUEST360, but a user/business will want to work with the different companies to determine which property management system best fits their needs. Property Management Systems are used in local government since authorities hold and manage large property estates ranging from schools, leisure centres, social housing and parks not to mention investment properties such as shops and industrial estates - even pubs. All of these are necessary income earners for a local authority, so the efficiency gained through an automated, computerised system is essential.

Property management systems are used to manage, control and account for personal property. Property is defined as the equipment, tooling and physical capital assets that are acquired and used to build, repair and maintain end item deliverables. Property Management involves the processes, systems and manpower required to manage the life cycle of all acquired property as defined above including Acquisition, Control, Accountability, Maintenance, Utilization, and disposition.

Property management is the operation of commercial, industrial or residential real estate. This is much akin to the role of management in any business. Property management is also the management of personal property, equipment, tooling and physical capital assets that are acquired and used to build, repair and maintain end item deliverables. Property management involves the processes, systems and manpower required to manage the life cycle of all acquired property as defined above including acquisition, control, accountability, responsibility, maintenance, utilization, and disposition. One important role is that of liaison between the landlord and/or the management firm operating on the landlord's behalf and tenant. Duties of property management include accepting rent, responding to and addressing maintenance issues, and providing a buffer for those landlords desiring to distance themselves from their tenant constituency. There are many facets to this profession, including managing the accounts and finances of the real estate properties, and participating in or initiating litigation with tenants, contractors and insurance agencies. Litigation is at times considered a separate function, set aside for trained attorneys. Although a person will be responsible for this in his/her job description, there may be an attorney working under a property manager. Special attention is given to landlord/tenant law and most commonly evictions, non-payment, harassment, reduction of pre-arranged services, and public nuisance are legal subjects that gain the most amount of attention from property managers.

This book will prove beneficial to the students, teachers and researchers in the field of this subject.

—Author

1

Airport Management

Airport security refers to the techniques and methods used in protecting airports and aircraft from crime.

Large numbers of people pass through airports. This presents potential targets for terrorism and other forms of crime due to the number of people located in a small area. Similarly, the high concentration of people on large airliners, the potential high death rate with attacks on aircraft, and the ability to use a hijacked airplane as a lethal weapon may provide an alluring target for terrorism.

Airport security attempts to prevent would-be attackers from bringing weapons or bombs into the airport. If they can succeed in this, then the chances of these devices getting on to aircraft are greatly reduced. As such, airport security serves several purposes: To protect the airport from attacks and crime and to protect the aircraft from attack, and to reassure the travelling public that they are safe. Monte R. Belger of the U.S. Federal Aviation Administration notes "The goal of aviation security is to prevent harm to aircraft, passengers, and crew, as well as support national security and counter-terrorism policy."

Airport Enforcement Authority

While some countries may have an agency that protects all of their airports (such as Australia, where the Australian Federal Police is responsible for security at major airports), in other countries like the United States, the protection is controlled at the state or local level. The primary personnel will vary and can include:

- A police force hired and dedicated to the airport
- A branch (substation) of the local police department stationed at the airport
- Members of the local police department assigned to the airport as their normal patrol area
- Members of a country's military
- Members of a country's airport protection service
- Police dog services for explosive detection, drug detection and other purposes

Other resources may include:

- Security guards
- Paramilitary forces
- Military forces

Process and Equipment

Some incidents have been the result of travellers being permitted to carry either weapons or items that could be used as weapons on board aircraft so that they could hijack the plane. Travellers are screened by *metal detectors*. Explosive detection machines used include X-ray machines and explosives trace-detection portal machines (a.k.a. "puffer machines"). In the United States the TSA is working on new scanning machines that are still effective searching for objects that aren't allowed in the airplanes but that don't depict the passengers in a state of undress that some find embarrassing. Explosive detection machines can also be used for both carry on and checked baggage. These detect volatile compounds given off from explosives using gas chromatography. A recent development is the controversial use of backscatter X-rays to detect hidden weapons and explosives on passengers. These devices, which use Compton scattering, require that the passenger stand close to a flat panel and produce a high resolution image. A technology released in Israel in early 2008 allows passengers to pass through metal detectors without removing their shoes, a process required as walk-though gate detectors are not reliable in detecting metal in shoes or on the lower body extremities. Alternately, the passengers step fully shod onto a device which scans in under 1.2 seconds for objects as small as a razor blade. In some countries, specially trained individuals may engage passengers in a conversation to detect threats rather than solely relying on equipment to find threats.

Generally people are screened through airport security into areas where the exit gates to the aircraft are located. These areas are often called "secure", "sterile" and airside. Passengers are discharged from airliners into the sterile area so that they usually will not have to be rescreened if disembarking from a domestic flight; however they are still subject to search at any time. Airport food outlets have started using plastic glasses and utensils as opposed to glasses made out of glass and utensils made out of metal to reduce the usefulness of such items as weapons.

In the United States non-passengers were once allowed on the concourses to meet arriving friends or relatives at their gates, but this is greatly restricted now in the United States. Non-passengers must obtain a gate pass to enter the secure area of the airport. The most common reasons that a non-passenger may obtain a gate pass is to assist children and the elderly as well as for attending business meetings that take place in the secure area of the airport. In the United States, at least 24 hours notice is generally required for those planning to attend a business meeting inside the secure area of the airport. Other countries, such as Australia do not yet restrict non-travellers from accessing the airside area, however non-travellers are typically subject to the same security scans as travellers.

Sensitive areas in airports, including airport ramps and operational spaces, are restricted from the general public. Called a SIDA (Security Identification Display Area), these spaces require special qualifications to enter.

Throughout the world, there have been a few dozen airports that have instituted a version of a "trusted traveler program". Proponents argue that security screening can be made more efficient by detecting the people that are threats, and then searching them. They argue that searching trusted, verified individuals should not take the amount of time it does. Critics argue that such programs decrease security by providing an easier path to carry contraband through. Another critical security measure utilized by several regional and international airports is the use of fiber optic perimeter intrusion detection systems. These security systems allow airport security to locate and detect any intrusion on the airport perimeter, ensuring real-time, immediate intrusion notification that allows security personnel to assess the threat and track movement and engage necceassary security procedures. This has notably been utilized at Dulles International Airport and U.S. Military JFPASS.

Notable Incidents

The world's first terrorist attack intending to indiscriminately kill civilians while in flight was Cubana Flight 455. It was a Cubana flight from Barbados to Jamaica that was brought down by a terrorist attack on October 6, 1976, killing 73 people. Evidence implicated several Central Intelligence Agency-linked anti-Castro Cuban exiles and members of the Venezuelan secret police DISIP, including Luis Posada Carriles.

The single deadliest airline catastrophe resulting from the failure of airport security to detect an on board bomb was Air India Flight 182 in 1985, which killed 329 people.

Another notable failure was the 1994 bombing of Philippine Airlines Flight 434, which turned out to be a test run for a planned terrorist attack called Operation Bojinka. The explosion was small, killing one person, and the plane made an emergency landing. Operation Bojinka was discovered and foiled by Manila police in 1995.

On May 30, 1972 three members of the Japanese Red Army undertook a terrorist attack, popularly called the Lod Airport massacre, at the Lod Airport, now known as the Ben Gurion International Airport, in Tel Aviv. Firing indiscriminately with automatic firearms and throwing grenades, they managed to kill 24 people and injure 78 others before being neutralized (one of them through suicide). One of the three terrorists, Kozo Okamoto, survived the incident.

The Rome and Vienna airport attacks in December 1985 were two more instances of airport security failures. The attacks left 20 people dead when gunmen threw grenades and opened fire on travellers at El Al airline ticket counters.

On July 5, 2002, a gunman opened fire at Los Angeles International Airport (Israel's El Al Ticket Counter). The shooter killed two people and injured four.

On August 10, 2006, security at airports in the United Kingdom, Canada, and the United States was raised significantly due to the uncovering by British authorities of a terror plot aimed at detonating liquid explosives on flights originating from these countries. This is also notable as it was the first time the U.S. Terror Alert Level ever reached "red". The incident also led to tighter restrictions on carrying liquids and gels in hand luggage in the EU, Canada, and the United States.

Explosives Trace-detection Portal Machine

An explosives trace-detection portal machine, also known as a trace portal machine or puffer machine, is a security device that seeks to detect explosives and illegal drugs at airports and other sensitive facilities as a part of airport security screening. The machines are intended as a secondary screening device, used as a complement to, rather than a substitute for, traditional X-ray machines.

The term "trace-detection" refers to the machine's ability to detect extremely small "traces" of these compounds. The exact sensitivities of these machines is not available information, but a mass spectrometer detects compounds on a molecular level and would only be limited by the efficiency of the collection from the air puffed to obtain a sample for analysis. The machines also have a low false alarm rate that can be less than 1%.

Available Models and Technologies

Entry Scan, developed by General Electric, and Ionscan Sentinel II, developed by Smiths Detection, use ion mobility spectrometry (IMS) technology and can detect explosives such as RDX, PETN, TNT, Semtex, and Nitroglycerin. It can also detect controlled substances such as cocaine, heroin, PCP, methamphetamine, and Ecstasy.

The Guardian, developed by Syagen Technology with preconcentration technology licensed from Sandia National Laboratories, is physically similar but internally different. The Guardian uses mass spectrometry (MS) technology, which can detect 16 explosive compounds with 10-100x more sensitivity than IMS, resolve multiple compounds at the same time, and perform shoe bomb detection without removing shoes. The collection technology licensed from Sandia Laboratories is also significantly different than those used in Entry Scan and the Sentinel II. Syagen offers a narcotics screening portal as a separate product.

Improvements

The Sentinel ll, unlike the Sentinel l, "requires less power, has a more modular frame design, which incorporates the compressor into the unit for easier installation and as a result, requires less space." It also "has a more ergonomic design, improved passenger interface and easier maintenance." According to the Transportation Security Administration's website, the machines "can be instantly updated through their vast information technology network to stay ahead of the curve."

The Guardian has been under development since 2001 but was introduced commercially after Entry Scan and The Sentinel. It improved the GE and Smiths Detection machines by providing a MS analyzer rather than IMS analyzer to do the sample analyses and detection. The National Academy of Sciences recommends the use of MS technology over IMS, calling it the "Gold Standard for resolving high-consequence analyses". The Guardian is the first and only trace portal machine that can perform shoe bomb detection as part of its scanning process, resulting in no removal of shoes is required. Most airports currently require passengers to remove their shoes, a common complaint about airport security hassles.

Process

The machine operates by releasing multiple puffs of air at a passenger who is standing upright within the machine. This will flush out any particles on the person inside the machine then analyze and identify them in seconds. According to an article in the 16 June, 2005, New York Times, it is capable of screening up to 180 passengers an hour. This sample is then analysed using IMS or MS technology to search for specific explosive or narcotic compounds. If a substance of concern is detected, the security personnel are notified by a visible and/or audible alarm.

Development

The machines were originally developed by Sandia National Laboratories in 1997. Prototypes have been under improvement since 2001 at the Science and Technology division of the Homeland Security Department of the United States. Sandia National Laboratories currently licenses its "puffer" preconcentration collection technology in collaboration with Syagen Technology in the production of the industry's only mass spectrometer-based puffer machine. According to an article in the 3 September, 2006, New York Times, they are also manufactured by General Electric and Smiths Detection based in London) using Ion Mobility Spectrometry (IMS) technology at a cost of about $160,000 each. Delays in testing at the Homeland Security Department laboratory and questions about reliability have hindered their deployment. Early models were loud and slow, and required a lot of power. Durability has also been a concern. Trace portal machines are currently the only airport screening devices that automatically examine passengers for explosives.

Usage

At their peak, about 95 machines were installed in 34 airports. The majority of these were GE's Entry Scan and a few were Smith's Sentinels. According to an article on the 10 October, 2007 in USA Today, the TSA had planned on installing 434 machines; however, due to maintenance problems, they have halted installation and "have no plans to acquire more." The Department of Homeland Security (DHS) has reported involvement with Syagen's MS trace portal machine recently, funding them in 2008 with one unit tested at Orange County Airport shortly afterwards. At some airports, the machines were replaced either by millimeter wave scanners or backscatter X-ray machines.

As well as having been implemented in US airports, there are also Puffer machines at the Statue of Liberty (GE EntryScan3), just before visitors enter the statue itself. This is one example of the many increased security measures taken for popular New York landmarks post September 11, 2001.

The Israeli Border Police use trace portal machines at border crossings into areas under their jurisdiction such as the Allenby Bridge.

Another machine is installed at the security check for the CN Tower in Toronto, Canada.

Five machines are also currently operating at the "Gentilly-2" nuclear plant in Quebec.

Airport Security by Country

Canada

All restrictions involving airport security are determined by Transport Canada and are enforced by the Canadian Air Transport Security Authority (CATSA). Since the September 11, 2001 attacks, as well as the Air India bombing in 1985 and other incidents, airport security has tightened in Canada in order to prevent any attacks in Canadian Airspace.

CATSA uses x-ray machines to verify the contents of all carry-ons as well as metal detectors, explosive trace detection (ETD) equipment and random physical searches of passengers at the pre-board screening points. X-ray machines, CTX machines, high-resolution x-rays and ETDs are also used to scan checked bags. All checked baggage is always x-rayed at all major commercial airports.

CATSA also completed the first phase of its Restricted Area Identity Credential (RAIC) program in January 2007. This program replaces the old Airport Restricted Area Passes issued to airport employees after security checks by the Canadian Security Intelligence Service, the Royal Canadian Mounted Police (RCMP) and Transport Canada with new cards (issued after the same checks are conducted) that contain biometric information (fingerprints and iris scans) belonging to the person issued the RAIC.

The RAIC has yet to be extended to the security perimeter of Canadian airports for vehicles and persons entering from checkpoints not within airport terminals. As of September 2010 it is being tested at the Vancouver International Airport. Vehicles and personnel entering near the domestic terminals from the YVR cargo and south side must drive through the new CATSA security screening booth.

While CATSA is responsible for pre-board passenger and random non-passenger screening, they contract out to third-party "service providers" such as Aeroguard and Garda to train, manage and employ the screening officers. In addition, individual airport authorities which were privatized in the 1990s by the

Canadian Government are responsible for general airport security rather than CATSA and normally contract out to private companies and in the case of large airports, pay for a small contingent of local police officers to remain on site as well.

Safety and security at Canada's airports are provided by local police forces. The RCMP once used to provide this service at most airports, but remains so for a few today:

- Toronto Pearson International Airport – Peel Regional Police Airport Division
- Winnipeg James Armstrong Richardson International Airport – Winnipeg Police Service
- Calgary International Airport – Calgary Police Service Airport Unit (1997)
- Edmonton International Airport – RCMP airport detachment
- Vancouver International Airport – RCMP airport detachment
- Halifax Stanfield International Airport – RCMP airport detachment
- Ottawa Macdonald-Cartier International Airport – Ottawa Police Service (1997)
- Montreal-Pierre Elliott Trudeau International Airport – Airport Unit of the SPVM for police services and Aeroports de Montreal's Airport Patrol for property security

European Union

Regulation (EC) No 300/2008 of the European Parliament and of the Council establishes common rules in the European Union to protect civil aviation against acts of unlawful interference. The regulation's provisions apply to all airports or parts of airports located in an EU country that are not used exclusively for military purposes. The provisions also apply to all operators, including air carriers, providing services at the aforementioned airports. It also applies to all entities located inside or outside airport premises providing services to airports.

The standards of regulation 300/2008 are implemented by Commission Regulation (EU) No 185/2010.

France

French security has been stepped up since terrorist attacks in France in 1986. In response France established the Vigipirate program. The program uses troops to reinforce local security and increases requirements in screenings and ID checks. Since 1996 security check-points have transferred from the Police Nationale/Gendarmerie de l'Air to private companies hired by the airport authorities.

Spain

Airport security in Spain is provided by police forces, as well as private security guards. The Policía Nacional provides general security as well as passport (in international airports) and documentation checking. In Catalonia and Basque Country, the Mossos d'Esquadra and the Ertzaintza, respectively, have replaced the Policía Nacional except for documentation functions. The Guardia Civil handles the security and customs checking, often aided by private security guards. Local police provide security and traffic control outside the airport building.

Safety measures are controlled by the state owned company Aena, and are bound to European Commission Regulations, as in other European Union countries.

United Kingdom

The Department for Transport (DFT) is the heart of airport security in the United Kingdom. In September 2004, with the Home Office, DFT started an initiative called the "Multi Agency Threat and Risk Assessment" (MATRA), which was piloted at five of the United Kingdom's major airports – Heathrow, Birmingham, East Midlands Airport, Newcastle and Glasgow. Following successful trials, the scheme has now been rolled out across 44 airports.

Since the September 11 attacks in New York, the United Kingdom has been assessed as a high risk country due to its support of the United States both in its invasion of Afghanistan and Iraq.

From January 7, 2000, travellers are no longer limited to a single piece of carry-on luggage at most of the UK's major airports Currently, hand luggage is not limited by size or weight by the DFT, although most airlines do impose their own rules.

Passengers are not permitted to take any liquids over 100 ml past security, although liquids in larger containers purchased in the secure area are allowed on flights. Any liquids under 100 ml must be placed in "a single, transparent, re-sealable plastic bag (about the size of a small freezer bag), which itself must not exceed 1 litre in capacity (approximately 20cm x 20cm)".

All bags are screened via X-ray before being put on the plane. All passengers must walk through metal detectors. Human airport security has also been increased and people are highly likely to be searched. There are also the usual checks of passports and boarding cards.

The UK is considering controversial new methods of screening passengers to further improve airport security, such as backscatter X-ray machines that provide a 360-degree view of a person, as well as "see" under clothes, right down to the skin and bones.

Hong Kong

The Hong Kong International Airport is secured by the Hong Kong Police Force and Aviation Security Company (AVSECO). Within the police force, the Airport District is responsible for the safety and security of the airport region. Airport Security Unit are deployed around the airport and are armed with H&K MP5 A3 Submachine Gun and Glock 17 handgun. The security of the restricted area is the responsibility of the police and AVSECO.

While the airport is under the control of the Airport Authority Hong Kong (AAHK), the security power has been delegated to the AVSECO staffs. All persons and baggages carried by them must be X-Rayed and checked at the security screening points of the AVSECO (with a few exceptions at the Tenant Restricted Area).

The Immigration Department will check incomers passport and other identities, while the Customs and Excise Department will check passengers and crews' luggages to discourage smuggling of drugs and contraband from entering Hong Kong.

India

India stepped up its airport security after the 1999 Kandahar hijacking. The Central Industrial Security Force, a paramilitary organization is in charge of airport security under the regulatory frame work of the Bureau of Civil Aviation Security (Ministry of Civil Aviation Security). CISF formed an Airport Security Group to protect Indian airports. Every airport has now been given an APSU (Airport Security Unit), a trained unit to counter unlawful interference with civil aviation. Apart from the CISF, every airline has an aviation security force which is a separate department.

Terrorist threats and narcotics are the main threats in Indian airports. Another problem that some airports face is the proliferation of slums around the airport boundaries in places like Mumbai. Before boarding, additional searching of hand luggage is likely.

Israel

El Al Airlines is headquartered in Israel. The last hijacking occurred on July 23, 1969, and no plane departing Ben Gurion Airport, just outside Tel Aviv, has ever been hijacked.

It was in 1972 that terrorists from the Japanese Red Army launched an attack that led to the deaths of at least 24 people at Ben Gurion. Since then, security at the airport relies on a number of fundamentals, including a heavy focus on what Raphael Ron, former director of security at Ben Gurion, terms the "human factor", which may be generalized as "the inescapable fact that terrorist attacks are carried out by people who can be found and stopped by an effective security methodology."

On December 27, 1985, terrorists simultaneously attacked El Al ticket counters at the Rome, Italy and Vienna, Austria airports using machine guns and hand grenades. Nineteen civilians were killed and many wounded. In response, Israel developed further methods to stop such massacres and drastically improved security measures around Israeli airports and even promised to provide plainclothes armed guards at each foreign airport. The last successful airline-related terrorist attack was in 1986, when a security agent found a suitcase full of explosives during the initial screening process. While the bag did not make it on board, it did injure 13 after detonating in the terminal.

As part of its focus on this so-called "human factor," Israeli security officers interrogate travellers using racial profiling, singling out those who appear to be Arab based on name or physical appearance. Additionally, all passengers, even those who do not appear to be of Arab descent, are questioned as to why they are travelling to Israel, followed by several general questions about the trip in order to search for inconsistencies. Although numerous civil rights groups have demanded an end to the profiling, Israel maintains that it is both effective and unavoidable. As stated by Ariel Merari, an Israeli terrorism expert, "it would be foolish not to use profiling when everyone knows that most terrorists come from certain ethnic groups. They are likely to be Muslim and young, and the potential threat justifies inconveniencing a certain ethnic group."

Passengers leaving Israel are checked against a computerized list. The computers, maintained by the Israeli Ministry of Interior, are connected to the Israeli police and Interpol in order to catch suspects or others leaving the country illegally.

Despite such tight security, an incident occurred on November 17, 2002 in which a man apparently slipped through airport security at Ben Gurion Airport with a pocketknife and attempted to storm the cockpit of El Al Flight 581 en route from Tel Aviv to Istanbul, Turkey. While no injuries were reported and the attacker was subdued by guards hidden among the passengers 15 minutes before the plane landed safely in Turkey, authorities did shut down Ben Gurion for some time after the attack to reassess the security situation and an investigation was opened to determine how the man, an Israeli Arab, managed to smuggle the knife past the airport security.

At a conference in May 2008, the United States Department of Homeland Security Secretary Michael Chertoff told Reuters interviewers that the United States will seek to adopt some of the Israeli security measures at domestic airports. He left his post in January 2009, a mere 6 months after this statement, which may or may not have been enough time to implement them.

On a more limited focus, American airports have been turning to the Israeli government and Israeli-run firms to help upgrade security in the post-9/11 world. Israeli officials toured Los Angeles Airport in November 2008 to re-evaluate the airport after making security upgrade recommendations in 2006, and Ron's company, New Age Security Solutions, based in Washington, D.C., consults on aviation security at Boston's Logan International Airport. Calling Ben Gurion "the world's safest airport," Antonio

Villaraigosa, mayor of Los Angeles, has implemented the Israeli review in order to bring state-of-the-art technology and other tactical measures to help secure LAX, considered to be the state's primary terrorist target and singled out by the Al Qaeda network.

Other U.S. airports to incorporate Israeli tactics and systems include Port of Oakland and the San Diego County Regional Airport Authority. "The Israelis are legendary for their security, and this is an opportunity to see firsthand what they do, how they do it and, as importantly, the theory behind it," said Steven Grossman, director of aviation at the Port of Oakland. He was so impressed with a briefing presented by the Israelis that he suggested a trip to Israel to the U.S. branch of Airports Council International in order to gain a deeper understanding of the methods employed by Israeli airport security and law enforcement.

Singapore

Security for the country's two international passenger airports comes under the purview of the Airport Police Division of the Singapore Police Force, although resources are concentrated at Singapore Changi Airport where scheduled passenger traffic dominate. Seletar Airport, which specializes in handling non-scheduled and training flights, is seen as posing less of a security issue. Since the September 11, 2001 attacks, and the naming of Changi Airport as a terrorism target by the Jemaah Islamiyah, the airport's security has been stepped up. Roving patrol teams of two soldiers and a police officer armed with machine guns patrol the terminals at random. Departing passengers are checked at the entrance of the gate rather than after immigration clearance like Hong Kong International Airport. This security measure is easily noticed by the presence of X-Ray machines and metal detectors at every gate which is not normally seen at other airports.

Assisting the state organizations, are the security services provided by the ground handlers, namely that of the ((Certis CISCO)), Singapore Airport Terminal Services's SATS Security Services, and the Aetos Security Management Private Limited, formed from a merger of the Changi International Airport Services's airport security unit and that of other companies to become a single island-wide auxiliary police company. These officers duties include screening luggage and controlling movement into restricted areas.

Since 2005, an upgrade in screening technology and rising security concerns led to all luggage-screening processes to be conducted behind closed-doors. Plans are also in place to install over 400 cameras to monitor the airport, to discourage bomb attacks similar to the 2005 Songkhla bombings in Southern Thailand where Hat Yai International Airport was targeted. Tenders to incorporate such a system were called in late September 2005.

United States

Prior to the 1970s American airports had minimal security arrangements to prevent aircraft hijackings. Measures were introduced starting in the late 1960s after several high-profile hijackings.

Sky marshals were introduced in 1970, but there were insufficient numbers to protect every flight and hijackings continued to take place. Consequently in late 1972, the Federal Aviation Administration required that all airlines begin screening passengers and their carry-on baggage by January 5, 1973. This screening was generally contracted to private security companies. Private companies would bid on these contracts. The airline that had operational control of the departure concourse controlled by a given checkpoint would hold that contract. Although an airline would control the operation of a checkpoint, oversight authority was held by the FAA. C.F.R. Title 14 restrictions did not permit a relevant airport authority to exercise any oversight over checkpoint operations.

The September 11 attacks prompted even tougher regulations, such as limiting the number of and types of items passengers could carry on board aircraft and requiring increased screening for passengers who fail to present a government issued photo ID.

The Aviation and Transportation Security Act generally required that by November 19, 2002 all passenger screening must be conducted by Federal employees. As a result, passenger and baggage screening is now provided by the Transportation Security Administration (TSA), part of the Department of

Homeland Security. Provisions to improve the technology for detecting explosives were included in the Terrorism Prevention Act of 2004. Often, security at category X airports, the U.S. largest and busiest as measured by volume of passenger traffic, are provided by private contractors. Because of the high volume of passenger traffic, category X airports are considered vulnerable targets for terrorism.

Noticing the demand for new technology in airport security, General Electric (GE) started to develop the Secure Registered Traveler System. The new system would use newly developed technology such as automated carry-on scanning, automatic biological pathogen detection, millimeter-wave full body scanning and a quadruple resonance carpet that would detect threats in shoes without having to take them off. The SRT program also works with smartcard technology along with fingerprint technology to help verify passengers. The fingerprint scanner also detects for explosive material traces on the person's fingers.

With the increase in security screening, some airports saw long queues for security checks. To alleviate this, airports created Premium lines for passengers travelling in First or Business Class, or those who were elite members of a particular airline's Frequent Flyer program.

The "screening passengers by observation techniques" (SPOT) program is operating at some U.S. airports. Airport racial profiling in the United States

Airport racial profiling in the United States, as the term has been referred to in recent public debates, refers to government activity directed at a suspect or group of suspects because of their race or ethnicity. Under Fourth Amendment analysis, objective factors measure whether law enforcement action is constitutional, and under the Fourteenth Amendment challenges to the practice are assessed under the customary strict scrutiny test for racial classifications.

Since September 11, 2001, there have been reports on increases in racial profiling at airports, particularly targeting people who appear to be Muslim or of South Asian or Middle Eastern descent. It has been a routine practice by law enforcement officials to stop individuals who are profiled because of their race and religious and ethnic appearance or who may appear to be "suspicious."

In the United States

In the weeks following September 11, 2001, federal, state and local law enforcement officials investigated those responsible for the September 11 attacks during which nearly 3,000 people died. They assessed the United States's vulnerability to future acts of terrorism. Conclusions found the suspects of the crime were by a group of foreign nationals of Middle Eastern descent.

In the wake of the September 11 attacks, US officials responded to fears of people travelling by air by beefing up security in and around the nation's airports. Despite more thorough investigation of baggage and increased security personnel, there were so many vast open spaces and exits and entrances at airport hubs to prevent possible incidents to occur.

Los Angeles International Airport was recently found to be the most vulnerable to infiltration in the US when it comes to smuggling weapons. Knives, guns, and explosives carried by federal undercover inspectors were missed by LA International airport screeners at checkpoints 41% of the time in an airport security test. The test, which checked security at America's 32 biggest airports, was carried out in June by the Transportation Security Administration (TSA), which assumed responsibility for airport security.

Criticism

A 2009 study published in the Proceedings of the National Academy of Sciences has shown that due to terrorists being vastly outnumbered by innocents, racial profiling is no more effective than random profiling. Moreover, any form of profiling is less secure than random profiling, because a terrorist cell can simply have a number of members go through airport security, until one is reliably not profiled, then use that individual to perform an attack. None of the 19 successful hijackers in the September 11 attacks was reported or even remembered by checkpoint supervisors.

Some critics ask if a rational reason exists to single out Arabic-looking men at airport. King Downing, the national coordinator of the American Civil Liberties Union's Campaign

Against Airport Racial Profiling, says he was the victim of profiling by police at Logan International Airport in Boston, MA. He was going to the federal court to challenge a screening technique used around the country that looks at suspicious behaviour patterns to identify potential terrorists.

Mr. Downing alleges he was stopped and questioned by state police after arriving on a flight to attend a meeting or racial profiling. Downing has sued the Massachusetts Port Authority, which operates the airport, and the Massachusetts State Police, citing they violated his constitutional rights. Downing, who is black and wears a short beard, believes he was targeted because of his race. In his lawsuit, Downing alleges the behavioral screening system used at Logan International Airport encourages racial profiling. His lawsuit also seeks a ruling to declare airport racial profiling as unconstitutional.

In 2002, after the September 11 attack on the US, Logan International Airport began a program called "Behaviour Assessment Screening System" which allows police to question passengers whose behaviour appears to be "suspicious". Logan was the first airport in the country to use the system.

The Transportation Security Act (TSA) has rolled out a similar system at more than 40 of the nation's largest airports.

Legality

Does the current situation facing America, the ongoing threat of terrorism, justify the inclusion of race, gender, and age in profiling procedures at airports and other ports of entry?

In an article published by The Atlantic they summarize "the mathematical probability that a randomly chosen Arab passenger might attempt a mass murder suicide hijacking is considerably higher than the probability that a randomly chosen white, black, Hispanic, or Asian passenger might do the same. In constitutional law, while racial profiling may be presumably unconstitutional, that presumption is overcome in the case of airline passengers, because the government has a compelling interest in preventing mass-murder-suicide hijackings and because close scrutiny of Arab-looking people is narrowly tailored to protect that interest."

"America faces a "clear and present danger" of hijackers taking control of airlines and either killing passengers of using these aircraft as flying bombs. All nineteen terrorists involved in the September 11 attacks belonged to the "Al-Qaeda terrorist network headed by Usama Bin Laden. These hijackers were exclusively adult males of Middle Eastern ethnicity."

US Support

The Obama administration's decision to heighten airport security for passengers while travelling to the US from 14 nations triggered a backlash of complaints from Muslim and privacy groups who say President Obama's response to terror threats amounted to little more than racial profiling.

Defenders of the policy say it is a carefully targeted way of zeroing in on those travellers who most likely pose a threat and hurt feelings should not matter after the US averted a midair bombing on an airliner heading to Detroit on Christmas day.

The TSA is dealing with these opposing arguments and continues to examine and adjust its screening policies in the best way to balance security and privacy.

Asa Hutchinson, former Homeland Security undersecretary, stated "it is important to draw a line between profiling based on race and profiling based on national origin." "If you're talking about profiling based upon geographic origin or where they're flying from, absolutely," he said. "If you're talking about simply because they're part of a particular racial origin, absolutely not..You have to be smart about who you are inspecting."

Frank Cilluffo, former special assistant for Homeland Security under President George W. Bush, said "airports need to be "profiling" based on behaviour even though its a "dirty word."

Despite evidence that ethnic profiling has yielded zero results in Europe, a recent poll by USA Today showed Americans are in favour of more intensive security check for people who fit a profile of terrorists based on age, ethnicity and gender.

United States Incidents

On February 27, 2006, at the Will Rogers World Airport in Oklahoma City, in an airliner cargo area (accessible only to authorized personnel), threatening graffiti was found. On March 6, 2006 at John F. Kennedy International Airport in New York, an elderly man drove his car onto the runway through two security gates. He made it to an active runway where an Air France aircraft was preparing to land. The man drove around for approximately 23 minutes before being stopped. On the same day a man made it on to the runway by running through a secure gate while it was being opened at Midway International Airport in Chicago. The man made it through one of the three perimeter entrances that did not have a camera, resulting in four different runways being closed down. This incident led to 222 aviation security officers being retrained and a redesign of all perimeter gates.

On March 11, 2006, after four years of continuous security breaches and staffing problems news reports indicated that federal officials removed the head of security at Newark Liberty International Airport.

Category X Airports in the United States

- Boston Logan International Airport
- John F. Kennedy International Airport
- Newark Liberty International Airport
- Philadelphia International Airport
- Baltimore/Washington International Thurgood Marshall Airport
- Washington Dulles International Airport
- Charlotte/Douglas International Airport
- Hartsfield–Jackson Atlanta International Airport
- Orlando Sanford International Airport
- Orlando International Airport
- Miami International Airport
- Cincinnati/Northern Kentucky International Airport
- Detroit Metropolitan Wayne County Airport
- Las Vegas McCarran International Airport
- O'Hare International Airport
- Minneapolis-Saint Paul International Airport
- Denver International Airport
- Dallas/Fort Worth International Airport

- George Bush Intercontinental Airport
- Phoenix Sky Harbor International Airport
- Seattle–Tacoma International Airport
- San Francisco International Airport
- Los Angeles International Airport
- Honolulu International Airport

Airline Security

Airline security refers to the procedures and infrastructure designed to avoid security problems aboard aircraft. A related area is airport security. Security for air travel is primarily based in airports. Exceptions include security measures aboard aircraft of the Israeli El Al airline which include undercover armed security guards, as well as secure cargo holds, and United States airlines that use sky marshals on some flights.

Precautions

Security devices include metal detectors, watch dogs, and guards that do random checks. Many airports now use advanced forms of identification such as a security identification display area. Identification cards that identify a person as an airline or airport employee, or authorized personnel are the most common measures (For example, the ASIC in Australia).

Another critical security measure utlised by several regional and international airports is the use of fiber optic perimeter intrusion detection systems. A perimeter intrusion detection security systems allow airport security to locate and detect any intrusion on the airport perimeter, ensuring real-time, immediate intrusion notification that allows security personnel to assess the threat and track movement and engage necceassary security procedures.

Sensitive areas in airports, including airport ramps and operational spaces, are restricted from the general public. Called a SIDA (Security Identification Display Area) in the US, these spaces require special authority to enter.

The issue of security aboard aircraft assumed prominence after the terrorist attacks of September 11, 2001. A controversial decision in the United States has been to allow pilots to carry handguns for personal safety. As well as proposals to strengthen airport security, United States Congress spent $250 million to reinforce the cockpit doors on commercial aircraft. However, in some aircraft, these cockpit doors remain open due to restricted ventilation in the cockpit.

Restricted Objects

Since September 11, restrictions have been placed on taking objects aboard planes that could be used as weapons or to make a bomb.

Knitting Needles

In the United States, knitting needles and all other objects used for knitting are permitted to be carried on airplanes with the exception of scissors and other cutting blades, which must be placed in checked baggage. They were banned after the September 11 attacks, but reinstated in 2002. In Canada, knitting needles are allowed on airplanes. In Great Britain, knitting on airplanes was banned after the September 11 attacks, but was allowed again in 2005 after airplanes had more secure doors. In France, knitting needles are considered dangerous and are not allowed on airplanes. In New Zealand, knitting needles were banned after the September 11 attacks but, in 2005, they were permitted again. Australia banned knitting needles after the September 11 attacks, and did not allow them again until 2009.

Sky Marshal

A sky marshal (also known as air marshal or flight marshal) is an undercover law enforcement or counter terrorist agent on board a commercial aircraft to counter aircraft hijackings. Sky marshals may be provided by airlines such as El Al (who provide sky marshals on every flight), or by government agencies such as the Royal Canadian Mounted Police, German Federal Police, United Kingdom Metropolitan Police or US Federal Air Marshal Service.

History: Australia

In response to the September 11 incidents, the Commonwealth instituted an Air Security Officer (ASO) Program under the Australian Federal Police in December 2001. These officers are generally referred to in the media as Sky Marshals.

The ASO Programme provides a discreet anti-hijacking capability for Australian civil aviation by providing armed security personnel on board aircraft. This involves both random and intelligence-led placement of armed ASOs on flights operated by Australian registered air carriers, including domestic and international flights into and out of Australia.

Officers are armed and trained and equipped for a variety of situations on both domestic and international flights.

Canada

The Canadian Air Carrier Protection/Protective Program (CACPP) began on September 17, 2002 when a Memorandum of Understanding was signed between the Royal Canadian Mounted Police with Transport Canada, the authority responsible for Canadian aviation security, and the Canadian Air Transport Security Authority (CATSA), for the implementation and administration of the CACPP.

The program is conducted by specially trained undercover, armed RCMP officers (known as Aircraft Protective OfficersAPOs) on selected domestic and international flights and all flights to the Ronald Reagan Washington National Airport. Pilots and flight attendants are advised of their presence and the officer will physically intervene should an unauthorized person attempt to gain control of an aircraft. APOs, however, will not be involved in controlling unruly passengers. While they are peace officer within Canadian territories, they rely on section 6(2) of the Tokyo Convention as a legal basis for intervening an incident outside of Canadian airspace.

By law, such officers are exempt from acquiring a permit for importing or exporting their duty firearms when crossing the border. However, the exact nature of their weaponry is not released to the public except they are "deadly and effective and should not damage the aircraft."

United States

The US Federal Aviation Administration began its "Sky Marshal" program in 1968, which eventually became the Federal Air Marshal Service in 1985. That year, an Egyptian security officer on board EgyptAir Flight 648 opened fire on three Abu Nidal Organization hijackers, killing one before being fatally shot himself. In 2005, Rigoberto Alpizar was shot dead by two sky marshals on a jetway at Miami International Airport.

Currently, Federal Air Marshal Officers are under Transportation Security Administration.

Under the Visible Intermodal Prevention Response (VIPR) system, started up circa 2005, FAMs began to patrol non-aviation sites like bus terminals and train stations.

Security Identification Display Area

Security Identification Display Area, or SIDA, is a special security area designated by an airport operator in the US to comply with Federal Aviation Administration (FAA) requirements directed by Federal Aviation Regulation (FAR) part 107.205. An identification system must be used in this area. Before allowing unescorted access to this area, a person must be trained and their background investigated. Normally, the flight ramp and other sensitive operational areas of a US commercial airport are designated as a SIDA.

Computer Assisted Passenger Prescreening System

The Computer Assisted Passenger Prescreening System (often abbreviated CAPPS) is a counter-terrorism system in place in the United States air travel industry. The United States Transportation Security Administration (TSA) maintains a watchlist, pursuant to 49 USC § 114 (h)(2), of "individuals known to pose, or suspected of posing, a risk of air piracy or terrorism or a threat to airline or passenger safety." The list is used to pre-emptively identify terrorists attempting to buy plane tickets or board planes travelling in the United States, and to mitigate perceived threats.

CAPPS systems rely on what is known as a Passenger Name Record, often abbreviated PNR. When a person books a plane ticket, certain identifying information is collected by the airline: full name, address, etc. This information is used to check against some data store (e.g., a TSA No-Fly list, the FBI ten most wanted fugitive list, etc.) and assign a terrorism "risk score" to that person. High risk scores require the airline to subject the person to extended baggage and/or personal screening, and to contact law enforcement if necessary.

CAPPS I

CAPPS I was first implemented in the late 1990s, in response to the perceived threat of U.S. domestic and international terrorism. CAPPS I was administered by the FBI and FAA. CAPPS screening selected passengers for additional screening of their checked baggage for explosives. CAPPS selectees did not undergo any additional screening at passenger security checkpoints.

September 11, 2001, Attacks

On the morning of the September 11, 2001 attacks, several of the hijackers were selected by CAPPS. Wail al-Shehri, and Satam al-Suqami were selected for extra screening of their checked bags, before they boarded American Airlines Flight 11 at Logan International Airport. Waleed al-Shehri was also selected, but since he had checked no bags, CAPPS selection had no effect on him. Mohamed Atta was selected by CAPPS when he checked in at Portland International Jetport.

All five of the hijackers on American Airlines Flight 77 were CAPPS selectees, with Hani Hanjour, Khalid al-Mihdhar, and Majed Moqed chosen by the CAPPS criteria. Nawaf al-Hazmi and Salem al-Hazmi were selected because they did not provide adequate identification, and had their checked bags held until they boarded the aircraft.

Ahmad al-Haznawi was the only hijacker selected of those on United Airlines Flight 93, and none of the hijackers of United Airlines Flight 175 were selected by CAPPS.

After 9/11

In November 2001, control was transferred to the TSA, where it has "...expanded almost daily as Intelligence Community (IC) agencies and the Office of Homeland Security continue to request the addition of individuals..."

In 2003, the Transportation Security Administration (TSA) presented a proposal for an expanded system (CAPPS II), which was reviewed by Congress and later canceled by the United States Department of Homeland Security (DHS).

The Computer Assisted Passenger Prescreening System II was a proposal for a new CAPPS system, designed by the Office of National Risk Assessment (ONRA), a subsidiary office of the TSA, with the contracted assistance of Lockheed Martin. Congress presented the TSA with a list of requirements for a successor to CAPPS I. Some of those requirements were:

- The government, not the airlines, would control and administer the system
- Every ticketed passenger would be screened, for instance not just those who check bags
- Every airline and every airport would be covered by the system

Like its predecessor, the CAPPS II proposal would rely on the PNR to uniquely identify people attempting to board aircraft. It would expand the PNR field to include a few extra fields, like a full street address, date of birth, and a home telephone number. It would then cross-reference these fields with government records and private sector databases to ascertain the identity of the person, and then determine a number of details about that person. Law enforcement would be contacted in the event that the person was either present on a terrorist or most-wanted list or had outstanding Federal or state arrest warrants for violent crime. Otherwise, the software would calculate a "risk score" and then print a code on the boarding pass indicating the appropriate "screening level" for that person: green (no threat) indicates no additional screening, yellow (unknown or possible threat) indicates additional screening, and red (high risk) indicates no boarding and deferral to law enforcement. Exactly how this risk score would be calculated was never disclosed nor subject to public oversight of any kind outside of the TSA.

The CAPPS II system was criticized in a report by the United States General Accounting Office in early 2004, and faced increased opposition from watchdog groups like the ACLU, ReclaimDemocracy.org, and Electronic Privacy Information Center. These advocacy groups believed it would undermine both privacy and safety. They expressed concern that the system would be unconstitutional and that terrorists could use it to their advantage.

CAPPS II was cancelled by the TSA in the summer of 2004. Shortly thereafter, the TSA announced a successor program, called Secure Flight, that would work much the same way as CAPPS II. TSA hoped to test Secure Flight in August 2005 using two airlines. Secure Flight has been blocked by Congress until the government can prove that the system can pass 10 tests for accuracy and privacy protection as follows:

Annex I: Legislatively Mandated Secure Flight Issues to be Certified by DHS and Reviewed by GAO.

Legislative mandated issue (number and short title) Description of mandated issue:

1. *Redress process:* A system of due process exists whereby aviation passengers determined to pose a threat are either delayed or prohibited from boarding their scheduled flights by TSA may appeal such decisions and correct erroneous information contained in CAPPS II or Secure Flight or other follow-on/successor programs.
2. *Accuracy of databases and effectiveness of Secure Flight:* The underlying error rate of the government and private databases that will be used to both establish identity and assign a risk level to a passenger will not produce a large number of false positives that will result in a significant number of passengers being treated mistakenly or security resources being diverted.
3. *Stress testing:* TSA has stress-tested and demonstrated the efficacy and accuracy of all search technologies in CAPPS II or Secure Flight or other follow-on/successor programs and has demonstrated that CAPPS II or Secure Flight or other follow-on/successor programs can make an accurate predictive assessment of those passengers who may constitute a threat to aviation.
4. *Internal oversight:* The Secretary of Homeland Security has established an internal oversight board to monitor the manner in which CAPPS II or Secure Flight or other follow-on/successor programs are being developed and prepared.
5. *Operational safeguards:* TSA has built in sufficient operational safeguards to reduce the opportunities for abuse.
6. *Security measures:* Substantial security measures are in place to protect CAPPS II or Secure Flight or other follow-on/successor programs from unauthorized access by hackers or other intruders.

7. *Oversight of system use and operation:* TSA has adopted policies establishing effective oversight of the use and operation of the system.
8. *Privacy concerns:* There are no specific privacy concerns with the technological architecture of the system.
9. *Modifications with respect to intrastate travel to accommodate states with unique air transportation needs:* TSA has, in accordance with the requirements of section 44903 (j)(2)(B) of title 49, United States Code, modified CAPPS II or Secure Flight or other follow-on/successor programs with respect to intrastate transportation to accommodate states with unique air transportation needs and passengers who might otherwise regularly trigger primary selectee status.
10. *Life-cycle cost estimates and expenditure plans:* Appropriate life-cycle cost estimates, and expenditure and program plans exist.

TSA expects that Secure Flight will begin operational testing at the end of 2008 for domestic passenger vetting, with full implementation in 2010. TSA is working with DHS to explore ways to efficiently accelerate the schedule to implement the program, as appropriate and within established lifecycle cost estimates.

Surveillance Detection Report (SDR)

On July 21, 2006, TV station ABC 7 in Denver, Colorado released a report, citing air marshals that were using a quota system of reporting one person per month as a requirement for advancement. These reports are filed as Surveillance Detection Reports: it is unclear how many such reports are required on a person to place them on the watch lists.

Terrorist Identities Datamart Environment

The Terrorist Identities Datamart Environment, (TIDE) is the U.S. Government's central database on known or suspected international terrorists, and contains highly classified information provided by members of the Intelligence Community such as CIA, DIA, FBI, NSA, and many others. There are about 550,000 names in TIDE. In 2008, more than 27,000 names were removed from the list when it was determined they no longer met the criteria for inclusion. According to the FBI, international terrorists include those persons who carry out terrorist activities under foreign direction. For this purpose, they may include U.S. persons (U.S. citizens and legal permanent residents). The *Terrorist Identities Group (TIG),* located in NCTC's *Information Sharing & Knowledge Development Directorate (ISKD),* is responsible for building and maintaining TIDE.

From the classified TIDE database, an unclassified, but sensitive, extract is provided to the FBI's Terrorist Screening Center, which compiles the Terrorist Screening Database (TSDB).

This database, in turn, is used to compile various watch lists such as the TSA's No Fly List, State Department's Consular Lookout and Support System, Homeland Security's Interagency Border Inspection System, and FBI's NCIC (National Crime Information Center) for state and local law enforcement.

Secondary Security Screening Selection

Secondary Security Screening Selection or Secondary Security Screening Selectee, known by its acronym SSSS, is an airport security measure in the United States and Canada which selects passengers for additional inspection. This may also be known as Selectee, Automatic Selectee or the Selectee list. The list contains 14,000 names, as of December 2009.

Selection Criteria

Neither the Transportation Security Administration (TSA) nor the airlines publish the criteria that are used when boarding passes are issued to identify passengers who will be given extra screening or be denied boarding.

Some criteria are:

- Passengers with a one-way reservation.
- Passengers who pay cash for their tickets.
- Passengers who book reservations the day of their flight.
- Passengers who "no show" a single leg of their flight.
- Random selection, according to TSA spokeswoman Amy Von Walter in 2004, and as suggested by a 2003 DOI newsletter.

- Flight to specific final destinations.
- Flying without ID
- Having one's name on a list of names supplied by the government to the airlines, according to an airline staff questioned.

Since neither the TSA nor the airline run a background check at the time boarding passes are issued, immigration status and criminal records are not taken into consideration during SSSS. Furthermore, personal information such as a passenger's addresses, employment history, and medical records are not taken into account during SSSS and may not even be readily available to government officials to modify the process and increase its validity.

Procedure when Selected

Passengers who have been selected for this secondary screening will have the letters SSSS or *S* (all capitals) printed on their boarding passes.

SSSS passengers will go through a more intensive screening process which may include puffer explosive detectors. Their carry-on luggage may be also be inspected by hand. In the case of film or other items that cannot be X-rayed, the agent may perform a test for possible explosive materials. The screener may also use a hand held metal detector to search the passenger for metal objects.

Randomness and Credibility

Since the process acts on the accumulation of certain criteria rather than mathematical probability, it is expected that subjects may be selected more than once or more often than others. This has caused the public to believe the process is not random but instead discriminatory as those individuals selected are predominantly minorities or people of color. The TSA states that SSSS is a selective process in which candidates who fall under a predetermined category are chosen. Nonetheless, the process may rely, intermittently, in randomness, when subjects do not fall under any category and this becomes the mathematical variable.

With British Airways and Alaska Airlines, the marking happens at check-in. Thus a potential miscreant is warned and has the opportunity to leave the public area of the airport or abandon an attempt to smuggle something on board, while other passengers will continue to be screened.

No Fly List

The No Fly List is a list, created and maintained by the United States government's Terrorist Screening Center (TSC), of people who are not permitted to board a commercial aircraft for travel in or out of the United States. The list has also been used to divert away from U.S. airspace aircraft not flying to or from the U.S. The number of people on the list rises and falls according to threat and intelligence reporting. As of summer 2010, the list contained about 8,500 names, according to the TSC. The list – along with the Secondary Security Screening Selection, which tags would-be passengers for extra inspection – was created after the September 11 attacks.

The No Fly List is different from the Terrorist Watch List, a much longer list of people suspected of some involvement with terrorism. The Terrorist Watch List contained around 400,000 names as of summer 2011, according to the TSC.

The list has been criticized on civil liberties and due process grounds, due in part to the potential for ethnic, religious, economic, political, or racial profiling and discrimination. It has also raised concerns about privacy and government secrecy. Finally, it has been criticized as costly, prone to false positives, and easily defeated.

The No Fly List, the Selectee List and the Terrorist Watchlist were created by the administration of George W. Bush and retained by the administration of Barack Obama. U.S. Senate Intelligence Committee Chairwoman Dianne Feinstein (D-CA) said in May 2010: "The no-fly list itself is one of our best lines of defence."

History

On September 11, 2001, the FBI had a list of 16 people deemed "no transport" because they "presented a specific known or suspected threat to aviation." The list had grown to more than 400 names by November 2001, when responsibility for keeping it was transferred to the Federal Aviation Administration. In mid-December 2001, two lists were created: the "No Fly List" of

594 people to be denied air transport, and the "Selectee" list of 365 people who were to be more carefully searched at airports. By December 2002, the No Fly List held more than 1,000 names. *60 Minutes* reported on 8 October 2006 that the news program had obtained a March 2006 copy of the list that contained 44,000 names. TSA officials said that, as of November 2005, 30,000 people in 2005 had complained that their names were matched to a name on the list via the name matching software used by airlines. In April 2007, the United States government "terrorist watch list" administered by the Terrorist Screening Center, which is managed principally by the FBI, contained 700,000 records. A year later, the ACLU estimated the list to have grown to over 1,000,000 names and continues to expand.

However, according to Homeland Security secretary Michael Chertoff, in October 2008 the No Fly list contained only 2,500 names, with an additional 16,000 "selectees", who "represent a less specific security threat and receive extra scrutiny, but are allowed to fly."

Failures

In an article in *The Atlantic,* security expert Bruce Schneier described a simple way for people to defeat the No Fly List:

> *Use a stolen credit card to buy a ticket under a fake name. Print a fake boarding pass with your real name on it and go to the airport. You give your real ID, and the fake boarding pass with your real name on it, to security. They're checking the documents against each other. They're not checking your name against the no-fly list—that was done on the airline's computers. Once you're through security, you rip up the fake boarding pass, and use the real boarding pass that has the name from the stolen credit card. Then you board the plane, because they're not checking your name against your ID at boarding.*

Umar Farouk Abdulmutallab

Umar Farouk Abdulmutallab, who was accused of trying to bomb Northwest Airlines Flight 253, was not on the No Fly List. Thirty-five days earlier, his father made a report to two Central Intelligence Agency officers at the U.S. Embassy in Abuja regarding his son's "extreme religious views", and told the embassy that Abdulmutallab might be in Yemen. Acting on the report, Abdulmutallab's name was added in November 2009 to the 550,000-name U.S. Terrorist Identities Datamart Environment, a database of the U.S. National Counterterrorism Center. It was not added to the 4,000-name U.S. No Fly List. Secretary of Homeland Security Janet Napolitano stated that the system "failed miserably", because Abdulmutallab had been able to board the flight. President Barack Obama called the U.S.'s failure to prevent the bombing attempt "totally unacceptable", and ordered an investigation.

Faisal Shahzad

Faisal Shahzad, who was convicted of planting a car bomb in Times Square, New York City, was arrested after he had boarded Emirates Flight 202 to Dubai. He had been placed on the No Fly List earlier in the day. The airline did not check the No Fly List for added names when Shahzad made his reservation that evening, when he later purchased the ticket, or when he was allowed to board the plane. Only after a routine post-boarding check revealed that he was on the No Fly List did agents board the plane and arrest him.

Controversy

Among the complaints about the No Fly List is the use of credit reports in calculating the risk score. In response to the controversy, Transportation Security Administration (TSA) officials said in 2005 that they would not use credit scores to determine passengers' risk score and that they would comply with all rights guaranteed by the First and Fourth Amendments.

The European Union and other non-U.S. government entities have expressed concern about allowing the CAPPS II proposal to be implemented within their borders. During the early testing of the No Fly List and CAPPS II, the TSA privately asked airlines to disclose massive amounts of private information about their passengers. This action has been said to be a violation of the Privacy Act of 1974, which forbids the government to compile secret databases on U.S. citizens. Spokespeople from several major airlines denied providing TSA the information, then admitted that they had done so. TSA and the United States Department of Homeland Security (DHS) admitted that the government had inappropriately requested and used this information. In the midst of this controversy, the Government Accountability Office of the U.S. Congress produced a report critical of the CAPPS II system. It characterized the proposal as incomplete and seriously behind schedule, and noted that the TSA had failed to address "developmental, operational, and privacy issues identified by Congress". On July 14, 2004, TSA officials announced that CAPPS II was being pulled from consideration without proceeding to full testing. Critics have alleged that the TSA has merely chosen to start with a less controversial entry point that they are calling the "Registered Traveler" program. TSA has also begun testing of another program called "Secure Flight", which is supposed to solve some of the problems of CAPPS I while avoiding the privacy issues of CAPPS II.

In January 2009, Marcus Holmes conservatively estimated the total cost of the program to be $536 million since 9/11, with a reasonable estimation range that approaches $1 billion, and he questioned whether the benefits of the list outweigh the costs.

False Positives

A "false positive" occurs when a passenger who is not on the No Fly List has a name that matches or is similar to a name on the list. False positive passengers will not be allowed to board a flight unless they can differentiate themselves from the actual person on the list, usually by presenting ID showing their middle name or date of birth. In some cases, false positive passengers have been denied boarding or have missed flights because they could not easily prove that they were not the person on the No Fly List.

When an airline ticket is purchased, the reservation system uses software to compare the passenger's name against the No Fly List. If the name matches, or is similar to a name on the No Fly List, a restriction is placed in their reservation that prevents them from being issued a boarding pass until the airline has determined if they are the actual person whose name is on the No Fly List. Passengers are not told when a restriction has been placed on their reservation, and they normally do not find out that anything is unusual until they attempt to check in. "False positive" passengers cannot use Internet check-in or the automatic check-in kiosks in airports. Any attempt to use them will normally result in a message that the check-in cannot be completed and that the passenger needs to see a live check-in agent.

In order to be issued a boarding pass, a "false positive" passenger must present identification that sufficiently differentiates them from the person on the No Fly List. This can include, but is not limited to, date and place of birth, middle name, citizenship, passport number, etc. Depending on the airline, this clearance can be done either electronically, with the check-in agent keying the information into the system, or a manual procedure where the agent telephones a centralized security office to obtain clearance. Once a "false positive" passenger has been cleared for a flight, the clearance will usually, but not always, apply to the remaining flights on that reservation, including the return. However, the next time this passenger purchases an airline ticket, they will have to be cleared all over again. If a passenger's identification is insufficient to differentiate that passenger from a name on the No-Fly List, the airline will refuse to issue a boarding pass and tell the passenger to contact the TSA.

Policies vary from airline to airline as to whether a check-in agent will tell passengers why they must always have additional steps performed when they check-in, or why they are unable to check-in via Internet, kiosk, or at curbside. In some cases, check-in agents will incorrectly tell passengers that they must be cleared because they are "on the No Fly List", when in fact they are simply a "false positive" (having the same name as someone on the No-Fly List). False positive passengers who are ultimately issued boarding passes are not on the No Fly List. In the majority of instances, passengers are not told anything, and it is only through the repeated experience of needing to be cleared or being unable to use curbside, Internet or automatic check-in that they come to suspect that they are a "false positive".

False positive passengers are at a disadvantage when travelling, due to the fact that their documents must be inspected by airline personnel before they can be issued a boarding pass. Because this permanently excludes them being able to use Internet, kiosk, or curbside check-in, they are, at best, required to appear at the airport earlier than they might normally have, because they must wait in line to be cleared. Some airlines provide a special counter for this purpose; others require the passenger to wait in the line for passengers with checked baggage, even if they have no baggage to check. At worst, passengers have actually missed flights because the flights were oversold and all of the available boarding passes were already claimed by other passengers who were able to check-in via the Internet, or because airline personnel could not contact the airline's security department to obtain a clearance, or because the passenger's identification didn't sufficiently differentiate them from a name on the No Fly List.

In an effort to reduce the number of false positives, DHS announced on April 28, 2008 that each airline will be permitted to create a system to verify and store a passenger's date of birth, to clear up watch list misidentifications. Passengers can voluntarily provide this information to the airline, which would have to be verified by presenting acceptable ID at the ticket counter. Once this data has been stored, travellers that were previously inconvenienced on every trip would be able to check-in online or at remote kiosks. It will be up to each individual airline to choose whether they wish to implement such a system.

False Positives and Other Controversial Cases

False positives and abuses that have been in the news include:

- Numerous children (including many under the age of five, and some under the age of one) have generated false positives.
- Daniel Brown, a United States Marine returning from Iraq, was prevented from boarding a flight home in April 2006 because his name matched one on the No Fly List.
- David Fathi, an attorney for the ACLU of Iranian descent and a plaintiff in the ACLU lawsuit.
- Asif Iqbal, a management consultant and legal resident of the United States born in Pakistan, plans to sue the U.S. government because he is regularly detained when he tries to fly, because he has the same name as a former Guantanamo detainee. Iqbal's work requires a lot of travel, and, even though the Guantanamo detainee has

been released, his name remains on the No Fly List, and Iqbal the software consultant experiences frequent, unpredictable delays and missed flights. He is pushing for a photo ID and birthdate matching system, in addition to the current system of checking names.

- Robert J. Johnson, a surgeon and a former lieutenant colonel in the U.S. Army, was told in 2006 that he was on the list, although he had had no problem in flying the month before. Johnson was running as a Democrat against U.S. Representative John McHugh, a Republican. Johnson wondered whether he was on the list because of his opposition to the Iraq War. He stated, "This could just be a government screw-up, but I don't know, and they won't tell me." Later, a *60 Minutes* report brought together 12 men named Robert Johnson, all of whom had experienced problems in airports with being pulled aside and interrogated. The report suggested that the individual whose name was intended to be on the list was most likely the Robert Johnson who had been convicted of plotting to bomb a movie theater and a Hindu temple in Toronto.
- In August 2004, Senator Ted Kennedy (D-MA) told a Senate Judiciary Committee discussing the No Fly List that he had appeared on the list and had been repeatedly delayed at airports. He said it had taken him three weeks of appeals directly to Homeland Security Secretary Tom Ridge to have him removed from the list. Kennedy said he was eventually told that the name "T Kennedy" was added to the list because it was once used as an alias of a suspected terrorist. There are an estimated 7,000 American men whose legal names correspond to "T Kennedy". (Senator Kennedy, whose first name was Edward and for whom "Ted" was only a nickname, would not have been one of them.) Recognizing that as a U.S. Senator he was in a privileged position of being able to contact Ridge, Kennedy said of "ordinary citizens": "How are they going to be able to get to be treated fairly and not have their rights abused?" Former mayor of New York City Rudy Giuliani pointed to this incident as an example for the necessity to "rethink aviation

security" in an essay on homeland security published while he was seeking the Republican nomination for the 2008 presidential election.

- U.S. Representative John Lewis (D-GA), widely known for his civil rights advocacy, has been stopped many times.
- Canadian journalist Patrick Martin has been frequently interrogated while travelling, because of a suspicious individual with the same name.
- Walter F. Murphy, McCormick Professor of Jurisprudence at Princeton, reported that the following exchange took place at Newark on 1 March 2007, where he was denied a boarding pass "because I [Professor Murphy] was on the Terrorist Watch list." The airline employee asked, "Have you been in any peace marches? We ban a lot of people from flying because of that." "I explained," said professor Murphy, "that I had not so marched but had, in September 2006, given a lecture at Princeton, televised and put on the web, highly critical of George Bush for his many violations of the constitution." To which the airline employee responded, "That'll do it."
- David Nelson, the actor best known for his role on *The Adventures of Ozzie and Harriet,* is among various persons named David Nelson who have been stopped at airports because their name apparently appears on the list.
- Jesselyn Radack, a former United States Department of Justice ethics adviser who argued that John Walker Lindh was entitled to an attorney, was placed on the No Fly List as part of what she believes to be a reprisal for her whistle-blowing.
- In September 2004, former pop singer Cat Stevens (who converted to Islam and changed his name to "Yusuf Islam" in 1978) was denied entry into the U.S. after his name was found on the list.
- In February 2006, U.S. Senator Ted Stevens (R-AK) stated in a committee hearing that his wife Catherine had been subjected to questioning at an airport as to whether she was Cat Stevens due to the similarity of their names.

- U.S. Representative Don Young (R-AK), the third-most senior Republican in the House, was flagged in 2004 after he was mistaken for a "Donald Lee Young".
- Some members of the Federal Air Marshal Service have been denied boarding on flights that they were assigned to protect because their names matched those of persons on the no-fly list.
- Until July 2008, Nelson Mandela and other members of the African National Congress were on the list, something that U.S. Secretary of State Condoleezza Rice called "rather embarrassing". On July 5, 2008, the U.S. removed Mandela and the ANC from the list.
- In August 2008, CNN reported that an airline captain and retired brigadier general for the United States Air Force has had numerous encounters with security officials when attempting to pilot his own plane.
- After frequent harassment at airport terminals, a Canadian businessman changed his name to avoid being delayed every time he took a flight.
- In October 2008, the Washington Post reported that Maryland State Police classified 53 nonviolent political activists as terrorists, and entered their names and personal information into state and federal databases, with labels indicating that they were terror suspects. The protest groups were also entered as terrorist organizations. During a hearing, it was revealed that these individuals and organizations had been placed in the databases because of a surveillance operation that targeted opponents of the death penalty and the Iraq war.
- In April 2009, TSA refused to allow an Air France flight from Paris to Mexico to cross U.S. airspace because it was carrying Colombian journalist Hernando Calvo Ospina, who has sharply criticized U.S. foreign policy.
- Bollywood actor Shah Rukh Khan was held for extensive questioning by US Immigration and Customs officials in August 2009, because as he reported, "his name came up on a computer alert list." Customs officials claimed he

"was questioned as part of a routine process that took 66 minutes." Ironically, Khan was visiting the United States to promote his film *My Name is Khan*, which concerns racial profiling of Muslims in the United States.

- In June 2010, The New York Times reported Yahya Wehelie, a 26 year-old Muslim-American man was being prevented from returning to the United States, and trapped in Cairo. Despite Wehelie's offer to FBI agents to allow them to accompany him in the plane, while shackled, he was not permitted to return. The ACLU has argued that this constitutes banishment.
- A U.S. citizen, stranded in Colombia after being placed on the no-fly list as a result of having studied in Yemen, sought to reenter the U.S. through Mexico but was returned to Colombia by Mexican authorities.

DHS Traveler Redress Inquiry Program

The DHS Traveler Redress Inquiry Program (TRIP) is a procedure for travellers who are delayed or denied boarding of an aircraft, consistently receive excess scrutiny at security checkpoints, or are denied entry to the U.S. because they are believed to be or are told that they are on a government watch list. The traveler must complete an online application at the Department of Homeland Security website, print and sign the application, and then submit it with copies of several identifying documents. After reviewing their records, DHS notifies the traveler that if any corrections of data about them were warranted, they will be made.

Travellers who apply for redress through TRIP are assigned a record identifier called a "Redress Control Number". Airline reservations systems allow passengers who have a Redress Control Number to enter it when making their reservation.

DHS TRIP may make it easier for an airline to confirm a traveler's identity. False-positive travellers, whose names match or are similar to the name of a person on the No Fly List, will continue to match that name even after using DHS TRIP, so it will not restore a traveler's ability to use Internet or curbside check-in or to use an automated kiosk. It does usually help the airline identify the traveler as not being the actual person on the No Fly List, after an airline agent has reviewed his identity documents at check-in. DHS TRIP is often accused of being defunct and existing only to appease civil rights organizations without having any actual effect.

ACLU Lawsuit

On April 6, 2004 the American Civil Liberties Union "filed a nationwide class-action challenge to the government's No Fly List", in which they charge that "many innocent travellers who pose no security risk whatsoever are discovering that their government considers them terrorists – and find that they have no way to find out why they are on the list, and no way to clear their names." The case was settled in 2006, when "the federal government agreed to pay $200,000 in attorneys' fees to the ACLU of Northern California" and to "[make] public, for the first time, hundreds of records about the government's secret 'no fly' list used to screen airline passengers after September 11, 2001."

Other Lawsuits

On August 18, 2008, the Ninth Circuit Court of Appeals in San Francisco issued a ruling on behalf of Rahinah Ibrahim, overturning a lower court decision and allowing her case against inclusion in the No Fly List to proceed through the court system.

No Fly Lists in Other Countries

The government of Canada has created its own no fly list as part of a program called Passenger Protect. The Canadian list incorporates data from domestic and foreign intelligence sources, including the U.S. No Fly List. It contains between 500 and 2,000 names.

Satirical Responses

- In the *Simpsons* episode "We're on the Road to D'ohwhere", it is revealed Bart is on the No Fly List. It is implied that this is because on a recent flight Bart removed his seat belt, in defiance of the captain's instruction.
- In an episode of *Boston Legal* entitled "Nuts", lawyer Denny Crane is prohibited from flying to Hawaii because his name is on the no-fly list. Attorney Alan Shore wins the lawsuit by filling the courtroom audience with people named "Denny Crane" and arguing that America is

capable of amazing technical innovation such as the iPod and should be able to develop a solution that does not result in so many false positives.

- In the movie *Due Date* the two primary characters Ethan Tremblay/Chase and Peter Highman were allegedly put in the no fly list by the airlines authorities due to their repeated talk about terrorism in the aircraft.

Flying While Muslim/ Racial Profiling

Racial profiling refers to the use of an individual's race or ethnicity by law enforcement personnel as a key factor in deciding whether to engage in enforcement (e.g. make a traffic stop or arrest). The practice is controversial and is illegal in some nations, and the empirical evidence is that it is an ineffective strategy.

Definition

The concept of racial profiling has been defined in many ways, including:

- "Any police-initiated action that relies on the race, ethnicity, or national origin rather than the behaviour of an individual or information that leads the police to a particular individual who has been identified as being, or having been, engaged in criminal activity." –Deborah Ramirez, Jack McDevitt, Amy Farrell for US DoJ
- "Racially-biased policing occurs when law enforcement inappropriately considers race or ethnicity in deciding with whom and how to intervene in an enforcement capacity."–Lorie Fridell, Robert Lunney, Drew Diamond and Bruce Kubu
- "Using race as a key factor in deciding whether to make a traffic stop."–General Accounting Office
- "In the literature to date, there appear to be at least two clearly distinguishable definitions of the term 'racial profiling': a narrow definition and a broad definition... Under the narrow definition, racial profiling occurs when a police officer stops, questions, arrests, and/or searches someone solely on the basis of the person's race or ethnicity... Under the broader definition, racial

profiling occurs whenever police routinely use race as a factor that, along with an accumulation of other factors, causes an officer to react with suspicion and take action."–Jim Cleary

- "Use by law enforcement personnel of an individual's race or ethnicity as a factor in articulating reasonable suspicion to stop, question or arrest an individual, unless race or ethnicity is part of an identifying description of a specific suspect for a specific crime."–Office of the Arizona Attorney General

In the United States: Legality

At a Federal level, racial profiling is challenged by the Fourth Amendment of the U.S. Constitution which guarantees the right to be safe from unreasonable search and seizure without probable cause and the Fourteenth Amendment which requires that all citizens be treated equally under the law.

In his February 27, 2001, address to a Joint Session of Congress, President George W. Bush declared, Racial Profiling is "wrong, and we will end it in America. In so doing, we will not hinder the work of our nation's brave police officers. They protect us every day — often at great risk. But by stopping the abuses of a few, we will add to the public confidence our police officers earn and deserve."

On February 28, 2002, Attorney General John Ashcroft said "This administration... has been opposed to racial profiling and has done more to indicate its opposition than ever in history. The President said it's wrong and we'll end it in America, and I subscribe to that. Using race… as a proxy for potential criminal behaviour is unconstitutional, and it undermines law enforcement undermining the confidence that people can have in law enforcement."

In June 2003, the Department of Justice issued its Guidance Regarding the Use of Race by Federal Law Enforcement Agencies forbidding racial profiling by federal law enforcement officials.

In June 2001, the Bureau of Justice Assistance, a component of the Office of Justice Programs, United States Department of Justice, awarded the Northeastern research team a grant to create this web-based Racial Profiling Data Collection Resource

Center. It now maintains a website designed to be a central clearinghouse for police agencies, legislators, community leaders, social scientists, legal researchers, and journalists to access information about current data collection efforts, legislation and model policies, police-community initiatives, and methodological tools that can be used to collect and analyze racial profiling data. The website contains information on the background of data collection, jurisdictions currently collecting data, community groups, legislation that is pending and enacted in states across the country, and has information on planning and implementing data collection procedures, training officers in to implement these systems, and analyzing and reporting the data and results.

Several U.S. states now have reporting requirements. Texas, for example requires all agencies to provide annual reports to its Law Enforcement Commission. The requirement began on September 1, 2001, when the State of Texas passed a law to require all law enforcement agencies in the State to begin collecting certain data in connection to traffic or pedestrian stops beginning on January 1, 2002. Based on that data, the law mandated law enforcement agencies to submit a report to the law enforcement agencies' governing body beginning March 1, 2003 and each year thereafter no later than March 1. The law is found in the Texas Code of Criminal Procedure beginning with Article 2.131. Additionally, on January 1, 2011, all law enforcement agencies began submitting annual reports to the Texas State Law Enforcement Officers Standards and Education Commission. The submitted reports can be accessed on the Commission's website for public review.

Support

Many in the law enforcement community argue that although unfortunate, the use of ethnic and racial profiling is both effective and necessary. The argument is made that due to socio-economic and demographic factors as unfortunate and undesirable as it might be, crime is simply higher in some communities that have a large minority population and that to ignore that fact due to a sense of moral integrity would be both morally and professionally wrong. As an example, an airport interdiction task force at Los Angeles International Airport compiled a report of those arrested based solely on officer observations, and when that report was compared to one of those arrested based on alerts driven by the airline passenger alert computer system the percentages were almost identical. Examples such as these support the conclusion that although factors such as race may be taken into account, it does not necessarily indicate that a prejudicial bias is present.

If the success of law enforcement is defined as identifying and taking action against violators, then racial profiling would allow officers to be more effective.

Criticism

Critics of racial profiling argue that the individual rights of a suspect are violated if race is used as a factor in that suspicion. Notably, civil liberties organizations such as the ACLU have stated that racial profiling is a form of discrimination, stating, "Discrimination based on race, ethnicity, religion, nationality or on any other particular identity undermines the basic human rights and freedoms to which every person is entitled."

Critics argue that individuals should not be more or less likely to encounter law enforcement officers or other government agents based on racial or ethnic traits.

Responding to such criticisms are local community groups who seek to collect data, analyze trends and how they might correspond to public perceptions of profiling, and solicit ideas aimed at diminishing cultural and racial biases.

In Practice

- The airline ticketing agent who checked in Mohamed Atta, the leader of the September 11th terrorist attacks, and a companion, would afterwards say that looking at the pair his first reaction was to think, "If this doesn't look like two Arab terrorists, I've never seen two Arab terrorists." But he immediately felt guilty, and had no legal grounds to search on the basis of their suspicious appearance had he wished to.
- In December 2001, an American citizen of Middle Eastern descent named Assem Bayaa cleared all the security checks at Los Angeles airport and attempted to board a flight to New York. Upon boarding, he was told that he made the passengers uncomfortable by being on board

the plane and was asked to leave. Once off the plane, he wasn't searched or questioned any further and the only consolation he was given was a boarding pass for the next flight. He filed a lawsuit on the basis of discrimination against United Airlines. United Airlines filed a counter motion which was dismissed by a district judge on October 11, 2002. In June 2005, the ACLU announced a settlement between Bayaa and United Airlines who still disputed Bayaa's allegations, but noted that the settlement "was in the best interest of all".

Empirical Evidence

For motor vehicle searches academic research showed that the probability of a successful search is very similar across races. This suggests that police officers are not motivated by racial preferences but by the desire to maximize the probability of a successful search. Similar evidence has been found for pedestrian stops, with identical ratios of stops to arrests for different races.

In Other Countries: Canada

Accusations of racial profiling of visible minorities who accuse police of targeting them due to their ethnic background is a growing concern in Canada. In 2005, the Kingston Police Service released the first study ever in Canada which pertains to racial profiling. The study focused on in the city of Kingston, a small city where most of the inhabitants are white. The study showed that black skinned people were 3.7 times more likely to be pulled over by police than white skinned people, while Asian people were less likely to be pulled over than whites or blacks. Several police organizations condemned this study and suggested more studies like this would make them hesitant to pull over visible minorities.

Although aboriginal persons make up 3.6% of Canada's population, they account for 20% of Canada's prison population. This may show how racial profiling increases effectiveness of police, or be a result of racial profiling, as they are watched more intensely than others.

In February 2010, an investigation of the *Toronto Star* daily newspaper found that black people across Toronto were three times more likely to be stopped and documented by police than white people. To a lesser extent, the same seemed true for people described by police as having "brown" skin. This was the result of an analysis of 1.7 million contact cards filled out by Toronto police officers in the period 2003 2008.

Infrastructure Security

Infrastructure security is the security provided to protect infrastructure, especially critical infrastructure, such as airports, highways rail transport, hospitals, bridges, transport hubs, network communications, media, the electricity grid, dams, power plants, seaports, oil refineries, and water systems. Infrastructure security seeks to limit vulnerability of these structures and systems to sabotage, terrorism, and contamination. Critical infrastructures naturally utilize information technology as this capability has become more and more available. As a result they have become highly interconnected, and interdependent. Intrusions and disruptions in one infrastructure might provoke unexpected failures to others. How to handle interdependencies becomes an important problem.

The most recent example of vulnerable infrastructure was the electrical grid in 2003, when Northeastern American areas experienced a power outage that appears to have originated in the Midwest, and possibly from a tree branch.

Potential Causes of Infrastructure Failure

Critical infrastructure is vital for essential functioning of a country. Incidental or deliberate damage will have serious impact on the economy as well as providing essential services to the communities it serves. There are a number of reasons why infrastructure needs to be heavily secured and protected.

- Terrorism person or groups deliberately targeting critical infrastructure for political gain. In the November 2008 Mumbai attacks, the Mumbai central station and hospital were deliberately targeted.
- Sabotage person or groups such as ex-employee, political groups against governments, environmental groups in defence of environment. Refer to Bangkok's International Airport Seized by Protestors.

- Information warfare private person hacking for private gain or countries initiating attacks to glean information and also damage a country's infrastructure. For example in cyberattacks on Estonia and cyberattacks during the 2008 South Ossetia war.
- Natural disaster hurricane or natural events which damage critical infrastructure such as oil pipelines, water and power grids. See Hurricane Ike and Economic effects of Hurricane Katrina.

Security Challenges for the Electricity Infrastructure

One of the fundamental foundations of modern society is the electrical power systems. An intentional disruption of electricity supplies would effect national security, the economy, and every person's life. Because power grids and their sources are widely dispersed, this is a challenge for the effectiveness of defensive organizations and structures.

Sabotage can damage electrical sources for the power grid, including civilian nuclear power stations. Sabotage in the form of cyberattacks can create havoc with computer, communication, and information systems, which could severely interrupt the electrical supply. This in turn can cause major disruptions to other infrastructure components of society. Comprehensive defence plans are proposed.

One method is to isolate load systems. Sophisticated defence systems should be wide-area, real-time protection, with control systems that are alerted and guided by sensing technologies. Communication and information must be capably routed.

Remedies

Many countries have initiated government agencies to directly manage the security of critical infrastructure usually through the Ministry of Interior/Home Affairs, dedicated security agencies to protect facilities such as United States Federal Protective Service and also creation of dedicated transport police such as the British Transport Police. There are also commercial transportation security units such as the Amtrak Police in the United States.

A number of government organizations has focus on infrastructure security and protection. The Technical Support

Working Group has the Infrastructure Protection Subgroup. The UK has the National Infrastructure Security Coordination Centre.

Several infrastructures also utilise fiber optic perimeter intrusion detection security systems, which enables the detection and location of intrusions over many miles of deployed fiber. This is commonly utilized at water utility sites and at other critical infrastructure sites globally.

Registered Traveler

The Registered Traveler Pilot Program was an airline passenger security assessment system tested in the United States air travel industry in 2005. It was used in several U.S. airports in a voluntary pilot phase and continues in operation in several airports around the country. It is administered by TTAC, the Transportation Security Administration (TSA) office responsible for Secure Flight, the replacement for the Computer Assisted Passenger Prescreening System (CAPPS) and the canceled CAPPS II counter-terrorism system. Registered Traveler is a public and private partnership between the TSA and the Registered Traveler Interoperability Consortium (RTIC) providing rules and standards for private Enrolment Providers that sign up participants. At 11:00 p.m. PST on June 22, 2009, Clear (the largest of the three companies offering the Registered Traveler program) ceased operations because Clear and its parent company, Verified Identity Pass, Inc., have filed for bankruptcy.

The program seeks to identify passengers who pose a minimal security risk, and then provide those passengers an enhanced security checkpoint experience. Passengers will voluntarily pay a fee and submit to a background check to become a Registered Traveler.

Passengers who pass the background check will be issued a smartcard credential for use at the security checkpoints of airports that participate in the program. Registered Travellers will have access to a reserved security lane and will enjoy a shorter wait at the security checkpoint. Other benefits, such as allowing Registered Travellers to keep their coats and shoes on and their laptops in their bags have also been discussed. Any U.S. citizen or lawful permanent resident over the age of 18 can apply for membership, as can minors over the age of 12 with parental or guardian sponsorship.

In order to prevent a terrorist with a clean background from compromising the system, the TSA requires that registered travellers undergo the normal TSA screening (baggage x-ray and personal metal detector), at the RT kiosk checkpoint. Additionally, Registered Travellers are not exempt from random secondary screening and may not bring prohibited items into secure areas of terminals.

Airports

These airports operated the Clear Registered Traveler program until June 22 and currently other Registered Traveler programs:

- Albany International Airport (ALB)
- Cincinnati Northern Kentucky International Airport (CVG), Terminal 3
- Denver International Airport (DEN)
- Gulfport-Biloxi International Airport (GPT)
- Hartsfield-Jackson Atlanta International Airport (ATL)
- Indianapolis International Airport (IND)
- Jacksonville International Airport (JAX)
- LaGuardia International Airport (LGA), Delta/Northwest Terminal and B gates in the Central Terminal
- Little Rock National Airport (LIT)
- Logan International Airport (BOS)
- John F. Kennedy Airport (JFK), Terminals 1, 4, and 7
- Newark Liberty International Airport, Terminal B (EWR)
- Norman Y. Mineta San Jose International Airport (SJC), Terminal A and C
- Oakland International Airport (OAK)
- Orlando International Airport (MCO)
- Reno/Tahoe International Airport (RNO)
- Ronald Reagan Washington National Airport (DCA)
- San Francisco International Airport (SFO), Terminals 1 and 3
- Salt Lake City International Airport (SLC)

- Washington Dulles International Airport (IAD)
- Westchester County Airport (HPN)

These airports are currently implementing RT programs:

- Toronto Pearson International Airport (YYZ)

These airports intend to implement RT programs in the near future:

The following airports have expressed interest and/or have requested TSA approval for the RT program:

- Baltimore-Washington International Thurgood Marshall Airport (BWI)
- Birmingham International Airport (BHM)
- Chicago Midway International Airport (MDW)
- Huntsville International Airport (HSV)
- Los Angeles International Airport (LAX)
- O'Hare International Airport (ORD)
- Pittsburgh International Airport (PIT)
- Springfield-Branson National Airport (SGF)
- Ted Stevens Anchorage International Airport (ANC).

Programs

These Registered Traveler programs are inter-operable and membership to one works with other corresponding RT programs that have TSA approval.

Clear

Clear, operated by Verified Identity Pass, was the largest Registered Traveler program participant with almost 200,000 members. Clear was founded by Steven Brill, the founder of Court TV. Clear had programs at Albany, Cincinnati, Denver, Dulles Washington D.C., Indianapolis, Little Rock, New York LaGuardia, New York JFK, Newark, Oakland, Orlando, Reagan Washington D.C., Salt Lake City, San Jose, San Francisco and Westchester Airports.

On May 3, 2010, Verified Identity Pass was purchased by Allclear LLC. AllClear LLC has now brought Clear back and is honoring the time left on all Clear's original customers whose membership may have been terminated before the end of their contracts. New Clear service opened at Orlando International Airport on November 9 and at Denver International Airport on November 30. Clear says it hopes to be in a dozen cities by end of 2011.

On July 26, 2008, a laptop containing the names, addresses, birth dates, driver's license numbers, and passport information of 33,000 Clear customers was reported stolen from a secured room in San Francisco International Airport. The information was on an unencrypted laptop, in contravention of TSA rules, although it was protected by two levels of password protection.

As a result of the theft, TSA officials ordered Clear to inform affected customers, suspend enrolment of new customers, and cease use of unencrypted computers as well as secure devices until encryption can be installed, as required by TSA rules. Verified Identity Pass must submit an independent audit of its systems to the TSA before the company can register new customers.

On August 4, 2008 TSA Suspends Verified Identity Pass, Inc. Clear Registered Traveler Enrolment

On August 5, 2008, the laptop was found in the same room where it went missing. Officials are currently investigating whether any personal data was accessed as well as the circumstances of the reappearance.

On June 22, 2009, Clear announced they would cease operations effective immediately, citing an inability of Verified Identity Pass, Inc to obtain necessary financing. The entire contents of Clear's Web site was removed and most pages redirected to this simple statement:

> *Clear Lanes Are No Longer Available. At 11:00 p.m. PST on June 22, 2009, Clear will cease operations. Clear's parent company, Verified Identity Pass, Inc. has been unable to negotiate an agreement with its senior creditor to continue operations.*

On July 6, 2009 Two law firms filed a class-action lawsuit on behalf of customers of Clear's parent company, Verified Identity Pass, Inc that suddenly shut down on June 22.

The lawsuit was filed in the U.S. District Court for the Southern District of New York against Verified Identity Pass

Inc., by Schneider Wallace Cottrell Brayton Konecky LLP and Kaplan Fox & Kilsheimer LLP. The suit claims that by ceasing operations and not offering refunds, VIP committed conversion, fraud, breach of contract, negligence and unjust enrichment. Additional lawsuits since have focused upon demanding the return or destruction of personal information, social security numbers, credit card numbers, fingerprints and iris scans in addition to refunding membership fees.

On April 16, 2010, Judge Stuart M. Bernstein of the U.S Bankruptcy Court in Manhattan granted approval to Alclear LLC to purchase the CLEAR assets after outbidding rival Henry Inc.

CLEAR re-opened on November 2010 in Denver and Orlando. . As of February 2011, CLEAR is engaged in vigorous expansion plans.

iQueue

FLO Corporation has partnered with Cogent and iQueue to deliver RT solutions and services. They expect to bring back the Registered Traveler program in the Fall of 2010 starting with Indianapolis International Airport, with further expansions planned after.

FLO

The FLO Corporation, in conjunction with FLO Alliance partners, provides biometric identification technologies and credentialing processes for use in airports in accordance with the Registered Traveler program. Final enrolment centres are located in the Washington, D.C. area, or by on-location appointment for corporate accounts.

RtGo

RtGo was operated by Unisys Corporation (It has now been bought out by FLO and being operated by IRAM Associates). Membership is $100 per year, with option to prepay for up to 5 years. Enrolment is currently conducted at Reno/Tahoe International Airport in Reno, Nevada.

Preferred Traveler

The Preferred Traveler program is run by Vigilant Solutions, a Jacksonville Beach based company. The company's program differentiates itself by adding a suite of value-added services for the traveler.

Identifying Information

Passengers who participate in this system must first provide personal biographical information including name, address, phone number, citizenship status, and previous addresses, along with other information. The biographical information will be collected by a commercial Registered Traveler service provider. The biographical portion of the enrolment may be accomplished via a secure web site. Next, the applicant will proceed to the biometric phase of the enrolment process. During biometric enrolment applicants will present identification documents and fingerprints. Applicants may also choose to have an image of their iris taken if they wish to use an iris image as an alternative to a fingerprint scan at the security checkpoint. The iris image is totally non-invasive to the eye. Once the biometric enrolment is complete, the service provider submits the collected data to the TSA which performs a Security Threat Assessment (STA) of the applicant. If the assessment does not indicate that the applicant is suspected of posing a risk to aviation security, the TSA will return an approved STA result to the service provider. The service provider will then provide the passenger with a Registered Traveler card. The card will be a smartcard, containing biometric information to prevent the card from being used by unauthorized persons. This card will then be inserted into a verification kiosk at the special checkpoints, which will verify the passengers biometrics (fingerprint or iris scan) and acknowledge membership and clearance to proceed to RT screening.

Controversy: Privacy

This system, like the related Secure Flight, has come under fire for its privacy implications although less so because Registered Traveler unlike Secure Flight is voluntary. The potential effectiveness has also been questioned. On the privacy front Registered Traveler collects far more information than Secure Flight including biometrics. While supporters assert that this program is voluntary, critics assert that RT's extensive background checks will be misused. The privacy safeguards and rules can be found in the RTIC specification and the TSA RT

Privacy Impact Assessment (PIA). Many airports and airlines already offer access to shorter "priority" security lines to first class or other status travellers without requiring any background checks.

Effectiveness

Similar to the concerns raised about CAPPS and CAPPS II, critics point out that any program designed to exclude certain passengers from scrutiny will provide a backdoor for potential terrorists, since they would likely seek Registered Traveler status. This criticism draws on the 9/11 Commission finding that 9 of the 19 hijackers involved in the September 11, 2001 attacks were flagged by the CAPPS I system but were not intercepted, because security was focused short sightedly on luggage bombs. However, those participating in the Registered Traveler Program currently pass through the same security checkpoints and are screened the same as any other individual, the main difference being RT members enjoy a much shorter wait before screening. Currently RT programs do not offer a reduced security check, but their announced plans indicate they intend to offer this if airport officials allow it.

Fairness

Because the Registered Travellers Program, in its current form, does not exempt members from any of the security checks of the TSA, it is often criticized as merely being a method by which frequent travellers can pay an annual fee to a private company in order to be permitted to move to the head of the TSA line and not wait their turn along with less frequent travellers. Since the TSA lines are a government program (funded by equal payments on tickets of frequent travellers and non-travellers), this strikes many as being unfair to less frequent travellers.

Secondary Security Screening Selection

Secondary Security Screening Selection or Secondary Security Screening Selectee, known by its acronym SSSS, is an airport security measure in the United States and Canada which selects passengers for additional inspection. This may also be known as Selectee, Automatic Selectee or the Selectee list. The list contains 14,000 names, as of December 2009.

Selection Criteria

Neither the Transportation Security Administration (TSA) nor the airlines publish the criteria that are used when boarding passes are issued to identify passengers who will be given extra screening or be denied boarding.

Some criteria are:

- Passengers with a one-way reservation.
- Passengers who pay cash for their tickets.
- Passengers who book reservations the day of their flight.
- Passengers who "no show" a single leg of their flight.
- Random selection, according to TSA spokeswoman Amy Von Walter in 2004, and as suggested by a 2003 DOI newsletter.
- Flight to specific final destinations.
- Flying without ID
- Having one's name on a list of names supplied by the government to the airlines, according to an airline staff questioned.

Since neither the TSA nor the airline run a background check at the time boarding passes are issued, immigration status and criminal records are not taken into consideration during SSSS. Furthermore, personal information such as a passenger's addresses, employment history, and medical records are not taken into account during SSSS and may not even be readily available to government officials to modify the process and increase its validity.

Procedure when Selected

Passengers who have been selected for this secondary screening will have the letters SSSS or *S* (all capitals) printed on their boarding passes. SSSS passengers will go through a more intensive screening process which may include puffer explosive detectors. Their carry-on luggage may be also be inspected by hand. In the case of film or other items that cannot be X-rayed, the agent may perform a test for possible explosive materials. The screener may also use a hand held metal detector to search the passenger for metal objects.

Randomness and Credibility

Since the process acts on the accumulation of certain criteria rather than mathematical probability, it is expected that subjects may be selected more than once or more often than others. This has caused the public to believe the process is not random but instead discriminatory as those individuals selected are predominantly minorities or people of color. The TSA states that SSSS is a selective process in which candidates who fall under a pre-determined category are chosen. Nonetheless, the process may rely, intermittently, in randomness, when subjects do not fall under any category and this becomes the mathematical variable.

With British Airways and Alaska Airlines, the marking happens at check-in. Thus a potential miscreant is warned and has the opportunity to leave the public area of the airport or abandon an attempt to smuggle something on board, while other passengers will continue to be screened.

Secure Flight

Secure Flight is an airline passenger pre-screening program to be implemented starting in August 2009 by the Transportation Security Administration (TSA). Secure Flight will match passenger information against blacklists maintained by the federal government. The initial implementation phase of Secure Flight will result in the complete transfer of responsibility for passenger watch list matching to TSA from aircraft operators whose flights operate within the United States. The second phase of Secure Flight will result in the transfer of responsibility for passenger watch list matching to TSA for flights into, out of, and over the United States.

Secure Flight will serve to prevent individuals on the No Fly List from boarding an aircraft, as well as to subject individuals on the Selectee List to enhanced screening to determine if they are permitted to board an aircraft.

History

The Intelligence Reform and Terrorism Prevention Act (IRTPA) of 2004 requires the Department of Homeland Security (DHS) to assume from aircraft operators the function of conducting pre-flight comparisons of airline passenger information to federal government watch lists for international and domestic flights. The final report of the National Commission on the Terrorist Attacks Upon the United States (9/11 Commission Report) recommends that this watch list matching function "should be performed by TSA and it should utilize the larger set of watch lists maintained by the Federal Government" (See 9/11 Commission Report p. 393).

To fulfill this recommendation, TSA published the Secure Flight Final Rule on October 28, 2008. The Final Rule went into effect on December 29, 2008.

Benefits

Currently, individual aircraft operators conduct watch list matching using lists provided by TSA. By assuming watch list matching responsibilities from the airlines, TSA will:

- decrease the chance for compromised watch list data by limiting its distribution
- provide earlier identification of potential matches, allowing for expedited notification of law enforcement and threat management
- provide a fair, equitable, and consistent matching process across all airlines
- reduce instances of misidentified individuals
- offer consistent application of an expedited and integrated redress process for misidentified individuals via the Department of Homeland Security's Travel Redress Inquiry Program (DHS TRIP), a method by which misidentified travellers can file an inquiry to have erroneous information corrected in DHS systems

Implementation

Secure Flight began implementation with select domestic aircraft operators at the beginning of 2009 and completed implementation for all covered domestic and international airlines in December 2010 .

TSA's Office of Threat Assessment and Credentialing is the lead for the program. Contractors supporting the program have included IBM, Accenture, ESR, InfoZen, and Deloitte. Infoglide Software provided the underlying identity resolution technology.

TSA's met its goal to vet 100 percent of all domestic commercial flights by early 2010 and 100 percent of all international commercials flights by the end of 2010.

Privacy

TSA has stated it will not collect or use commercial data to conduct Secure Flight watch list matching. It has also released a Privacy Impact Assessment (PIA). The TSA policy, however, makes no mention of any limitations on what the *airlines themselves*, who collect the sensitive (birth date, etc.) information, may do with this.

Secure Flight has many similarities with CAPPS II and the No Fly List, and therefore raises the same validated concerns about civil liberties and due process. Specifically, Civil Libertarians argue that under the Secure Flight program there are insufficient redress mechanisms for innocent citizens on watch lists. Additionally, the content and quantity of the watch lists has fallen under scrutiny.

Multistate Anti-Terrorism Information Exchange

The Multistate Anti-Terrorism Information Exchange Program, also known by the acronym MATRIX, was a federally funded data mining system originally developed for the Florida Department of Law Enforcement described as a tool to identify terrorist subjects.

The system was reported to analyze government and commercial databases to find associations between suspects or to discover locations of or completely new "suspects". The database and technologies used in the system were housed by Seisint, a Florida-based company since acquired by Lexis Nexis.

The Matrix program was shut down in June 2005 after federal funding was cut in the wake of public concerns over privacy and state surveillance.

History

Matrix was the brain child of Hank Asher a serial businessman in the data aggregation field. Asher reportedly contacted Florida police immediately after the September 11 terrorist attacks claiming he could find the hijackers as well as other potential terrorists. Asher reportedly offered to make available the database and technology that could do the job quickly, for free, supplied by the company he owned and operated, Seisint. Control of the system was handed over to law enforcement officials, although Seisint continued to house and operate it on their behalf. After a demonstration of the system at the White House in January 2003 Matrix received US$4 million in grants from the Justice Department and the program was earmarked US$8 million by Homeland Security.

The program snowballed, as states signed up to participate including Alabama, Connecticut, Florida, Georgia, Kentucky, Louisiana, Michigan, New York, Oregon, Pennsylvania, South Carolina, Ohio and Utah. California and Texas joined then exited the program citing privacy and security concerns. The federal government and the CIA was cited as likely future users.

The program's similarity to the Total Information Awareness (TIA) federally funded initiative that was terminated following public concerns contributed to Matrix's demise. Matrix came under scrutiny by the American Civil Liberties Union (ACLU) which made Freedom of Information Act requests in Florida, where the program originated, and to the federal government on 30 October 2003. The ACLU followed this up with simultaneous information requests in Connecticut, Michigan, New York, Ohio and Pennsylvania for information about those states' participation in Matrix.

The ACLU's requests sought to find out the information sources that Matrix was drawing upon, who had access to the database and how it is being used. As well as the funding and operational described here, the ACLU's requests revealed that the Matrix would perform an almost identical function to the banned TIA. Matrix would bind together government and commercial databases to allow federal and state law enforcement entities to conduct detailed searches on individuals.

Public revelation of the projects funding caused an uproar in the media and states began withdrawing their support. The Matrix program was finally shut down in June 2005 after federal funding was cut in the wake of public concerns over privacy and state surveillance.

Seisint retained the technology used to operate Matrix. Both Seisint and its Matrix technology are now owned by Lexis Nexis

Function

The Matrix website stated that the data would include criminal histories, driver's license data, vehicle registration records, and public data record entries. Other data was thought to include credit histories, driver's license photographs, marriage and divorce records, social security numbers, dates of birth, and the names and addresses of family members, neighbors and business associates. The ACLU pointed out that the type of data that the Matrix compiles could be expanded to include information in commercial databases encompasses such as purchasing habits, magazine subscriptions, income and job histories.

Matrix would combine these government records and information from commercial databases in a data warehouse. Dossiers would be reviewed by specialized software to identify anomalies using 'mathematical analysis.' When anomalies are spotted, they would be scrutinized by personnel who would search for evidence of terrorism or other crimes.

Like the TIA, Matrix would use data mining where searches for patterns in this data (including the 'anomalies') would be used to identify individuals possibly involved in terrorist or other criminal activity. Congressional critic Paula B. Dockery pointed out that like the TIA, this kind of 'data mining' may be ineffective, and have severe downsides, including its privacy costs.

Data from Matrix would be transferred through the Regional Information Sharing Systems network , an existing secure law enforcement network used to transmit sensitive information among law enforcement agencies. The network was linked to High Intensity Drug Trafficking Areas, United States Attorneys' Offices, other federal agencies and several state law enforcement systems.

Travel Technology

Travel technology is a term used to describe applications of Information Technology (IT), or Information and Communications Technology (ICT), in travel, tourism and hospitality industry. Travel technology may also be referred to as tourism technology, hospitality automation, travel tracking and flight tracking.

Definition

Since travel implies locomotion, travel technology was originally associated with the computer reservations system (CRS) of the airlines industry, but now is used more inclusively, incorporating the broader tourism sector as well as its subset the hospitality industry. While travel technology includes the computer reservations system, it also represents a much broader range of applications, in fact increasingly so. Travel technology includes virtual tourism in the form of virtual tour technologies. Travel technology may also be referred to as *e-travel / etravel* or *e-tourism / etourism* (eTourism), in reference to "electronic travel" or "electronic tourism".

Travel technology is increasingly being used to describe systems for managing and monitoring travel, including travel tracking and flight tracking systems.

In other contexts, the term "travel technology" can refer to technology intended for use by travellers, such as light-weight laptop computers with universal power supplies or satellite Internet connections. That is not the sense in which it is used here.

Applications

Travel technology includes many processes such as dynamic packaging which provide useful new options for consumers. Today the tour guide can be a GPS tour guide, and the guidebook could be an audioguide, podguide or I-Tours, such as City audio guides. The biometric passport may also be included as travel technology in the broad sense.

XML-based technologies have become increasingly important for the travel industry. XML can be used to support air reservation booking or to implement optional services and merchandising functions in the booking process. Another important application of XML is the establishing of direct connections between Airlines and Travel Agencies. In order to create a generally accepted XML-standard, the Open Axis Group was founded.

History

Certainly travel technology was born on the coat-tails of the airline industry's use of automation and their need to extend this out to the travel agency partners. It should be kept in mind that there was an online world before the advent of the world wide web in the form of private and commercial online services, via packet switched network using X.25. Travel technology played a significant role in the so-called dot-com boom and bust, circa 1997-2001.

Tracking (commercial airline flight)

Tracking commercial aviation flights is an activity by enthusiasts or concerned citizens. Tracking is not limited to aircraft activity, it can include tracking of airport activity. Flight tracking via software is a relatively new activity.

Flight/airline tracking, that is the use of flight trackers has been growing due to the obvious reason to know whether a flight has safely landed or whether everything goes according to the schedule so it is indeed the time to go to the airport.

With development of cell phones and other small PDA devices, flight trackers have become a must-have for people who are concerned about arrivals and departures of airplanes. Indeed, modern trackers can track airlines virtually all around the world and inform concerned parties via such commonplace mediums as SMS. The integration of flight tracking into travel management and travel tracking services is a new frontier, allowing increased automation of travel software. This application of flight tracking is currently in its infancy, but is set to grow significantly as systems get more connected.

Despite all the progress, many abrupt events like sudden weather changes are not captured by existing flight trackers because they take their information not from the airplane itself but from dispatcher centres which often do not know the actual status of plane's whereabouts.

Security Theater

Security theater is a term that describes security countermeasures intended to provide the feeling of improved security while doing little or nothing to actually improve security. The term was coined by computer security specialist and writer Bruce Schneier for his book *Beyond Fear*, but has gained currency in security circles, particularly for describing airport security measures. It is also used by some experts such as Edward Felten to describe the airport security repercussions due to the September 11 attacks. Security theatre gains importance both by satisfying and exploiting the gap between perceived risk and actual risk.

Disadvantages

Security theatre has real monetary costs but does not necessarily provide tangible security benefits. Security theatre typically involves restricting certain aspects of people's behaviour in very visible ways, that could involve potential restrictions of personal liberty and privacy, ranging from negligible (where bottled water can be purchased) to significant (prolonged screening of individuals to the point of harassment).

The direct costs of security theatre may be lower than that of more elaborate security measures. However, it may divert portions of the budget for effective security measures without resulting in an adequate, measurable gain in security. In many cases, intrusive security theatre measures also create secondary negative effects whose real cost is hard to quantify and likely to dwarf the direct expenses.

Such ripple effects are often connected to fear; visible measures such as armed guards and highly intrusive security measures may lead people to believe that there must be a real risk associated with their activity. Other reasons for ripple effects may be that people are simply unwilling to undergo such intrusions as would be required for some activity by the security measures imposed on it.

An example for both issues is that after a recent increase in restrictions in air travel, many frequent air travellers have expressed that they will try to avoid flying in the future. Incongruously, car travel, which is often considered as the alternative, is in fact riskier than air travel.

Security theatre encourages people to make uninformed, counterproductive political decisions. The feeling of (and wished for) safety can actually increase the real risk.

The disruption, cost, and fear caused by security theatre acts as positive feedback for those who wish to exploit it: even if they fail to take lives, they can cause large economic costs. Critics such as the American Civil Liberties Union have argued that the benefits of security theatre are temporary and illusory since after such security measures inevitably fail, not only is the feeling of insecurity increased, but there is also loss of belief in the competence of those responsible for security.

Benefits

While it may seem that security theatre must always cause loss, it may actually be beneficial, at least in a localised situation. This is because *perception* of security is sometimes more important than security itself. If the potential victims of an attack feel more protected and safer as a result of the measures, then they may carry on activities they would have otherwise avoided. In addition, if the security measures in place appear effective, potential attackers may be dissuaded from proceeding or may direct their attention to a target perceived as less secure. Unsophisticated adversaries in particular may be frightened by superficial impressions of security (such as seeing multiple people in uniform or observing cameras) and not even attempt to find weaknesses or determine effect.

Security theatre may also be useful where a threat is perceived to be more likely than it really is; in these cases, it can bring the risk's perception in line with its reality. For example, a gated community might have weak enough security that the gates don't really reduce the risk of crime, but if it is in a low-crime area anyway the gates can help ensure that people feel as safe as they ought to.

Security theatre has also proven itself effective in reducing shoplifting, particularly for businesses too small or otherwise unwilling to spend money on actual security measures. Examples of this include the use of mock surveillance cameras and empty camera housings; attachment of devices with blinking indicator lamps (and no other function) to high theft goods; and placing periodic make-believe security-related announcements on the store's public address system such as, "Inventory control...Please zoom cameras, focus and record zones 5, 8, and 9."

Examples

It is inherently difficult to give examples of security theatre that are clear and uncontroversial, because once it is agreed *by all* that a measure is ineffective, the measure seldom has any noticeable influence on perceived risk. As such the following are examples of alleged security theatre.

- National Guardsmen carrying automatic weapons in airport lobbies in the months following the September 11 attacks. Reports varied on whether the weapons were loaded or unloaded; loaded weapons would apparently pose an extreme danger to the dense crowds found at an airport in the case of an actual incident.
- The announcement after the September 11th suicide attacks that airports would be discontinuing curbside check-in, which had no relationship to the tactics Al Qaeda employed in hijacking the aircraft and would pose no barrier to a suicide bomber who fully intended to board the aircraft with a bomb bag anyway.
- The air travel industry uses a screening system called Computer Assisted Passenger Prescreening System. This system relies on static screening of passenger profiles to choose which people should be searched. Systems of this nature have been demonstrated to *reduce* the effectiveness of searching below that of random searches since terrorists can test the system and use those who are searched least often for their operations.
- With the aim of preventing individuals on a No Fly List from flying in commercial airliners, U.S. airports require all passengers to show valid picture ID (e.g. a passport or driver's license) along with their boarding pass before entering the boarding terminal. At this checkpoint, the name on the ID is matched to that on the boarding pass, but is not recorded. In order to be effective, this practice must assume that 1) the ticket was bought under the passenger's real name (at which point the name was recorded and checked against the No Fly List), 2) the boarding pass shown is real, and 3) the ID shown is real. However, the rise of print-at-home boarding passes, which can be easily forged, allows a potential attacker to buy a ticket under someone else's name, to go into the boarding terminal using a real ID and a fake boarding pass, and then to fly on the ticket that has someone else's name on it. Additionally, recent investigations show

that obviously false IDs can be used when claiming a boarding pass and entering the departures terminal, so a person on the No Fly List can simply travel under a different name.

- Random searches on subway systems, such as those taking place on the New York City Subway system, have been criticized by the American Civil Liberties Union and others as security theatre. They allege that since such searches are only at some stations and that people may decline such a search and simply leave that station, a terrorist could simply find a station where no searches were occurring and board there.
- The 1950s "duck and cover" drills in U.S. public schools – which suggested that ducking under a desk is a reasonable way to protect oneself from the detonation of an atomic bomb – have been cited as an example of security theatre.
- Australian airline authorities now prohibit any liquids, aerosols, and gels in a container larger than 100 ml in luggage hand carried onto international flights. They would prohibit a tube of toothpaste labelled able to contain more than 100 ml, even if it were squeezed empty. They would, however, allow the carrying on of 2 or 3 tubes of paste provided each is labelled to carry less than 100 ml.
- As demonstrated on the Discovery Channel show It Takes a Thief, most low-end locks and security systems provide very minimal actual protection against an experienced burglar. Commercially constructed doors without deadbolts can be simply overpowered by human kicks, and police response times to security alarms are frequently far too slow to catch a thief before he is finished ransacking the house and in flight.
- The use of Virus Scanners to detect malware on computer systems. In order to be "scanned" a piece of malware (be it a virus, trojan horse, spyware, rootkit, etc...) needs to be identified and recognized by the company developing the software to create a "signature" for it and deploy this to machines running its software.

This reveals some considerable doubts about the approach in general in that:

- First, if a virus or piece of malware is not identified it will not be detected in time to prevent it from delivering its payload. In the case of a rootkit it is usually insufficient to simply "scan and remove" it, requiring a restore or reinstall to guarantee a clean system.
- Second, if the antivirus company refuses to identify a virus or other piece of malware or acknowledge it the malware gets a free pass, regardless of damage caused or data compromised. This was the case in the Sony Rootkit fiasco.
- Third, a computer system which can be compromised via an automated method such as viruses or malware has inherent security flaws which could just as easily be exploited by an individual looking to exploit the flaw.

Usage

Theatre of the Absurd at the T.S.A. For theatre on a grand scale you can't do better than the audience-participation dramas performed at airports, under the direction of the Transportation Security Administration. ... The T.S.A.'s profession of outrage is nothing but 'security theatre,' Mr. Schneier said, using the phrase he coined in 2003 to describe some of the agency's procedures. *The New York Times*; December 17, 2006. Report: Plane Lighter Ban to Be Lifted. Airline passengers will be able to bring many types of cigarette lighters on board again starting next month after authorities found that a ban on the devices did little to make flying safer, a newspaper reported Friday. 'Taking lighters away is security theatre,' Transportation Security Administration chief Kip Hawley told The (New York) Times in an interview. Associated Press; July 20, 2007.

2

Hotel Property Management

A hotel is an establishment that provides paid lodging on a short-term basis. The provision of basic accommodation, in times past, consisting only of a room with a bed, a cupboard, a small table and a washstand has largely been replaced by rooms with modern facilities, including en-suite bathrooms and air conditioning or climate control. Additional common features found in hotel rooms are a telephone, an alarm clock, a television, a safe, a mini-bar with snack foods and drinks, and facilities for making tea and coffee. Luxury features include bathrobes and slippers, a pillow menu, twin-sink vanities, and jacuzzi bathtubs. Larger hotels may provide additional guest facilities such as a restaurant, swimming pool, fitness center, business center, childcare, conference facilities and social function services.

Hotel rooms are usually numbered (or named in some smaller hotels and B&Bs) to allow guests to identify their room.

Some hotels offer meals as part of a room and board arrangement. In the United Kingdom, a hotel is required by law to serve food and drinks to all guests within certain stated hours. In Japan, capsule hotels provide a minimized amount of room space and shared facilities.

Etymology

The word *hotel* is derived from the French *hôtel* (coming from *hôte* meaning *host*), which referred to a French version of a townhouse or any other building seeing frequent visitors, rather than a place offering accommodation. In contemporary French usage, *hôtel* now has the same meaning as the English term, and *hôtel particulier* is used for the old meaning. The French spelling, with the circumflex, was also used in English, but is now rare. The circumflex replaces the 's' found in the earlier *hostel* spelling, which over time took on a new, but closely related meaning. Grammatically, hotels usually take the definite article – hence "The Astoria Hotel" or simply "The Astoria."

Types

Hotel operations vary in size, function, and cost. Most hotels and major hospitality companies that operate hotels have set widely accepted industry standards to classify hotel types. General categories include the following;

- Upscale Luxury
  - o *Examples include Conrad Hotels, Ritz-Carlton, Four Seasons Hotels and Resorts, Dorchester Collection, and JW Marriott Hotels*
- Full Service
  - o *Examples include Hilton, Marriott, Doubletree, and Hyatt*
- Select Service
  - o *Examples include Courtyard by Marriott and Hilton Garden Inn*
- Limited Service
  - o *Examples include Hampton Inn, Fairfield Inn, Days Inn, and La Quinta Inns & Suites*
- Extended Stay
  - o *Examples include Homewood Suites by Hilton, Residence Inn by Marriott, and Extended Stay Hotels*
- Timeshare
  - o *Examples include Marriott Vacation Club International, Westgate Resorts, and Disney Vacation Club*
- Destination Club.

Management

Hotel management is a significant career. Larger hotels may operate with an extensive management structure consisting of a General Manager which serves as the head executive, department heads that oversee various departments, middle managers, administrative staff, and line-level supervisors. Degree programs such as hospitality management studies, a business degree, and/or certification programs prepare hotel managers for industry practice.

Historic Hotels

Some hotels have gained their renown through tradition, by hosting significant events or persons, such as Schloss Cecilienhof in Potsdam, Germany, which derives its fame from the Potsdam Conference of the World War II allies Winston Churchill, Harry Truman and Joseph Stalin in 1945. The Taj Mahal Palace & Tower in Mumbai is one of India's most famous and historic hotels because of its association with the Indian independence movement. Some establishments have given name to a particular meal or beverage, as is the case with the Waldorf Astoria in New York City, United States where the Waldorf Salad was first created or the Hotel Sacher in Vienna, Austria, home of the Sachertorte. Others have achieved fame by association with dishes or cocktails created on their premises, such as the Hotel de Paris where the crepe Suzette was invented or the Raffles Hotel in Singapore, where the Singapore Sling cocktail was devised.

A number of hotels have entered the public consciousness through popular culture, such as the Ritz Hotel in London, through its association with Irving Berlin's song, 'Puttin' on the Ritz'. The Algonquin Hotel in New York City is famed as the meeting place of the literary group, the Algonquin Round Table, and Hotel Chelsea, also in New York City, has been the subject of a number of songs and the scene of the stabbing of Nancy Spungen (allegedly by her boyfriend Sid Vicious). The Waldorf Astoria and Statler hotels in New York City are also immortalized in the names of Muppets Statler and Waldorf.

Unusual Hotels

Many hotels can be considered destinations in themselves, by dint of unusual features of the lodging or its immediate environment:

Treehouse Hotels

Some hotels are built with living trees as structural elements, for example the Costa Rica Tree House in the Gandoca-Manzanillo Wildlife Refuge, Costa Rica; the Treetops Hotel in Aberdare National Park, Kenya; the Ariau Towers near Manaus, Brazil, on the Rio Negro in the Amazon; and Bayram's Tree Houses in Olympos, Turkey.

Bunker Hotels

The Null Stern Hotel in Teufen, Appenzellerland, Switzerland and the Concrete Mushrooms in Albania are former nuclear bunkers transformed into hotels.

Shoe Hotels

Shoe hotels are hotels built into a giant shoe. The idea was inspired by the "Old Woman who lived in a shoe" myth. The largest such hotel is currently in Hokkaido, Japan. The most popular shoe hotels are modelled after a woman's platform dancing shoe.

Cave Hotels

The Cuevas Pedro Antonio de Alarcon (named after the author) in Guadix, Spain, as well as several hotels in Cappadocia, Turkey, are notable for being built into natural cave formations, some with rooms underground. The Desert Cave Hotel in Coober Pedy, South Australia is built into the remains of an opal mine.

Capsule Hotels

Capsule hotels are a type of economical hotel that are found in Japan, where people sleep in stacks of rectangular containers.

Ice and Snow Hotels

An ice hotel is a temporary hotel made up of snow, sculpted blocks of ice, and some steel framing. They are promoted by their sponsors and have special features for travellers who are interested in novelties and unusual environments, and thus are in the class of destination hotels. Their lobbies are often filled with ice sculptures, and food and beverages are specially chosen for the circumstances.

All of the ice hotels are reconstructed every year, and are dependent upon constant sub-freezing temperatures during construction and operation. The walls, fixtures, and fittings are made entirely of ice, and are held together using a substance known as snice, which takes the place of mortar in a traditional brick-built hotel.

Sweden

Existing each year between December and April, the Icehotel in the village of Jukkasjarvi, about 17 km from Kiruna, Sweden was the world's first ice hotel. In 1989, Japanese ice artists visited the area and created an exhibition of ice art.

In Spring 1990, French artist Jannot Derid held an exhibition in a cylinder-shaped igloo in the area. One night there were no rooms available in the town, so some of the visitors asked for permission to spend the night in the exhibition hall. They slept in sleeping bags on top of reindeer skin - the first guests of the "hotel".

The entire hotel is made out of snow and ice blocks taken from the Torne River - even the glasses in the bar are made of ice. Each spring, around March, Icehotel harvests tons of ice from the frozen Torne River and stores it in a nearby production hall with room for over 10,000 tons of ice and 30,000 tons of snow. The ice is used for creating Icebar designs and ice glasses, for ice sculpting classes, events and product launches all over the world while the snow is used for building a strong structure for the building. About 1,000 tons of what is left is used in the construction of the next Icehotel.

History

In 1989, Japanese ice artists visited the area and created an exhibition of ice art. In Spring 1990, French artist Jannot Derid held an exhibition in a cylinder-shaped igloo in the area. One night there were no rooms available in the town, so some of the visitors asked for permission to spend the night in the exhibition hall. They slept in sleeping bags on top of reindeer skin - the first guests of the "hotel".

The entire hotel is made out of snow and ice blocks taken from the Torne River - even the glasses in the bar are made of ice. Each spring, around March, Icehotel harvests tons of ice from the frozen Torne River and stores it in a nearby production hall with room for over 10,000 tons of ice and 30,000 tons of snow. The ice is used for creating Icebar designs and ice glasses, for ice sculpting classes, events and product launches all over the world while the snow is used for building a strong structure for the building. About 1,000 tons of what is left is used in the construction of the next Icehotel.

When the temperature drops and the snow guns start humming on the Torne River shore, usually in mid-November, the building process begins. The snow is sprayed on huge inverted catenary shaped steel forms and allowed to freeze. After a couple of days, the forms are removed, leaving a maze of free-standing corridors of snow. In the corridors, dividing walls are built in order to create rooms and suites. Ice blocks are now being transported into the hotel where selected artists start creating the art and design of the perishable material. Icehotel in Jukkasjarvi opens in phases, the first phase opens in the beginning of December and for each week, another part of the hotel opens up for visitors and guests until the beginning of January when the entire construction is completed.

When completed, the hotel features a bar, church, main hall, reception area and rooms and suites for over 100 guests to sit and sleep on blocks of sculpted ice in the form of chairs and beds. There is also warm accommodation available next to the hotel. The Icehotel in Jukkasjarvi is known to be the biggest hotel of ice and snow in the world, spanning over some 6 000 m². Each suite is unique and the architecture of the hotel is changed each year, as it is rebuilt from scratch. Each year artists submit their ideas for suites and a jury selects about 50 artists to create the church, Absolut Icebar, reception, main hall and suites. When spring comes, everything melts away and returns to the Torne River. The Icehotel only exists between December and April, and has been listed as one of the Seven Wonders of Sweden.

Documentaries that focus on this hotel can be seen from time to time on Discovery Channel and National Geographic. The Icehotel has guests from many countries and there are many charter flights to the nearby Kiruna Airport directly from London.

The Icebars

Icehotel AB searched for business partners during the early and mid 1990, and the founder Yngve Bergqvist decided upon Absolut Vodka. The first Absolut Icebar opened in Icehotel in Jukkasjarvi 1994, and today is the concept in three cities: London, Stockholm and Jukkasjarvi.

Several high-profile events around the Icehotel has since been initiated by Absolut Vodka. In 1994, the extension was an advertising shoot for Absolut Vodka to Jukkasjarvi with photographer Herb Ritts. Models, Kate Moss, Naomi Campbell, Mark Findlay and Marcus Schenkenberg was photographed surrounded by ice wearing creations of fashion designer Gianni Versace.

Guests are served vodka in glasses made of ice from the Torne River, often described as a drink "in the rocks". Ice glasses at the bars are sent from the production hall in Jukkasjarvi. This is also the case with the interior of every six months be replaced on site by staff from the ice production and artists. This is done to ensure quality and safety.

Icebar by Icehotel is a franchise concept for ice bar. The concept was launched in spring 2009 with the opening of the Ice Bar CPH by Icehotel in Copenhagen, Denmark. The bar was followed in June of that year the Ice Bar Tokyo by Icehotel in Tokyo, Japan, and shortly after – Icebar Oslo by Icehotel in Oslo, Norway.

Canada

The Ice Hotel opened on New Year's Day in 2001. For its first year it was located in Montmorency Falls Park, which is on the outskirts of Quebec City, with plans right from the beginning to move to the nearby Duchesnay resort for its next year, where it has been built ever since.

The hotel is located 5 km north of Quebec City, on the first slopes of the Laurentian mountains, in the Charlesbourg borough. It is the first ice hotel in North America and is built each December for an opening date in early January. The hotel has a four-month lifespan each year before being brought down in April. It had 22 beds when it first opened in 2000. In its last iteration it had 85 beds, all made of ice but lined with deer furs and covered with mattresses and Arctic sleeping bags. Only the bathrooms are heated and located in a separate insulated structure.

It takes about a month and a half to build with 60 workers. The Hotel makes its own snow using a special mixture to adjust the humidity. It is built with metal frames, it is allowed to harden for a few days, and then the cranes are removed. The hotel is made of 15,000 tons of snow and 500,000 tons of ice and the walls are up to four feet thick.

Description

The hotel is usually made (the architecture and size may vary from season to season) in arches over rooms with 16 foot (5 m) and larger and higher spaces for one art galleries a club dubbed the N'Ice Club, an "Ice Cafe" and a 60-feet slide. The walls are over 4 feet (1.2 m) thick on average. All furniture is made of ice. In addition to using ice glasses as in the Kiruna ice hotel, the bar (and room service) also serves cold cuts on ice plates.

Amenities include a nightclub, movie theatre, indoor heated washrooms and outdoor hot tubs.

Tourist Site

The hotel has been described as a "tourist hotspot" and is backed by Quebec's tourism department. For its first year, it costs $350,000 to build, including $125,000 from the Quebec government.

Tours are available in French or English, seven days a week, and the hotel is otherwise open to the public. After the fourth season, the official statistics reported 220,000 visitors and 10,500 overnight guests. In its fifth season, it hosted around 70,000 tourists.

Weddings

There is a chapel where weddings are celebrated. The Ice Hotel has been described as one of the "10 dream wedding locations."

Eighteen weddings were conducted for the 2003 season, and the Ice Hotel had its first same-sex wedding in February 2005, after same-sex marriages became legal in Quebec in April of the previous year.

The Hôtel de Glace is celebrating it's 11th year anniversary in 2011. It is located on the shores of Lac-Saint-Joseph, Quebec, just 30 minutes north of Quebec City. It operates from the first week in January to the last week in March. It was the first ever in the world to make a bed and everything else out of ice.

The hotel de glace is now located at Hôtel de Glace Quebec-Canada inc. 9530, rue de la Faune Quebec Quebec Canada G1G 5H9 Telephone : 418 623.2888 Toll free : 1 877 505.0423 (Canada et Etats-Unis)

Google maps still shows it on Lac-Saint Joseph but it has since moved closer to the city and is 10 minutes away from Old Town Quebec.

Norway

Kirkenes Snow Hotel

Kirkenes Snow Hotel is situated in the eastmost town of Norway, close to the Norwegian-Russian border. The hotel had its first season during winter 2006/2007, the hotel had 20 rooms and the largest snow dome in Norway (8 metres high and 12 metres in diameter). All the rooms were individually decorated by the ice artists from Finland and Japan. The west Snow Hall was decorated by a local sculptor Arild Wara. A night in the snow hotel is combined with a special dinner prepared on an open fire, the visitors can also get a sauna before or after staying at the hotel. There is also a reindeer park and a husky farm in the hotel area.

Ice Lodge

The Ice Lodge is one of the largest in Norway and part of the Bjorligard Hotel. It has a longer season than most ice hotels because of its altitude (1,250 meters above sea level).

Sorrisniva Igloo Hotel, Alta

Sorrisniva Igloo hotel, Alta has been rebuilt yearly since 2000. It is Europe's northernmost ice hotel, as it is located in the Finnmark region and is approximately 250 km from North Cape. The 2000 square meter hotel has 30 rooms, including 2 suites and it is decorated with numerous ice sculptures and ice furnishings, including lighting systems which enhance the different types of crystalline formations. Besides the bedrooms the hotel also contains an ice chapel, ice gallery and ice bar where drinks are served in glasses made of ice. The Sorrisniva Igloo Hotel in Alta has a changing theme every year. In 2004, it was a Viking theme, in 2005, Norwegian fairytales, and in 2006, the theme was wild animals of the region. The guests use sleeping bags that sit on top of reindeer hides.

Romania

In 2006, the first ice hotel in Eastern Europe was built in

Romania, deep in the Fagaraº Mountains, at an altitude of 2034 m. Due to its altitude and remote location the Ice Hotel is only accessible via cable car in the winter.

This picturesque setting is next to Balea Lake, where each year local craftsmen wait for the lake to freeze, before using the ice to build the small 14 room Ice Hotel and its adjacent Ice Church. Local artists imitate sculptures by Romanian modernist sculptor, Constantin Brancuºi. Typically the hotel is completed in December and is open until it melts in late April or early May.

Bedding, furs, specialist sleeping bags are all provided, with bathroom facilities nearby. There are also two chalets within walking distance, which also provide accommodation. Activities such as skiing, sledging or perhaps a ride on a snow bike are on offer. For those who are more organized and adventurous you can even arrange heliskiing.

The Balea Lake Ice Hotel is Romanian owned, but has a relationship with a travel company Untravelled Paths Limited, based in the United Kingdom.

Finland

Lainio Snow Village

Snow Village is located in Western part of Finnish Lapland, in close proximity of Yllas and Levi ski-resorts and easily reachable from the international airport of Kittila.

The annual construction of the Snow Village begins when the temperature drops to about "10 °C (14 °F) which is usually at the end of October or the beginning of November. Approximately 1500 tonnes (1650 US tons) of snow and 300 tonnes (330 US tons) of crystal clear, natural ice are used for the construction. The constructors, specialized in using snow and ice as building material, are constantly developing new tools and instruments for snow construction and exploring innovative ways of taking this artform into new levels.

Snow Village is built entirely of snow and ice covering approximately an area of 20,000 square metres (220,000 sq ft). During the winter season, about 3,000 square metres (32,000 sq ft) of covered indoor spaces are built as a combination of different snow and ice structures. The architectural design and the themes of interior decoration vary from year to year. Visitors can find in there for example the biggest ice dome of Europe and an a la carte restaurant with ice carved tables and bar, in addition to snow galleries full of beautifully illuminated ice art.

At Snow Village the visitors can also spend a night in a room made of snow and ice. Because of the good insulating qualities of snow, the indoor temperature of Snow Village remains always between -2 and -5 °C (28 and 23 °F), regardless of the outdoor temperature.

There are approximately 30 rooms, all made of ice and snow. Individually decorated suites with different themes are also available.

The Ice Hotel in Jukkasjarvi, Sweden, and the Hotel de Glace in Duschenay, Canada, melt every spring and are rebuilt each winter; the Mammut Snow Hotel in Finland is located within the walls of the Kemi snow castle; and the Lainio Snow Hotel is part of a snow village near Yllas, Finland.

Garden Hotels

Garden hotels, famous for their gardens before they became hotels, include Gravetye Manor, the home of garden designer William Robinson, and Cliveden, designed by Charles Barry with a rose garden by Geoffrey Jellicoe.

Underwater Hotels

Some hotels have accommodation underwater, such as Utter Inn in Lake Malaren, Sweden. Hydropolis, project cancelled 2004 in Dubai, would have had suites on the bottom of the Persian Gulf, and Jules Undersea Lodge in Key Largo, Florida requires scuba diving to access its rooms.

Other Unusual Hotels

- The Library Hotel in New York City, is unique in that each of its ten floors is assigned one category from the Dewey Decimal System.
- The Burj al-Arab hotel in Dubai, United Arab Emirates, built on an artificial island, is structured in the shape of a boat's sail.
- The Jailhotel Löwengraben in Lucerne, Switzerland is a converted prison now used as a hotel.

- The Luxor, a hotel and casino on the Las Vegas Strip in Paradise, Nevada, United States due to its pyramidal structure.
- The Liberty Hotel in Boston, used to be the Charles Street Jail.
- Built in Scotland and completed in 1936, The former ocean liner RMS *Queen Mary* in Long Beach, California, United States uses its first-class staterooms as a hotel, after retiring in 1967 from Transatlantic service.
- There are several hotels throughout the world built into converted airliners.

Resort Hotels

Some hotels are built specifically to create a captive trade, example at casinos and holiday resorts. Though of course hotels have always been built in popular desinations, the defining characteristic of a resort hotel is that it exists purely to serve another attraction, the two having the same owners.

In Las Vegas there is a tradition of one-upmanship with luxurious and extravagant hotels in a concentrated area known as the Las Vegas Strip. This trend now has extended to other resorts worldwide, but the concentration in Las Vegas is still the world's highest: nineteen of the world's twenty-five largest hotels by room count are on the Strip, with a total of over 67,000 rooms.

In Europe Center Parcs might be considered a chain of resort hotels, since the sites are largely man-made (though set in natural surroundings such as country parks) with captive trade, whereas holiday camps such as Butlins and Pontin's are probably not considered as resort hotels, since they are set at traditional holiday destinations which existed before the camps.

Railway Hotels

Frequently, expanding railway companies built grand hotels at their termini, such as the Midland Hotel, Manchester next to the former Manchester Central Station and in London the ones above St Pancras railway station and Charing Cross railway station also in London is the Chiltern Court Hotel above Baker Street tube station and Canada's grand railway hotels. They are or were mostly, but not exclusively, used by those travelling by rail.

Motels

A motel is a hotel designed for motorists, and usually has a parking area for motor vehicles. In the United States, the term is considered somewhat outdated; few motel chains still exist (Motel 6 and Super8 are two of the most popular still in existence). Motels peaked in popularity in the 1960s with rising car travel. In the year 2000, the American Hotel-Motel Association removed 'motel' from its name after considerable market research, and is now the American Hotel and Lodging Association. The association felt that the term 'lodging' more accurately reflects the large variety of different style hotels, including luxury and boutique hotels, suites, inns, budget, and extended stay hotels.

Entering dictionaries after World War II, the word motel, a portmanteau of *motor* and *hotel* or *motorists' hotel,* referred initially to a type of hotel consisting of a single building of connected rooms whose doors faced a parking lot and, in some circumstances, a common area; or a series of small cabins with common parking. As the United States highway system began to develop in the 1920s, long distance road journeys became more common and the need for inexpensive, easily accessible overnight accommodation sited close to the main routes, led to the growth of the motel concept.

History

Auto camps predated motels by a few years. Unlike motels, auto camps and tourist courts typically provided bed and breakfast or hotel-style service, usually with stand-alone cabins. After the introduction of the motel, auto camps continued in popularity through the Depression years and after World War II, their popularity finally starting to diminish with the construction of freeways and changes in consumer demands. Examples include the Rising Sun Auto Camp in Glacier National Park and Blue Bonnet Court in Texas. Such facilities were "mom-and-pop" facilities, on the outskirts of a town, that were as quirky as their owners. The 1935 City Directory for San Diego, CA lists "motel" type accommodations under Tourist Camps.

In contrast, though they remained "Mom and Pop"

operations, motels quickly adopted a more homogenized appearance and were designed from the start to cater purely to motorists. The motel concept originated with the Motel Inn of San Luis Obispo, constructed in 1925 by Arthur Heineman. In conceiving of a name for his hotel Heineman abbreviated *motor hotel* to *mo-tel*. Motels are typically constructed in an 'I'- or 'L'- or 'U'-shaped layout that includes guest rooms, an attached manager's office, a small reception and, in some cases, a small diner. Post-war motels sought more visual distinction, often featuring eye-catching neon signs which employed themes from popular culture, ranging from Western imagery of cowboys and Indians to contemporary images of spaceships and atomic era iconography.

Motels differ from hotels in their location along highways, as opposed to the urban cores favored by hotels, and their orientation to the outside (in contrast to hotels whose doors typically face an interior hallway). Motels almost by definition include a parking lot, while older hotels were not usually built with automobile parking in mind. With the 1952 introduction of Kemmons Wilson's Holiday Inn, the mom-and-pop motels of that era started to decline. The emergence of the interstate highway system, along with other factors, led to a blurring of the motel and the hotel, though family-owned motels with as few as five rooms may still be found, especially along older highways. In the late 20th century, a majority of motels in the United States came under the ownership of people of Indian descent, particularly Gujaratis.

Long-term

Motels/hotels with low rates sometimes serve as housing for people who are not able to afford an apartment or have recently lost their home and need somewhere to stay until further arrangements are made. Motels catering to long-term stays often have kitchenettes. However, even though most of these establishments that were previously called motels may still look like motels, most are now called hotels, inns, lodges, etc.

Film, TV and Stage Depictions

The Bates Motel is an important part of *Psycho*, a 1959 novel by Robert Bloch and Alfred Hitchcock's 1960 film, *Psycho*. Film sequels, *Psycho II* and *Psycho III*, also feature the motel as does the

1987 television movie, *Bates Motel*. The motel makes appearances in *Psycho IV: The Beginning*, but is not featured as much as in previous films. The Bates Motel returned to prominence in the 1998 remake of the original film.

The scenario of an isolated motel being operated by a serial killer, whose guests subsequently become victims, has been exploited in a number of other horror films, notably *Motel Hell* (1980) and *Mountaintop Motel Massacre* (1986). More recently, the genre has been revived with such films as *Mayhem Motel* (2001), *Murder Inn* (2005), *Vacancy* (2007), and its direct-to-video prequel, *Vacancy 2: The First Cut* (2009).

Several of these horror films also incorporate the sub-theme of voyeurism, whereby the motel owner spies on (or even films) the sexual exploits of the guests. This plays on the long-established connotations of motels and illicit sexual activity, which has itself formed the basis for numerous other films, variously representing the thriller, comedy, teen film and sexploitation genres. Stephen C. Apostolof's *Motel Confidential* (1967) and the porn film *Motel for Lovers* (1970) were two notable early examples. More recent manifestations include *Paradise Motel* (1985), *Talking Walls* (1987), *Desire and Hell at Sunset Motel* (1991) and the Korean films *Motel Cactus* (1997) and *The Motel* (2005).

In countless other movies and TV series, the motel - invariably depicted as an isolated, rundown and seedy establishment - has served as the setting for sordid events often involving equally sordid characters. Examples include *Pink Motel* (1982), *Motel Blue 19* (1993), *Backroad Motel* (2001), *Stateline Motel* (2003), *Niagara Motel* (2006) and *Motel 5150* (2008). In the film *Sparkle Lite Motel* (2006) and the TV miniseries *The Lost Room* (2006), the motel made forays into the realms of science fiction.

In the theatre, the seedy motel room has been the setting for two-hander plays, *Same Time, Next Year* (1975) and *Bug* (2006). Both were later adapted as films. Broadway musicals have also paid homage to the lowbrow reputation of motel culture, demonstrated by songs such as 'The No-Tel Motel' from *Prettybelle* and 'At the Bed-D-by Motel' from *Lolita, My Love*.

Legal Problems

Motels have also served as a haven for fugitives from the law. In the past, the anonymity and a simple registration process helped fugitives to remain ahead of the law. However, several changes have reduced the capacity of motels to serve this purpose. Credit card transactions, which in the past were more easily approved and took days to report, are now approved or declined on the spot and are instantly recorded in a database, thereby allowing law enforcement access to this information. This system was implemented in 1993 after the abduction and murder of Donna Martz, whose credit card was used by her killers following her death to purchase food, gasoline and to pay for overnight motel stays. The story of Martz's disappearance, leading to the development of this system, was described on *The FBI Files*. Laws in many places now require registering guests to present a government-issued photo ID, even when paying with cash. Local law enforcement agencies frequently check motels when they suspect a wanted fugitive is within their jurisdiction.

World Record Setting Hotels

Largest

In 2006, Guinness World Records listed the First World Hotel in Genting Highlands, Malaysia as the world's largest hotel with a total of 6,118 rooms. Similarly, the Venetian Palazzo Complex, in Las Vegas, has the most number of rooms. It has 7,117 rooms followed by MGM Grand Hotel, which contains 6,852 rooms.

Oldest

According to the Guinness Book of World Records, the oldest hotel still in operation is the Hoshi Ryokan, in the Awazu Onsen area of Komatsu, Japan which opened in 718.

Tallest

The Rose Tower in United Arab Emirates is the tallest building used exclusively as a hotel. Originally, the tower was to be 380 m (1,250 ft) high, but design modification reduced it to 333 m (1,093 ft).

Hotel Rooms as an Investment

Some hotels sell individual rooms to investors. Timeshare is an example of this kind of investment. The buyer is allowed to stay in the room without charge or at a reduced rate for a given number of days each year. The investor is paid a share of the takings for the room. Rooms can be sold on a leasehold basis, sometimes on a 999 year lease. Room owners are free to sell at any time.

Living in Hotels

A number of public figures have notably chosen to take up semi-permanent or permanent residence in hotels.

- Actor Richard Harris lived at the Savoy Hotel while in London. Hotel archivist Susan Scott recounts an anecdote that when he was being taken out of the building on a stretcher shortly before his death he raised his hand and told the diners "it was the food."
- Inventor Nikola Tesla lived the last 10 years of his life at the New Yorker Hotel until 1943 when he died in the hotel room.
- Millionaire Howard Hughes lived his last few years in a Las Vegas hotel.
- Egyptian actor Ahmad Zaki lived his last 15 years in Ramses Hilton Hotel – Cairo.
- Larry Fine (of the Three Stooges) and his family lived in hotels, due to his extravagant spending habits and his wife's dislike for housekeeping. They first lived in the President Hotel in Atlantic City, New Jersey, where his daughter Phyllis was raised, then the Knickerbocker Hotel in Hollywood. Not until the late 1940s did Larry buy a home in the Los Feliz area of Los Angeles, California.
- General Douglas McArthur lived his last 14 years in the penthouse of the Waldorf Towers, a part of the Waldorf-Astoria Hotel.
- American actress Elaine Stritch lived in the Savoy Hotel in London for over a decade.
- Fashion designer Coco Chanel lived in the Hotel Ritz Paris on and off for more than 30 years.
- Vladimir Nabokov and his wife Vera lived in the Montreux Palace Hotel in Montreux, Switzerland from 1961 until his death in 1977.
- British entrepreneur Jack Lyons lived in the Hotel Mirador Kempinski in Switzerland for several years until his death in 2008.

Fictitious Hotels

Hotels have been used as the settings for television programmes such as the British situation comedies Fawlty Towers and I'm Alan Partridge, the British soap opera Crossroads, and in films such as the Bates Motel in Hitchcock's 1960 film Psycho and The Dolphin Hotel in 1408, a short story by Stephen King which was adapted into a 2007 film.

Another is Tipton Hotel; a fictitious hotel in Disney's "The Suite Life of Zack and Cody." When the show later became a spinoff into "The Suite Life on Deck," the Tipton evolved into the SS Tipton, run by the same company.

Vacation Rental

Vacation rental is the renting out of a furnished apartment or house on a temporary basis to tourists as an alternative to a hotel. The term *vacation rental* is mainly used in the US. In Europe the term villa rental or villa holiday is preferred for rentals of detached houses in warm climates. Other terms used are self-catering rentals, holiday homes, holiday lets (in the United Kingdom), cottage holidays (for rentals of smaller accommodation in rural locations) and gites (in rural locations in France).

Vacation rentals have long been a popular travel option in Europe (especially in the UK) as well as in Canada and are becoming increasingly popular across the world.

Types of Accommodation

Vacation rentals usually occur in privately owned vacation properties (holiday homes), so the variety of accommodation is broad and inconsistent. The property is a fully furnished property, such as a holiday cottage, condominium, townhome or single-family-style home. The client/traveler arranges to rent the vacation rental property for a designated period of time. Some rent on nightly basis similar to hotel rooms, although the more prevalent vacation rental industry practice is typically weekly rentals.

Vacation rentals can range from budget studio apartments to lavish, expensive private villas in the world's most desirable locations, some with pricetags of many thousands per night and all the amenities you would find in any luxury accommodation (fully staffed, private beaches, boats, chefs, cooking lessons, etc) to cater to the guests. Some vacation rentals, particularly condominiums or apartments, offer many of the same services hotels offer to their guests, e.g., front desk check-in, 24-hour maintenance, in-house housekeeping, concierge service.

Locations

Villa holidays are very popular in Europe, and main destinations include Spain, France, Greece, and Turkey.

Vacation rentals are available in most states of the US and is prevalent in major tourist areas such as Florida, Hawaii and California. The vacation rental market is much larger in Europe than it is in the United States, and Florida is a popular destination for villa holidays for Europeans.

Differences between Villa/vacation Rentals and Timeshares

Consumers unfamiliar with the concept of a vacation rental may confuse it with the seemingly similar, but distinctly different, timeshare. A timeshare can still be rented as a vacation rental should an owner decide to put his owned week(s) on a vacation rental program. Many timeshare resorts offer quarter-ownership which offers the owner 13-weeks of ownership and, therefore, more weeks to offer for rental.

A timeshare is a piece of real estate—often a fully furnished condominium—that is jointly shared by multiple owners. While different types of timeshare ownerships exist, in general, each owner bears a portion of the responsibility, along with the right to a segment of time in which he or she is granted sole use of the property. Timeshare resorts allow financially qualified guests to rent and tour their unowned properties and then make those properties available to the guest for purchase. Timeshare owners can also choose to bank their week with and exchange company such as RCI, or rent the unit

Pros and cons of Vacation Rentals

Vacation and villa rentals are generally appealing for many reasons, some of the foremost being cost savings, more space, and no tips or service charges that are associated with hotel rooms. Villa and vacation rentals have kitchens for cooking, living rooms for gathering together and offer the appeal of living in a real neighborhood and soaking up the rhythm of the locals.

Rental properties are usually privately owned vacation properties with the facilities that owners need for their own enjoyment such as sports and beach equipment, games, DVD libraries and books, and in warmer locations a swimming pool. Hotels often enjoy the advantages of brand recognition, familiar reservation processes, and on-site staff for problem resolution. For a guest, booking a vacation rental may mean stepping out of that comfort zone in order to garner some of the advantages they offer. Perceived cons of vacation rentals can include being unfamiliar with the property, lack of on-site staff, and concerns about quality or cleanliness—however, these are most often mitigated by dealing directly with the villa or vacation rental owner, who can address such concerns and provide references.

The benefits generally outweigh the potential negatives, with many vacation rentals offering more space (multiple bedrooms and bathrooms, separate living areas), more amenities (fully equipped kitchens, fireplaces, private hot tubs), convenient locations (on the beach, ski-in/ski-out, city centres in real neighbourhoods) and greater privacy than a hotel, including the fact that many villa/vacation rentals give travellers the option of inhabiting real neighbourhoods in their destination and living like the locals. As of 2006, vacation rental management has become a $10 billion industry and continues to become more popular.

Listing Services, agencies and Management Companies

Vacation and villa rentals are arranged either direct with the owner or through an agency, usually via the internet. Many owners have their own websites, but most also use listing services, which display property information and photos provided by the homeowner. Because each property owner has his or her own deposit and payment requirements, cancellation policies, key-pick-up procedures, etc., a guest contacts the property owner directly in order to book.

In contrast vacation rental agencies handle reservations and billing on the homeowner's behalf, and there is no direct contact between the guest and the owner. Because the fee or commission charged to an owner by an agency is higher than that charged by a listing service, the rent tends to be higher. In the United Kingdom villa holidays are also sold by tour operators as packages including flights and car hire. This is convenient for guests who prefer not to make their own arrangements, but may not be cheaper and does not usually allow the guest to choose a specific property.

Most property owners contract a vacation rental management company to manage their vacation rentals. These companies handle housekeeping and property maintenance. Some management companies also act as agencies, marketing the vacation rental property, and handling reservations and billing.

Traveler Concerns

Some travellers still hold back fear to the phenomenon industry insiders call SNAD: significantly not as described. This involves a property that looks like paradise in the photos, only to showcase leaky roofs and blocked views upon arrival. As a result, vacation rental companies offer user reviews.

Another significant concern is that people can create false accounts pretending to be a vacation rental owner and create an advert advertising a home which in reality is not owned by them. This can lead to innocent individuals booking and paying for a vacation only to find that on arrival the home doesn't exist. Given the nature of the transaction, booked and paid for many months in advance the culprit can disappear without trace leaving the client out of pocket To address these concerns, many websites listing vacation rental properties offer assurance that the existence and ownership of listed properties have been independently verified.

Restrictions

In some cities local authorities determined that vacation rentals were becoming a threat to the hotel industry and passed some legislation placing regulations and limits on the industry. In the U.S. New York City, Chicago and other cities have introduced restrictions on short term rentals.

RevPAR

RevPAR, or revenue per available room, is a performance metric in the hotel industry, which is calculated by multiplying a hotel's average daily room rate (ADR) by its occupancy rate. It may also be calculated by dividing a hotel's total guestroom revenue by the room count and the number of days in the period being measured.

Since it is only a measurement for a point in time (say a day, or month or year) it is most often compared to the same time frame. It is often used in comparison to competitors within a custom defined market, trading area, or DMA or a self-selected competitive set as defined the hotel's owner or manager. Also, comparisons are usually best considered between hotels of the same type, or with target customers. (e.g. Full Service, Luxury, Extended Stay, Economy)

A few syndicated data companies compile RevPAR information across markets via voluntary survey, and provide compiled blinded information back to the industry.

Other Caveats:

- Successful RevPAR numbers differ from market to market based on demand and other factors.
- Best compared across like time periods. For example, it is proper to compare RevPAR on a Friday only versus other Fridays.
- Best compared across similar seasonal time periods. For example, comparing results from the Christmas week with the same a year previous is more credible than with a non-holiday week.

Calculation

- *RevPAR* is revenue per available room,
- *Rooms Revenue* is the revenue generated by rooms sales
- *Rooms Available* is the number of rooms available for sale in the time period

An often used short cut to estimate RevPAR is to multiply Occupancy % times Average Daily Rate (ADR)

- So, Revpar (estimated) = Occ% * ADR

Transient Occupancy Tax

Transient Occupancy Tax (TOT) is charged in California when occupying a room or rooms or other living space in a hotel, inn, tourist home or house, motel or other lodging (defined below) for a period of 30 days or less.

Other lodging includes, but is not limited to:

- Camping sites
- Space at a campground or recreational vehicle park.

The authority to levy TOT is granted to the legislative bodies of both cities and counties by California Revenue and Taxation Code 7280. The authority to collect TOT is generally granted to the County Tax Collector by the Board of Supervisors by means of an ordinance. An ordinance passed by a Board is specific to that County.

Hotel Booking/Reservation

In accordance to the Tourism Board of Italy, there are roughly 40,000 hotels in Italy. In fact, this is a lot to opting for when you are tripping from abroad. In case you are planning to try any hotel in this wonderful country, then there are a few things that you should know in order to make your hotel reservations in a correct and successful way:

> *At first, while using hotel reservation service, you should pay your deposit. In accordance with Italian law, hotel reservations are valid on deposit payment. Your deposit is refundable on abrogation of your hotel reservations at least two weeks beforehand of the stay, or one month in advance in case you are tripping during travel season. If you are looking for good deals, visit Expedia.co.uk for cheap holidays Europe and worldwide cheap holidays.*

At second, it is highly recommended to time your journey. In resorts and cities, the off-season is regarded from November to March. Then April and May, September plus November are regarded the off-season for various ski resorts and, correspondingly, hotel reservations. Hotel reservations deals and rates will be much less in the off season.

In addition, you should take into account the ratings of the hotel. The tourism bureau of the country provides one-five hotels ratings, with 5 stars signifying luxury hotel reservations. Bed and breakfast hotel reservations are accessible throughout Italy, though they are not provided ratings.

You can decide on cheap day hotel reservations. When you are on the move and need a spot to freshen up, then Italy provides cheap hotel reservations. With baths, beauty salons, showers, baggage checking, as well as private rooms, such hotel reservations are typically found near train stations and in cities.

After you have made your hotel reservations in the country, it is high time to take pleasure of your holidays. The Tourism Board of Italy provides some tips and hints to help guarantee that your hotel reservations vacation will be unforgettable experience that you deserve:

1. You should avoid fake products - A 2005 law sets heavy fines on the persons who buy such goods. In case you are seeking for knock-offs supplied with luxury labels, then you may wish to think twice. Acquiring such things carries a penalty of about 10,000 Euro.
2. Also, you have to know the duty-free restrictions - The American allows citizens coming back from Italy may bring in roughly $400 worth of goods duty free. In fact, a duty charge of 10% of $1,000 worth of products will be fined.
3. You need no visa as American citizens who stay in the country fewer than 3 months do not need to have a visa.
4. Police and hotel reservations required - Travellers are demanded to registering with the police in three days of their arrival. Hotels generally ask hotel reservations on behalf of the guests, though it is great to double check while making your hotel reservations in Italy. In case you are staying in any private home or together with your friends, you need to go to the local police station in order to register.

Hotel Consolidator

Hotel consolidator (also called a hotel broker or discounter) is a travel company or business that buys up blocks of hotel rooms in top destinations and then resells them at discounted rates to the final customer. Hotel consolidators' seemingly to brokers buy in bulk and then resell at a predetermined discount thus creating a big push search for discounted hotel deals online and passing the savings on to their customers.

Global hotel consolidators usually offer discounted rooms in almost every major tourist destination, big city or popular resort while local consolidators focus only on a particular geographic area trying to be most competitive on a key for the company market. Hotel consolidator's activity can be separated into two main operations: 1) Buying blocks of rooms at volume discounts in certain major cities 2) Distributing "excess rooms" offered by hotels not anticipating full occupancy for given dates.

The Strength in Numbers

In comparison to individuals who contact hotels directly and ask for discounts, the consolidators are able to achieve deep discounts due to their buying power. Hotels are willing to offer dramatically reduced room rates to consolidators because they know it will yield a greater number of reservations. Many hotels are interested in selling room blocks (allotments) to consolidators, because they know that discounted rooms mean more business in the long run and subsequently a greater profit for them.

Final Client Benefits

When booking through a hotel consolidator or from hotel consolidator's retailer you can either get the least appealing room in the hotel, or you can get a surprising free upgrade to a higher class room if all other standard rooms have been sold out. The key advantage of booking a hotel room through a hotel consolidator is that just one call or just one website visit can get you a room at a 20 to 35 % discounted price. The key disadvantage is that prices are not negotiable and the cancellation and amendment charges can be pretty harsh. Additional benefit of hotel consolidators is that they have rooms available when all other hotels are sold out during conventions and trade fairs.

Price War

A new Cornell survey on the effectiveness of tactics that revenue management professionals around the globe used to survive the economic downturn showed that while discounting was the most frequent strategy used, marketing approaches were considered to be the most effective.

Drops in occupancies, ADR and RevPAR in 2009 have been widespread in the hotel industry and the trade press has been filled with articles discussing the downturn and proposing possible tactics for surviving it. Not surprisingly, hotel owners and hotel operators have disagreed on how best to manage during a recession as owners try to maintain sufficient cash flow to cover their costs while operators attempt to maintain service levels and long-term brand equity.

One of the keys to success in a down market is to avoid offering across the board price cuts, but to instead focus on particular market segments and distribution channels. An ADR is just that, an average, and care should be taken to keep your ADR at near or above the average of your competitive set.

Research has shown that hotels with an ADR significantly lower than that of their competitive set have an inferior RevPAR performance relative to their competitors. This relationship has been shown to hold true across all hotel market levels.

For example, in the luxury market, hotels that have an ADR that is higher than their competitive set have the same or slightly lower occupancies, but have a 8- to 14 % higher RevPAR than their competitive set. Conversely, hotels that have a lower ADR than their competitive set have about the same to slightly higher occupancy levels, but report a RevPARs of 3- to 9-percent lower than their competitive set. Given that knowledge, the challenge for hotel managers is how to compete in a price war. Essentially the two ways this can be done involve either non-price methods or price-related methods. Non-price methods include competing on the basis of quality, creating strategic partnerships, leveraging your loyalty program, developing additional revenue sources and developing ad

Visitor Center

A visitor center or centre (visitor information center, tourist information center) is a physical location that provides tourist information to the visitors who tour the place or area locally . It may be:

- A visitor center at a specific attraction or place of interest, such as a landmark, national park, national forest, or state park, providing information (such as trail maps, and about camp sites, staff contact, restrooms, etc.) and in-depth educational exhibits and artifact displays (for example, about natural or cultural history). Often a film or other media display is used. If the site has permit requirements or guided tours, the visitor center is often the place where these are coordinated.

- A tourist information center, providing visitors to a location with information on the area's attractions, lodgings, maps, and other items relevant to tourism. Often, these centres are operated at the airport or other port of entry, by the local government or chamber of commerce. Often a visitor center is called simply an information center.

Europe

In the United Kingdom, there is a nationwide network of Tourist Information Centres run by the British Tourist Authority (BTA), represented online by the VisitBritain website and public relations organisation. Other TICs are run by local authorities or through private organisations such as local shops in association with BTA.

The English Tourism Council is a subsidiary part of the British Tourist Authority and promotes domestic tourism under the Enjoy England banner.

In Wales, the National Assembly for Wales supports TICs through Visit Wales.

In Scotland, the Scottish Government supports VisitScotland, the official tourist organization of Scotland, which also operates Tourist Information Centres across Scotland.

North America

In North America, a welcome center is a rest area with a visitor center, located after the entrance from one state or province to another state or province or in some cases another country, usually along an interstate highway. These information centres are operated by the state they are located in.

South America

Peru: features iperu, tourist information and assistance, a free service that provides tourist information for domestic and foreign travellers, the information covers destinations, attractions, recommended routes and licensed tourism companies in Peru. It also provides assistance on various procedures or where tourists have problems of various kinds. iperu receive complaints and suggestions for destinations and tourism companies operating in Peru (lodging, travel agencies, airlines, buses, etc.). iperu, tourist information and assistance has a nationwide network represented online by the Peru.info website, the 24/7 line (51 1) 5748000, and 31 local offices in 13 regions in all over Peru: Lima-Callao, Amazonas, Piura, Lambayeque, La Libertad, Ancash, Arequipa, Tacna, Puno, Ayacucho, Cusco, Tumbes and Iquitos.

The official tourist organization or national tourist board of Peru is PromPerú, a national organization that promotes both tourism and international commerce of this country worldwide.

Oceania: In Australia, most Visitor Centres are local or state government-run, or in some cases as an association of tourism operators on behalf of the government, usually managed by a board or executive. Those that comply with a national accreditation program use the italic "i" as pictured above. These Visitor Information Centres (often abbreviated as VICs) provide information on the local area, and usually perform services such as accommodation and tour bookings, flight/bus/train/hire car options, and act as the first point of contact a visitor has with the town or region.

Accessible Tourism

Accessible tourism is the ongoing endeavour to ensure tourist destinations, products and services are accessible to all people, regardless of their physical limitations, disabilities or age. It encompasses publicly and privately owned tourist locations. The term has been defined by Darcy and Dickson (2009, p34) as:

> *Accessible tourism enables people with access requirements, including mobility, vision, hearing and cognitive dimensions of access, to function independently and with equity and dignity through the delivery of universally designed tourism products, services and environments. This definition is inclusive of all people including those travelling with children in prams, people with disabilities and seniors .*

Modern society is increasingly aware of the concept of integration of people with disabilities. Issues such as accessibility, design for all and universal design are featured in the international symposia of bodies such as the European Commission. Steps have been taken to promote guidelines and best practices, and major resources are now dedicated to this field.

A greater understanding of the accessible tourism market has been promoted through research commissioned by the European Commission where a stakeholder analysis has provided an insight into the complexities of accessible tourism. Similarly, the Australian Sustainable Tourism Cooperative Research Centre funded an Accessible Tourism Research Agenda that sought to outline a research base on which to develop the supply, demand and coordination/regulation information required to develop the market segment. The research agenda has now seen three other funded projects contribute towards a research base on which the tourism industry and government marketing authorities can make more informed decisions.

As of 2008, there were more than 50 million persons with disabilities in Europe, and more than 600 million around the world. When expanded to include all beneficiaries of accessible tourism, as defined above, the number grows to some 130 million people affected in Europe alone. In addition to the social benefits, the market represents an opportunity for new investment and new service requirements, rarely provided by key players in the tourism sector.

According to ENAT, the European Network for Accessible Tourism, accessible tourism includes:

- Barrier-free destinations: infrastructure and facilities
- Transport: by air, land and sea, suitable for all users
- High quality services: delivered by trained staff
- Activities, exhibits, attractions: allowing participation in tourism by everyone
- Marketing, booking systems, web sites & services: information accessible to all

Specific Needs and Requirements

Specific problems found by travellers or tourists with disabilities include:

- Inaccessible, or only partly accessible, web sites
- Lack of accessible airport transfer
- Lack of wheelchair accessible vehicles

- Lack of well-adapted hotel rooms
- Lack of professional staff capable of dealing with accessibility issues
- Lack of reliable information about a specific attraction's level of accessibility
- Lack of accessible restaurants, bars, and other facilities
- Lack of adapted toilets in restaurants and public places
- Inaccessible streets and sidewalks
- Lack of technical aids and disability equipment such as wheelchairs, bath chairs and toilet raisers

Brief History

Europe and the United States of America are home to the majority of the existing companies in this niche. However, companies worldwide are starting to appear as the result of a growing need, largely driven by senior tourism, due to increasing life expectancy in developed countries.

Portugal, Spain, the United Kingdom, Germany, France and other northern European countries are increasingly prepared to receive tourists in wheelchairs, and to provide disability equipment and wheelchair accessible transport.

Bed and Breakfast

A bed and breakfast (or B&B) is a small lodging establishment that offers overnight accommodation and breakfast, but usually does not offer other meals. Typically, bed and breakfasts are private homes with fewer than 10 bedrooms available for commercial use.

Generally, guests are accommodated in private bedrooms with private bathrooms, or in a suite of rooms including an en suite bathroom. Some homes have private bedrooms with a bathroom which is shared with other guests. Breakfast is served in the bedroom, a dining room, or the host's kitchen.

B&Bs and guest houses may be operated either as a secondary source of income or a primary occupation. Usually the owners themselves prepare the breakfast and clean the room etc., but some bed and breakfasts hire staff for cleaning or cooking. Although some bed and breakfast owners hire professional staff, a property which hires professional management is usually no longer considered a bed and breakfast, but enters the category of inn or hotel.

Some B&Bs operate in a niche market. Floating bed and breakfasts for example are a concept originating in Seattle in which a boat or houseboat offers B&B accommodation.

Regional Differences

Australia

Despite the cultural similarities and a population more than twenty times greater, there are far fewer B&Bs in the whole of Australia than there are in just the South Island of New Zealand.

Since the 1960s the average per capita disposable income of Australians has been greater than that of New Zealanders and this has mitigated the powerful incentive to let out rooms in their homes to travellers. Another factor may be that Australia has, apart from City States such as Singapore, the greatest concentration of city dwellers anywhere on the globe and these cities are amply supplied with budget hotels and motels.

British Isles

B&Bs, and frequently guest houses, are a budget option where owners often take pride in the high service levels, local knowledge and personal touch that they are able to offer.

There tend to be concentrations of B&Bs in seaside towns where, historically, the working classes holidayed such as County Down, Northern Ireland, and Blackpool, England, and isolated rural areas such as the Highlands of Scotland and Connemara where there is not the year-round concentration of travellers that would sustain an hotel. They are present in most towns and cities, and their numbers vary on trade such as for business travellers and tourists: York and Edinburgh for example both have several hundred establishments known as either B&Bs or guest houses. In very busy areas, B&Bs may display a sign saying "VACANCIES" (rooms available) or "NO VACANCIES", to save both the hosts and potential guests the trouble of them having to enquire within.

Breakfast is usually cooked on demand for the guest and is usually some kind of full breakfast, but some offer a continental breakfast. In recent years B&Bs in the UK have struggled against budget hotel chains such as Premier Inn and Travelodge. Traditionally, business travellers used B&Bs but many of these clients now tend to stay in budget hotel chains. However, in holiday areas the B&B and guest house still prevail. Unlike the hotel chains, they provide a more comprehensive service and breakfast is included in the price, and some who stay regularly may simply like knowing their hosts.

B&Bs tend to place their bedrooms within three different categories:

- *Deluxe*: This standard of B&B accommodation in Ireland is considered to be very high and deluxe rooms would be available in high-end B&Bs and guesthouse accommodation. Deluxe rooms would often have additional furniture or Jacuzzis in the bathroom. Check the description.
- *En-Suite*: There is a private bathroom within the bedroom. This will always contain a WC and washbasin, and a shower or bath or both.
- *Standard*: There is not a bathroom within the bedroom. In this case there will be shared bathroom facilities in another room on the corridor. Usually there will be a washbasin within the room.

Cuba

In Cuba, which opened up to tourism in the 1990s after the financial support of the Soviet Union ended, a form of B&B called *casa particular* ("private home") became the main form of accommodation outside the tourist resorts.

Israel

The Israeli B&B is known as a *zimmer* (German for *room*). All over the country, but especially in northern Israel (Galilee, Upper Galilee and Golan Heights) the zimers has developed an extensive industry, settlements belonging to private families and Rural Settlements, rents them for a short period. Industry began to develop in the '90s of the 20th century, when profits from Agriculture became Less profitable, and many families with farms in community, kibbutzim, farms and individual seats decided to try their strength in the business of hospitality. In the last decade there has been development of bed and breakfasts also in southern Israel in the Negev.

Italy

In Italy, regional law regulates B&Bs.

India

In India, the government is promoting the concept of bed & breakfast. The government is doing this to increase tourism, especially keeping in view the expected demand for hotels during the 2010 Commonwealth Games in Delhi. They have classified B&B in 2 categories - Gold & Silver B&B. All B&B will be approved by the Ministry of Tourism who will then categorize it as Gold or Silver based upon the predefined criteria.

Kyrgyzstan

The tourism industry in Kyrgyzstan includes some B&Bs. One group, called CBT, organises homestays with people who own homes and rent rooms by the night. They help tourists and travellers in Kyrgyzstan find places to stay.

Pakistan

The trend of B&Bs in Pakistan is quite widespread. Popular resorts like Murree, which attract many tourists from different parts of the country, have a number of such resthouses. The expenses can vary, depending on the quality of facilities. Most bed and breakfast facilities tend to expediently cater to families, given the high level of group tourism, and offer suitable overnight lodging.

New Zealand

As in the USA, bed and breakfasts in New Zealand tend to be more expensive than motels and often feature historic homes and furnished bedrooms at a commensurate price.

North America

Many B&Bs in North America try to create a historical ambiance, with old properties turned into guesthouses decorated with antique furniture. For example, the Holladay House in Orange, Virginia is an 1830s Federal-style brick building that has been converted into a bed and breakfast. In the last ten years, B&B and Inn owners have been launching upscale amenities to improve business and move "up-market." It is not uncommon now to find free wireless Internet access, free parking, spa services, or nightly wine and cheese hours. Due to the need to stay competitive with the rest of the lodging industry, larger bed and breakfast inns have expanded to offer wedding services, business conference facilities, and meeting spaces as well as many other services a large hotel might offer.

The custom of opening one's home to travellers dates back the earliest day of Colonial America. Lodging establishments were few and far between in the 18th century, and apart from a limited number of coaching inns (a few of which survive as inns today), wayfarers relied on the kindness of strangers to provide a bed for the night. Hotels became more common with the advent of the railroad, and later, the automobile, and most towns had at least one prominent hotel.

During the Great Depression, tourist homes provided an economic advantage to both the traveller and the host. Driving through town (no Interstates then), travellers stopped at houses with signs reading Tourists or Guests, indicating that travellers could rent a room for the night for about $2. The money generated needed income for the home owner and saved money for the traveller.

After World War II, middle-class Americans began travelling in Europe in large numbers, many experiencing the European-style B&Bs (Zimmer frei in Germany, chambres d'hotes in France) for the first time. Some were inspired to open B&Bs in the U.S.; tourist home owners updated their properties as B&Bs. The interest in B&Bs coincided with an increasing interest in historic preservation, spurred by the U.S. Bicentennial in 1976 and assisted by two crucial pieces of legislation: the National Historic Preservation Act of 1966, and the Tax Reform Act of 1976, which provided tax incentives for the restoration and reuse of historic structures.

Through the 1980s and 1990s, B&Bs increased rapidly in numbers and evolved from homestay B&Bs with shared baths and a simple furnishings to beautifully renovated historic mansions with luxurious decor and amenities. The next big change started in the mid 1990s when the Internet became a major marketing force, making it affordable for innkeepers to promote their properties worldwide. Email marketing, in particular, serves as a useful tool for the Bed & Breakfast industry, for it proactively builds relationships with the existing guests after their stay. In addition, online reservation software has helped bed and breakfasts to capture more reservations and stay in touch with a rapidly changing technological world. At present, travellers research and book B&Bs online, checking out detailed photos, videos, and reviews. B&Bs are found in all states, in major cities and remote rural areas, occupying everything from modest cottages to opulent mansions, and in restored structures from schools to cabooses to churches. There are currently more than 18,000 bed and breakfast inns in North America.

Spain

In Spain, B&Bs are often run by people who place personal or family needs ahead of wealth and profit maximization. The business attracts numerous entrepreneurs with predominantly lifestyle motives, yet challenges them in specific ways. Spain does not have a B&B culture like Great Britain. As anything "modern" rules, locals usually shake their head at tourists visiting B&Bs when they could stay at a "proper hotel" for the same money or less. A study of the years 1997–2000, using a sample of 1131 Spanish firms, suggests that marketing must be done over the medium to long term to be effective.

Regulations

Regulations and laws vary considerably between jurisdictions both in content and extent and in enforcement.

The most common regulations B&Bs must follow pertain to safety. They are usually required by local and national ordinances to have fire resistance, a sufficient fire escape plan in place, and smoke detectors in each guest room. Kitchens and equipment used to serve meals are also often required to be monitored for hygienic operation, but there are significant national and local differences.

In Hawaii, it is illegal to open a new bed & breakfast on Oahu as of 1989. The reason for the moratorium is to force home owners with extra room to rent out their extra space to low income residents who otherwise cannot afford housing on crowded Oahu.

Professional and Trade Associations

Many inns and bed and breakfasts are members of professional associations. There are international, national, regional, and local associations, all of which provide services to both their members and the travelling public. Many require their members to meet specific standards of quality, while others simply require a lodging establishment to pay dues. These associations also facilitate marketing of the individual B&Bs and provide a stamp of approval that the business in question is reputable.

While various local governments have regulations and inspect lodging establishments for health and safety issues, membership in a state/provincial/national bed and breakfast association can indicate a higher standard of hospitality. Associations sometimes review their members' properties and tend to have additional standards of care.

In the US for example, each state has an innkeeping association (usually non-profit) that exists to promote the industry and tourism. Within those state associations, many city and regional bed and breakfast associations can be found. Many state, city and regional associations, have inspection criteria that often exceed government requirements for safety and cleanliness.

In Australia, the industry is represented by the Bed & Breakfast, Farmstay and Accommodation Australia Ltd (BBFAA).

In the British Isles the national approval boards set up by governments are far more stringent than others,while in Ireland there is an association that will only use the national tourist board's approved members (Almara Accommodations Dublin)

Studies

Tourism Queensland Study

In January 2003 Tourism Queensland conducted a review of current research to gain a better understanding of the Bed & Breakfast (B&B) market:

> *"Key needs that must be met for people staying at bed and breakfast style accommodation include: pampering and personalised service in an attractive location in an attractive house, opposed to more 'standard' hotelrooms.*

The following attributes are also appealing:

- Homely or wholesome atmosphere (older segments) or luxurious/heritage surrounds
- Home style meals
- Area for conversing with other guests
- Ability to tap into local knowledge of attractions and activities in local area.

Guests at B&Bs were asked to identify the features and factors which motivated them to choose the establishment they were staying at. The friendliness of the host was the most important factor, followed by easy access to other places, the site being the most appealing place in the region. Usually B & B's are privately owned, and therefor very different from standard commercial hotels.

Bed & Breakfasts provide mutual benefits for both the visitor and the operator. Visitors have the opportunity for a relaxing break in a homely environment. Operators have the opportunity to develop a profitable business, make new friends and contacts, understand the cultures andlifestyles of others, and to educate guests about their way of life.

Income and leisure time have changed so that shorter breaks with greater choice of leisure activities are sought. Changing work patterns have increased the popularity of shorter breaks that minimize the absence from work and the effect of absences on workflow and involvement. Bed & Breakfast holidays tend to be short break holidays and could benefit from the increased popularity of short breaks, sought by people who aim for authenticity and personal service. "

Michigan State University Study

According to a study by Michigan State University:

> *"The profile of B&B guests confirms widely held impressions that this is a middle-aged, well-educated, (moderately) high income, professional market. On the last reported B&B trip, couples comprised two thirds of the travel parties.*

Eighty-two percent of those sampled are married, and about half (44 percent) have children living at home. Average age for a travel party (respondent and spouse/partner ages are merged) is 40 years, with 60 percent under this age. This indicates that many B&B guests are at a mid-point in the traditional family cycle, when raising children is a primary activity. Newlyweds and "empty nesters" account for a smaller proportion. In fact, only 9 percent of the market is attributed to adults over 59 years of age.

Education levels are high, with the largest response category being completion of a college degree (31 percent). In addition, another one third had some graduate school or an advanced degree. It follows that the occupational profile is dominated by professionals and managers. Note that several categories such as business, health, education, and science are large enough for B&B's to consider promotion aimed specifically at these segments.

The unique touches that distinguish a B&B are clearly a primary reason for selecting this lodging option. Words like "charm," ambience," "quaintness," and "atmosphere" were often used by respondents to describe this intangible appeal. The importance of the "getaway" aspect demonstrates that B&B's have been well positioned to take advantage of shorter, more frequent weekend trips preferred by many two-income families. The lure of B&B's as a more personal alternative to the standard hotel/motel experience was reconfirmed by the 10 percent who called this the single most important reason for staying at a B&B, the most frequent response to this open-ended question. Customers were for the most part satisfied with their most recent B&B experience, with 80 percent giving the experience an .. excellent" rating and another 17 percent calling it "good." Over 90 percent would both consider a return visit and recommend the B&B to friends and family." According to this study, many bed and breakfast visitors make use of evaluations, given by other guests. This system of independent reviews is one of the fastest growing consumer content oriented sites on the net.

Com Score Study

Another study suggests that people trust online reviews posted by previous guests:

> *"People are willing to pay up to 99 percent more for services after reading positive online reviews about them, according to new research.*

The study, conducted in October by comScore and The Kelsey Group, found that online, consumer-created reviews have a big impact on prospective buyers. The researchers said 24 percent of those who eventually pay for local services – such as restaurants, bed & breakfasts and automotive shops – read online reviews before making a choice.

The study showed consumers were so trusting of online reviews, they were willing to pay at least 20 percent, and up to 99 percent, more if a company was rated excellent or five-star than if a business received a good, or four-star, rating. The study was based on 2,078 survey respondents, including 508 who used online consumer reviews.

Professional critics, and owners of companies that receive less-than-excellent online reviews by laypersons, might question the ability of regular people to adequately judge a service. However, the comScore/Kelsey Group study found that 90 percent of the people who trusted consumer-written reviews found the critiques to be accurate. In fact, noted the researchers, "reviews generated by fellow consumers had a greater influence than those generated by professionals."

The study included specific bed & breakfasts among others services. At least 75 percent of those using online reviews for nearly every category of business included in the study said the amateur field reports significantly impacted their decision. Eighty-seven percent of those in search of hotels said the reviews played a big part in their choice.

The take-away message for service providers, according to a statement issued by The Kelsey Group's research director, Steve Marshall: "With such a large percentage of review users subsequently purchasing, it's vital that local service providers have a positive presence on these review sites."

The fact that one-in-four of those contacted said they use reviews should come as good news for those in the online consumer review space, said Brian Jurutka, senior director at comScore Marketing Solutions.

"That's a sizeable chunk," he said. "This helps them in having discussions with folks looking to advertise; it says a sizeable portion of the online population is going to be visiting these sites."

Journal of Travel Research Study

A study by the Journal of Travel Research stated:

> *"While the hedonic price model has been used to evaluate willingness to pay in a variety of markets, its use in the tourism industry is limited. This research note highlights the usefulness of the hedonic price technique in this industry by evaluating willingness to pay for specific characteristics of bed and breakfast accommodations.*
>
> *Heterogeneity in price and amenities offered by bed and breakfast accommodations enables us to generate estimates of willingness to pay for specific characteristics. Using data on price and amenities collected from bed and breakfast accommodations, the findings show a willingness to pay for specific characteristics such as sunny balconies, a five star Champagne breakfast, and a room furnished with antique treasures..."*

Prince Edward Island Study

A 2007 study on Prince Edward Island:

> *"The vast majority of visitors to B & B are pleasure travellers. The most important reasons why travellers choose a B & B are personalised service and hospitality, price and value ratio, physical element, atmosphere, image and location."*

TIME Magazine

According to TIME magazine:

> *"Americans have a wide array of lodgings to choose from when they take a vacation: high-rise hotels, rustic resorts, motels by the bay. Yet more and more people are flocking to bed-and-breakfast inns, the most old-fashioned homes away from home. Just 20 years ago, there were only 1,000 B and Bs, as they are nicknamed, scattered throughout the country. Today there are more than 28,000 serving more than 50 million guests each year.*

What's the appeal? Bed-and-breakfasts, often situated in elegant, historic homes, tap into everyone's fantasy of living another life. Many have been lovingly renovated with period decorations, inviting visitors to step back in time. Others carry a theme throughout the house. Since on average they have only seven or eight rooms, they offer peace and quiet, a rare commodity in the average home.

The hosts, who nearly always live on the premises, provide plenty of coddling. They will recommend local attractions, help with dinner reservations, often provide an afternoon tea or glass of sherry—and, yes, prepare a delicious homemade breakfast.

Prices at bed-and-breakfasts, which average $104 to $133 a night, depending on the region, rival the rates of good hotels. While some 10,000 B and Bs are private homes in which the owners offer a room or two, most are serious businesses, complete with websites and toll-free numbers.

The clientele tends to be couples, most of them affluent and well educated. Most are tourists or people who are in town to visit family or to celebrate a special occasion. Bed-and-breakfasts are popular with many foreign travellers, mostly from Britain, Germany, Canada, France and Australia, who have grown up going to B and Bs in their own countries."

Destination Hotel

A destination hotel is a hotel whose location and amenities make the hotel itself a destination for tourists, rather than merely a convenient place to stay while travelling through or visiting the area for other reasons. Destination hotels are also called destination lodgings and sometimes destination resorts. The market for destination hotels is the subject of academic and business analysis.

A destination hotel is often characterized by:

- Upscale lodging, dining, and activities
- Recreation and entertainment on the hotel's own property
- Distinctive characteristics of the building, gardens, and sometimes history

History

Since the 1800s, the traditional concept of a destination hotel has been based upon a venue which is typically remote and has a natural feature as its attraction. For example, the Kviknes

Hotel in Norway is a difficult to reach remote location which provides visitors access to the scenic fjord at Balestrand. Historically there were certain built-in amenities such as gourmet cuisine, music recitals and shoreline trails; however, the amenities of modern (post 1980) destination hotels dwarf the scale of these earlier models. Many of the Las Vegas and Caribbean resort hotels have complete shopping malls, conference centres and large entertainment halls on site; thus, the contemporary version of a destination often features large on-site capital investment in activities, although the access to a local natural feature is still retained by many newer destination hotels (e.g. Hotel l'Anjajavy in Madagascar).

Historic Examples

There are numerous historic venues which were well known in the 19th century, some of which survive to the present. Examples of these properties include:

- Eastern & Oriental Hotel, George Town, Penang, Malaysia
- Raffles Hotel, Singapore
- Kviknes Hotel, Balestrand, Norway
- Metropole Hotel, Avalon, California, USA, circa 1887 Victorian style hotel
- Gilroy Yamato Hot Springs, Gilroy, California, USA
- Ahwahnee Hotel, Yosemite National Park, California
- Hotel Metropole, Vienna, Austria
- Mohonk Mountain House, New Paltz, New York. Owned and operated by the Smiley family since 1869.
- Greenbrier Resort, White Sulphur Springs, W. Va., USA
- Grand Hotel-Mackinac, Mackinac Island, Mich.
- Hotel del Coronado, Coronado, California

Types of Destination Hotels

There are several distinct types of destination hotels including:

- Geographically remote locations often associated with a noteworthy natural feature such as a volcano or rainforest

- Urban settings
- Conference center oriented
- Specialized activity settings (e.g. Disneyland Hotel)
- Hotels of unusual construction by virtue of being built into a specialized environment (e.g. ice hotels, cave hotels or treehouse hotels)
- Boutique hotels

Destination Spa

A destination spa is a short term residential/lodging facility with the primary purpose of providing individual services for spa-goers to develop healthy habits. Historically many such spas were developed at the location of natural hot springs or sources of mineral waters. Typically over a seven-day stay, such facilities provide a comprehensive program that includes spa services, physical fitness activities, wellness education, healthy cuisine and special interest programming.

Some destination spas offer an all-inclusive program that includes facilitated fitness classes, healthy cuisine, educational classes and seminars as well as similar services to a beauty salon or a day spa. Guests reside and participate in the program at a destination spa instead of just visiting for a treatment or pure vacation. Some destination spas are in exotic locations or in spa towns.

Destination spas have been in use for a considerable time, and some are not used actively, but rather are historically preserved as elements of earlier history; for example, Gilroy Yamato Hot Springs in California is such a historically used spa whose peak patronage occurred in the late 19th and early 20th century.

Resort spas are generally located in resorts and offer similar services via rooms with services, meals, body treatments and fitness a la carte.

Spa

The term spa is associated with water treatment which is also known as balneotherapy. Spa towns or spa resorts (including hot springs resorts) typically offer various health treatments. The belief in the curative powers of mineral waters goes back to prehistoric times. Such practices have been popular worldwide, but are especially widespread in Europe and Japan. Day spas are also quite popular, and offer various personal care treatments.

Origins of the Term

The term is derived from the name of the town of Spa, Belgium, whose name is known back to Roman times, when the location was called Aquae Spadanae, perhaps related to the Latin word "spargere" meaning to scatter, sprinkle or moisten.

Since medieval times, illnesses caused by iron deficiency were treated by drinking chalybeate (iron-bearing) spring water (in 1326, the ironmaster Collin le Loup claimed a cure, when the spring was called *Espa,* a Walloon word for "fountain").

In 16th century England, the old Roman ideas of medicinal bathing were revived at towns like Bath, and in 1571 William Slingsby who had been to the Belgian town (which he called *Spaw*) discovered a chalybeate spring in Yorkshire. He built an enclosed well at what became known as Harrogate, the first resort in England for drinking medicinal waters, then in 1596 Dr Timothy Bright called the resort *The English Spaw,* beginning the use of the word *Spa* as a generic description.

It is commonly claimed, in a commercial context, that the word is an acronym of various Latin phrases such as "Salus Per Aquam" or "Sanitas Per Aquam" meaning "health through water". This is very unlikely: the derivation doesn't appear before the early 21st century and is probably a "backronym" as there is no evidence of acronyms passing into the language before the 20th century; nor does it match the known Roman name for the location.

History

The practice of travelling to hot or cold springs in hopes of effecting a cure of some ailment dates back to pre-historic times. Archaeological investigations near hot springs in France and Czech Republic revealed Bronze Age weapons and offerings. In Great Britain, ancient legend credited early Celtic kings with the discovery of the hot springs at Bath, England.

Many people around the world believed that bathing in a particular spring, well, or river resulted in physical and spiritual purification. Forms of ritual purification existed among the native

Americans, Persians, Babylonians, Egyptians, Greeks, and Romans. Today, ritual purification through water can be found in the religious ceremonies of Jews, Muslims, Christians, Buddhists, and Hindus. These ceremonies reflect the ancient belief in the healing and purifying properties of water. Complex bathing rituals were also practiced in ancient Egypt, in prehistoric cities of the Indus Valley, and in Aegean civilizations. Most often these ancient people did little building construction around the water, and what they did construct was very temporary in nature.

Bathing in Greek and Roman Times

Some of the earliest descriptions of western bathing practices came from Greece. The Greeks began bathing regimens that formed the foundation for modern spa procedures. These Aegean people utilized small bathtubs, wash basins, and foot baths for personal cleanliness. The earliest such findings are the baths in the palace complex at Knossos, Crete, and the luxurious alabaster bathtubs excavated in Akrotiri, Santorini; both date from the mid-2nd millennium BC. They established public baths and showers within their gymnasium complexes for relaxation and personal hygiene. Greek mythology specified that certain natural springs or tidal pools were blessed by the gods to cure disease. Around these sacred pools, Greeks established bathing facilities for those desiring healing. Supplicants left offerings to the gods for healing at these sites and bathed themselves in hopes of a cure. The Spartans developed a primitive vapour bath. At Serangeum, an early Greek *balneum* (bathhouse, loosely translated), bathing chambers were cut into the hillside from which the hot springs issued. A series of niches cut into the rock above the chambers held bathers' clothing. One of the bathing chambers had a decorative mosaic floor depicting a driver and chariot pulled by four horses, a woman followed by two dogs, and a dolphin below. Thus, the early Greeks used the natural features, but expanded them and added their own amenities, such as decorations and shelves. During later Greek civilization, bathhouses were often built in conjunction with athletic fields.

The Romans emulated many of the Greek bathing practices. Romans surpassed the Greeks in the size and complexity of their baths. This came about by many factors: the larger size and population of Roman cities, the availability of running water following the building of aqueducts, and the invention of cement, which made building large edifices easier, safer, and cheaper. As in Greece, the Roman bath became a focal center for social and recreational activity. As the Roman Empire expanded, the idea of the public bath spread to all parts of the Mediterranean and into regions of Europe and North Africa. With the construction of the aqueducts, the Romans had enough water not only for domestic, agricultural, and industrial uses, but also for their leisurely pursuits. The aqueducts provided water that was later heated for use in the baths. Today, the extent of the Roman bath is revealed at ruins and in archaeological excavations in Europe, Africa, and the Middle East.

The Romans also developed baths in their colonies, taking advantage of the natural hot springs occurring in Europe to construct baths at Aix and Vichy in France, Bath and Buxton in England, Aachen and Wiesbaden in Germany, Baden, Austria, and Aquincum in Hungary, among other locations. These baths became centres for recreational and social activities in Roman communities. Libraries, lecture halls, gymnasiums, and formal gardens became part of some bath complexes. In addition, the Romans used the hot thermal waters to relieve their suffering from rheumatism, arthritis, and overindulgence in food and drink. The decline of the Roman Empire in the west, beginning in AD 337 after the death of Emperor Constantine, resulted in Roman legions abandoning their outlying provinces and leaving the baths to be taken over by the local population or destroyed.

Thus, the Romans elevated bathing to a fine art, and their bathhouses physically reflected these advancements. The Roman bath, for instance, included a far more complex ritual than a simple immersion or sweating procedure. The various parts of the bathing ritual – undressing, bathing, sweating, receiving a massage, and resting – required separated rooms which the Romans built to accommodate those functions. The segregation of the sexes and the additions of diversions not directly related to bathing also had direct impacts on the shape and form of bathhouses. The elaborate Roman bathing ritual and its resultant architecture served as precedents for later European and American bathing facilities. Formal garden spaces and opulent architectural arrangement equal to those of the Romans reappeared in Europe by the end of the eighteenth century. Major American spas followed suit a century later.

Bathing in Medieval Times

With the decline of the Roman Empire, the public baths often became places of licentious behaviour, and such use was responsible for the spread rather than the cure of diseases. A general belief developed among the European populace was that frequent bathing promoted disease and sickness. Medieval church authorities encouraged this belief and made every effort to close down public baths. Ecclesiastical officials believed that public bathing created an environment open to immorality and disease. Roman Catholic Church officials even banned public bathing in an unsuccessful effort to halt syphilis epidemics from sweeping Europe. Overall, this period represented a time of decline for public bathing.

People continued to seek out a few select hot and cold springs, believed to be holy wells, to cure various ailments. In an age of religious fervor, the benefits of the water were attributed to God or one of the saints. In 1326, Collin le Loup, an ironmaster from LiEge, Belgium, discovered the chalybeate springs of Spa, Belgium. Around these springs, a famous health resort eventually grew and the term "spa" came to refer to any health resort located near natural springs. During this period, individual springs became associated with the specific ailment that they could allegedly benefit.

Bathing procedures during this period varied greatly. By the 16th century, physicians at Karlsbad, Bohemia, prescribed that the mineral water be taken internally as well as externally. Patients periodically bathed in warm water for up to 10 or 11 hours while drinking glasses of mineral water. The first bath session occurred in the morning, the second in the afternoon. This treatment lasted several days until skin pustules formed and broke resulting in the draining of "poisons" considered to be the source of the disease. Then followed another series of shorter, hotter baths to wash the infection awayclose the eruptions.

In the English coastal town of Scarborough in 1626, a Mrs. Elizabeth Farrow discovered a stream of acidic water running from one of the cliffs to the south of the town. This was deemed to have beneficial health properties and gave birth to Scarborough Spa. Dr Wittie's book about the spa waters published in 1660 attracted a flood of visitors to the town. Sea bathing was added to the cure, and Scarborough became Britain's first seaside resort. The first rolling bathing machines for bathers are recorded on the sands in 1735.

Bathing in the 18th Century

In the 17th century, most upper-class Europeans washed their clothes with water often and washed only their faces (with linen), feeling that bathing the entire body was a lower-class activity; but the upper-class slowly began changing their attitudes toward bathing as a way to restore health later in that century. The wealthy flocked to health resorts to drink and bathe in the waters. In 1702, Queen Anne of England traveled to Bath, the former Roman development, to bathe. A short time later, Richard (Beau) Nash came to Bath. By the force of his personality, Nash became the arbiter of good taste and manners in England. He along with financier Ralph Allen and architect John Wood transformed Bath from a country spa into the social capital of England. Bath set the tone for other spas in Europe to follow. Ostensibly, the wealthy and famous arrived there on a seasonal basis to bathe in and drink the water; however, they also came to display their opulence. Social activities at Bath included dances, concerts, playing cards, lectures, and promenading down the street.

A typical day at Bath might be an early morning communal bath followed by a private breakfast party. Afterwards, one either drank water at the Pump Room (a building constructed over the thermal water source) or attended a fashion show. Physicians encouraged health resort patrons to bathe in and drink the waters with equal vigor. The next several hours of the day could be spent in shopping, visiting the lending library, attending concerts, or stopping at one of the coffeehouses. At 4:00 pm, the rich and famous dressed up in their finery and promenaded down the streets. Next came dinner, more promenading, and an evening of dancing or gambling.

Similar activities occurred in health resorts throughout Europe. The spas became stages on which Europeans paraded with great pageantry. These resorts became infamous as places full of gossip and scandals. The various social and economic classes selected specific seasons during the year's course, staying from one to several months, to vacation at each resort. One season aristocrats occupied the resorts; at other times, prosperous farmers or retired military men took the baths. The wealthy and the criminals that preyed on them moved from one spa to the next as the fashionable season for that resort changed.

During the 18th century, a revival in the medical uses of spring water took place among some Italian, German, and English physicians. This revival changed the way of taking a spa treatment. For example, in Karlsbad the accepted method of drinking the mineral water required sending large barrels to individual boardinghouses where the patients drank physician-prescribed dosages in the solitude of their rooms. Dr. David Beecher in 1777 recommended that the patients come to the fountainhead for the water and that each patient should first do some prescribed exercises. This innovation increased the medicinal benefits obtained and gradually physical activity became part of the European bathing regimen. In 1797, in England, Dr. James Currier published *The Effects of Water, Cold and Warm, as a Remedy in Fever and other Diseases*. This book stimulated additional interest in water cures and advocated the external and internal use of water as part of the curing process.

Bathing in the 19th and 20th Centuries

In the 19th century, bathing became a more accepted practice as physicians realized some of the benefits that cleanliness could provide. A cholera epidemic in Liverpool, England in 1842 resulted in a sanitation renaissance, facilitated by the overlapping hydropathy and sanitation movements, and the implementation of a series of statutes known collectively as "The Baths and Wash-houses Acts 1846 to 1896". The result was increased facilities for bathing and washed clothes, and more people participating in these activities.

Also in 1842, a house in Cincinnati, Ohio, received the first indoor bathtub in the United States. Bathing, however, was still not a universal custom. Only one year later – in 1843 – bathing between November 1 and March 15 was outlawed in Philadelphia, Pennsylvania, as a health measure, and in 1845 bathing was banned in Boston, Massachusetts, unless under the direct orders of a physician. The situation improved, however, and by 1867 in Philadelphia most houses of the well-to-do had tubs and indoor plumbing. In England, hot showers were installed in barracks and schools by the 1880s. The taboos against bathing disappeared with advancements in medical science; the worldwide medical community was even promoting the benefits of bathing. In addition, the Victorian taste for the exotic lent itself perfectly to seeking out the curative powers of thermal water.

In most instances, the formal architectural development of European spas took place in the 18th and 19th centuries. The architecture of Bath, England, developed along Georgian and Neoclassical lines, generally following Palladian structures. The most important architectural form that emerged was the "crescent" – a semi-elliptical street plan used in many areas of England. The architecture of Carlsbad, Marienbad, Franzensbad, and Baden-Baden was primarily Neoclassical, but the literature seems to indicate that large bathhouses were not constructed until well into the 19th century. The emphasis on drinking the waters rather than bathing in them led to the development of separate structures known as *Trinkhallen* (drinking halls) where those taking the cure spent hours drinking water from the springs.

By the mid-19th century, the situation had changed dramatically. Visitors to the European spas began to stress bathing in addition to drinking the waters. Besides fountains, pavilions, and Trinkhallen, bathhouses on the scale of the Roman baths were revived. Photographs of a 19th century spa complex taken in the 1930s, detailing the earlier architecture, show a heavy use of mosaic floors, marble walls, classical statuary, arched openings, domed ceilings, segmental arches, triangular pediments, Corinthian columns, and all the other trappings of a Neoclassical revival. The buildings were usually separated by function – with the Trinkhalle, the bathhouse, the inhalatorium (for inhaling the vapors), and the *Kurhaus* or *Conversationhaus* that was the center of social activity. Baden-Baden featured golf courses and tennis courts, "superb roads to motor over, and drives along quaint lanes where wild deer are as common as cows to us, and almost as unafraid." The European spa, then, started with structures to house the drinking function – from simple fountains to pavilions to elaborate Trinkhallen. The enormous bathhouses came later in the 19th century as a renewed preference for an elaborate bathing ritual to cure ills and improve health came into vogue. European architects looked back to Roman civilizations and carefully studied its fine architectural precedents. The Europeans copied the same formality, symmetry, division of rooms by function, and opulent interior design in their bathhouses. They emulated the fountains and formal garden spaces in their resorts, and they also added new diversions. The tour books always mentioned the roomy, woodsy offerings in the vicinity and the faster-paced evening diversions.

By the beginning of the 19th century, the European bathing regimen consisted of numerous accumulated traditions. The bathing routine included soaking in hot water, drinking the water, steaming in a vapour room, and relaxing in a cooling room. In addition doctors ordered that patients be douched with hot or cold water and given a select diet to promote a cure. Authors began writing guidebooks to the health resorts of Europe explaining the medical benefits and social amenities of each. Rich Europeans and Americans traveled to these resorts to take in cultural activities and the baths.

Each European spa began offering similar cures while maintaining a certain amount of individuality. The 19th century bathing regimen at Karlsbad can serve as a general portrayal of European bathing practices during this century. Visitors arose at 6:00 am to drink the water and be serenaded by a band. Next came a light breakfast, bath, and lunch. The doctors at Karlsbad usually limited patients to certain foods for each meal. In the afternoon, visitors went sight-seeing or attended concerts. Nightly theatrical performances followed the evening meal. This ended around 9:00 pm with the patients returning to their boardinghouses to sleep until six the next morning. This regimen continued for as long as a month and then the patients returned home until the next year. Other 19th century European spa regimens followed similar schedules.

At the beginning of the 20th century, European spas combined a strict diet and exercise regimen with a complex bathing procedure to achieve benefits for the patients. One example will suffice to illustrate the change in bathing procedures. Patients at Baden-Baden, which specialized in treating rheumatoid arthritis, were directed to see a doctor before taking the baths. Once this occurred, the bathers proceeded to the main bathhouse where they paid for their baths and stored their valuables before being assigned a booth for undressing. The bathhouse supplied bathers with towels, sheets, and slippers.

The Baden-Baden bathing procedure began with a warm shower. The bathers next entered a room of circulating, 140-degree hot air for 20 minutes, spent another ten minutes in a room with 150-degree temperature, partook of a 154-degree vapour bath, then showered and received a soap massage. After the massage, the bathers swam in a pool heated approximately to body temperature. After the swim, the bathers rested for 15 to 20 minutes in the warm "Sprudel" room pool. This shallow pool's bottom contained an 8-inch (200 mm) layer of sand through with naturally carbonated water bubbled up. This was followed by a series of gradually cooler showers and pools. After that, the attendants rubbed down the bathers with warm towels and then wrapped them in sheets and covered them with blankets to rest for 20 minutes. This ended the bathing portion of the treatment. The rest of the cure consisted of a prescribed diet, exercise, and water-drinking program.

The European spas provided various other diversions for guests after the bath, including gambling, horse racing, fishing, hunting, tennis, skating, dancing, golf, and horseback riding. Sight-seeing and theatrical performances served as further incentives for people to go to the spa. Some European governments even recognized the medical benefits of spa therapy and paid a portion of the patient's expenses.

A number of these spas catered to those suffering from obesity and overindulgence in addition to various other medical complaints. In recent years, elegance and style of earlier centuries may have diminished, but people still come to the natural hot springs for relaxation and health. In Germany, the tradition survives to the present day. 'Taking a cure' at a spa is covered by both public and private health care insurance, as mandated by federal legislation. Typically, a doctor prescribes a few weeks stay at a mineral spring or other natural setting where a patient's condition will be treated with healing spring waters and natural therapies.

Spas in Colonial America

Some European colonists brought with them knowledge of the hot water therapy for medicinal purposes, and others learned the benefits of hot springs from the Native Americans. Europeans gradually obtained many of the hot and cold springs from the various Indian tribes. They then developed the spring to suit European tastes. By the 1760s, British colonists were travelling to hot and cold springs in Connecticut, Pennsylvania, New York, and Virginia in search of water cures. Among the more frequently visited of these springs were Bath, Yellow, and Bristol Springs in Pennsylvania; and Warm Springs, Hot Springs, and White Sulphur Springs, West Virginia (now in West Virginia) in Virginia. In the last decade of the 1700s, New York spas were beginning to be frequented by intrepid travellers, most notably Ballston Spa. Nearby Saratoga Springs and Kinderhook were yet to be discovered.

Colonial doctors gradually began to recommend hot springs for ailments. Dr. Benjamin Rush, American patriot and physician, praised the springs of Bristol, Pennsylvania, in 1773. Dr. Samuel Tenney in 1783 and Dr. Valentine Seaman in 1792 examined the water of Ballston Spa in New York and wrote of possible medicinal uses of the springs. Hotels were constructed to accommodate visitors to the various springs. Entrepreneurs operated establishments where the travellers could lodge, eat, and drink. Thus began the health resort industry in the United States.

Bathing in 19th and 20th Century America

After the American Revolution, the spa industry continued to gain popularity. The first truly popular spa was Saratoga Springs, which, by 1815, had two large, four-story, Greek revival hotels. It grew rapidly, and by 1821 it had at least five hundred rooms for accommodation. Its relative proximity to New York city and access to the country's most developed steamboat lines meant that by the mid-1820s the spa became the country's most popular tourist destination, serving both the country's elite and a more middle-class audience. Although spa activity had been central to Saratoga in the 1810s, by the 1820s the resort had hotels with great ballrooms, opera houses, stores, and clubhouses. The Union Hotel (first built in 1803 but steadily expanded over the coming decades) had its own esplanade, and by the 1820s had it's own fountain and formal landscaping, but with only two small bathhouses. As the resort developed as a tourist destination mineral bathhouses became auxiliary structures and not the central features of the resort, although the drinking of mineral water was at least followed as a pro-forma activity by most in attendance, despite nightly dinners that were elaborate and extensive. Although Saratoga and other spas in New York centered their developments around the healthful mineral waters, their real drawing card was a complex social life and a cultural cachet. However, the wider audience it garnered by the late 1820s began to take some of the bloom off the resort, and in the mid-1830s, as a successful bid to revive itself, it turned to horse racing.

By the mid 1850s hot and cold spring resorts existed in 20 states. Many of these resorts contained similar architectural features. Most health resorts had a large, two-story central building near or at the springs, with smaller structures surrounding it. The main building provided the guests with facilities for dining, and possibly, dancing on the first floor, and the second story consisted of sleeping rooms. The outlying structures were individual guest cabins, and other auxiliary buildings formed a semicircle or U-shape around the large building.

These resorts offered swimming, fishing, hunting, and horseback riding as well as facilities for bathing. The Virginia resorts, particularly White Sulphur Springs, proved popular before and after the Civil War. After the Civil War, spa vacations became very popular as returning soldiers bathed to heal wounds and the American economy allowed more leisure time. Saratoga Springs in New York became one of the main centres for this type of activity. Bathing in and drinking the warm, carbonated spring water only served as a prelude to the more interesting social activities of gambling, promenading, horse racing, and dancing.

During the last half of the 19th century, western entrepreneurs developed natural hot and cold springs into resorts – from the Mississippi River to the West Coast. Many of these spas offered individual tub baths, vapour baths, douche sprays, needle showers, and pool bathing to their guests. The various railroads that spanned the country promoted these resorts to encourage train travel. Hot Springs, Arkansas, became a major resort for people from the large metropolitan areas of St. Louis and Chicago.

The popularity of the spas continued into the 20th century. Some medical critics, however, charged that the thermal waters in such renowned resorts as Hot Springs, Virginia, and Saratoga Springs, New York, were no more beneficial to health than ordinary heated water. The various spa owners countered these arguments by developing better hydrotherapy for their patients. At the Saratoga spa, treatments for heart and circulatory disorders, rheumatic conditions, nervous disorders, metabolic diseases, and skin diseases were developed. In 1910, the New York state government began purchasing the principal springs to protect them from exploitation. When Franklin Delano Roosevelt was governor of New York, he pushed for a European type of spa development at Saratoga.

The architects for the new complex spent two years studying the technical aspects of bathing in Europe. Completed in 1933, the development had three bathhouses — Lincoln, Washington, and Roosevelt — a drinking hall, the Hall of Springs, and a building housing the Simon Baruch Research Institute. Four additional buildings composed the recreation area and housed arcades and a swimming pool decorated with blue faience terra-cotta tile.

Saratoga Spa State Park's Neoclassical buildings were laid out in a grand manner, with formal perpendicular axes, solid brick construction, and stone and concrete Roman-revival detailing. The spa was surrounded by a 1,200-acre (4.9 km) natural park that had 18 miles (29 km) of bridle paths, "with measured walks at scientifically calculated gradients through its groves and vales, with spouting springs adding unexpected touches to its vistas, with the tumbling waters of Geyser Brook flowing beneath bridges of the fine roads. Full advantage has been taken of the natural beauty of the park, but no formal landscaping". Promotional literature again advertised the attractions directly outside the spa: shopping, horse races, and historic sites associated with revolutionary war history. New York Governor Herbert Lehman opened the new facilities to the public in July 1935.

Other leading spas in the country during this period were French Lick, Indiana; Hot Springs and White Sulphur Springs, West Virginia; Hot Springs, Arkansas; and Warm Springs, Georgia. French Lick specialized in treating obesity and constipation through a combination of bathing and drinking the water and exercising. Hot Springs, Virginia, specialized in digestive ailments and heart diseases, and White Sulphur Springs, Virginia, treated these ailments and skin diseases. Both resorts offered baths where the water would wash continuously over the patients as they lay in a shallow pool. Warm Springs, Georgia, gained a reputation for treating infantile paralysis by a procedure of baths and exercise. President Franklin D. Roosevelt, who earlier supported Saratoga, became a frequent visitor and promoter of this spa.

Spa Treatment

A body treatment, spa treatment, or cosmetic treatment is non-medical procedure to help the health of the body. It is often performed at a resort, destination spa, day spa, beauty salon or school.

Typical treatments include:

- Aromatherapy
- Bathing or soaking in any of the following:
  - o Hot spring
    - * Onsen (Japanese Hot Springs)
    - * Thermae (Roman Hot Springs)
  - o Hot tub
  - o Mud bath
  - o Peat pulp bath
  - o Sauna
  - o Steam bath
- Body wraps, wrapping the body in hot linens, plastic sheets and blankets, or mud wraps, often in combination with herbal compounds.
- Facials, facial cleansing with a variety of products
- Massage
- Nail care such as manicures and pedicures

- Nutrition and weight guidance
- Personal training
- Skin exfoliation, including chemical peels and microdermabrasion
- Yoga and meditation
- Waxing, the removal of body hair with hot wax

Recent Trends

By the late 1930s more than 2,000 hot- or cold-springs health resorts were operating in the United States. This number had diminished greatly by the 1950s and continued to decline in the following two decades. In recent past, spas in the U.S. emphasized dietary, exercise, or recreational programs more than traditional bathing activities.

Up until recently, the public bathing industry in the U.S. remained stagnant. Nevertheless, in Europe, therapeutic baths have always been very popular, and remain so today. The same is true in Japan, where the traditional hot springs baths, known as *onsen,* always attracted plenty of visitors.

But also in the U.S., with the increasing focus on health and wellness, such treatments are again becoming popular.

Resort or Place of Treatment

- Day spa, a form of beauty salon.
- Destination spa, a resort for personal care treatments.
- Spa town, a town visited for the supposed healing properties of the water.

Medication or Equipment

- Foot spa
- Hot tub, in United States usage.
- Soda fountain, in United States usage.
- Spa (mineral water), from the sources in Spa.
- Spas usually offer mud baths for general health, or to address a variety of medical conditions. This is also known as 'fangotherapy'. A variety of medicinal clays and peats is used.

International Spa Association Definitions

Spa - places devoted to overall well-being through a variety of professional services that encourage the renewal of mind, body and spirit.

Types of Spa

- Ayurvedic spa, a spa in which all treatments and products are natural and it's often used as alternative medicine.
- Club spa, a facility whose primary purpose is fitness and which offers a variety of professionally administered spa services on a day-use basis.
- Cruise ship spa, a spa aboard a cruise ship providing professionally administered spa services, fitness and wellness components and spa cuisine menu choices.
- Day spa, a spa offering a variety of professionally administered spa services to clients on a day-use basis.
- Dental spa, a facility under the supervision of a licensed dentist that combines traditional dental treatment with the services of a spa.
- Destination spa, a facility with the primary purpose of guiding individual spa-goers to develop healthy habits. Historically a seven-day stay, this lifestyle transformation can be accomplished by providing a comprehensive program that includes spa services, physical fitness activities, wellness education, healthful cuisine and special interest programming.
- Garden spa, an outdoor spa used for bathing and self cleansing
- Medical spa, a facility that operates under the full-time, on-site supervision of a licensed health care professional whose primary purpose is to provide comprehensive medical and wellness care in an environment that integrates spa services, as well as traditional, complimentary and/or alternative therapies and treatments. The facility operates within the scope of practice of its staff, which can include both aesthetic/ cosmetic and prevention/wellness procedures and

services. These spas typically use balneotherapy, employing a variety of peloids.

"Balneotherapy treatments can have different purposes. In a spa setting, they can be used to treat conditions such as arthritis and backache, build up muscles after injury or illness or to stimulate the immune system, and they can be enjoyed as a relief from day-to-day stress."

- Mineral springs spa, a spa offering an on-site source of natural mineral, thermal or seawater used in hydrotherapy treatments.
- Resort/hotel spa, a spa owned by and located within a resort or hotel providing professionally administered spa services, fitness and wellness components and spa cuisine menu choices.
- Mobile spa, a spa which provides services at home, hotels, or wherever you are.

General Manager

General manager (sometimes abbreviated GM) is a descriptive term for certain executives in a business operation. It is also a formal title held by some business executives, most commonly in the hospitality industry.

Generic Usage

A manager may be responsible for one functional area, but the general manager is responsible for all areas. Sometimes, most commonly, the term *general manager* refers to any executive who has overall responsibility for managing both the revenue and cost elements of a company's income statement. This is often referred to as profit & loss (P&L) responsibility. This means that a general manager usually oversees most or all of the firm's marketing and sales functions as well as the day-to-day operations of the business. Frequently, the general manager is responsible for effective planning, delegating, coordinating, staffing, organizing, and decision making to attain desirable profit making results for an organization (Sayles 1979).

In many cases, the general manager of a business is given a different formal title or titles. Most corporate managers holding the titles of chief executive officer (CEO) or president, for example, are the general managers of their respective businesses. More rarely, the chief financial officer (CFO), chief operating officer (COO), or chief marketing officer (CMO) will act as the general manager of the business. Depending on the company, individuals with the title managing director, regional vice president, country manager, product manager, branch manager, or segment manager may also have general management responsibilities.

In consumer products companies, general managers are often given the title brand manager or category manager. In professional services firms, the general manager may hold titles such as managing partner, senior partner, or managing director.

In non-profit enterprises, the general manager is often given the title executive director.

Industry-specific Usages

Hotels

In hotels, the General Manager is the executive manager responsible for the overall operation of a hotel establishment. The General Manager holds ultimate authority over the hotel operation and usually reports directly to a corporate office or hotel owner. Common duties of a General Manager include hiring and management of a management team, overall management of hotel staff, budgeting and financial management, creating and enforcing business objectives and goals, managing projects and renovations, management of emergencies and other major issues involving guests, employees, or the facility, public relations with the media, local governments, and other businesses, and many additional duties. The extent of duties of a hotel General Manager vary significantly depending on the size of the hotel and company; for example, General Managers of smaller hotels may have additional duties such as accounting, human resources, payroll, purchasing, and other duties that would usually be handled by other managers or departments in a larger hotel.

Sports Teams

In most professional sports, the general manager is a team executive responsible for acquiring the rights to player personnel, negotiating their contracts, and reassigning or dismissing players no longer desired on the team. The general manager may also have responsibility for hiring the head coach of the team.

For many years in U.S. professional sports, coaches often served as general managers for their teams as well, deciding which players would be kept on the team and which ones dismissed, and even negotiating the terms of their contracts in cooperation with the ownership of the team. In fact, many sports teams in the early years of U.S. professional sports were coached by the owner of the team, so in some cases the same individual served as owner, general manager and head coach.

As the amount of money involved in professional sports increased, many prominent players began to hire agents to negotiate contracts on their behalf. The intensified contract negotiations that resulted, as well as the overall increased need for professional business management, drove many sports teams to separate the positions of coach and general manager. Some coaches, however, still insist on being allowed to fill both positions as a condition of employment.

In some sports leagues salary caps have been adopted to maintain a competitive balance and in these leagues it is one of the functions of the general manager to ensure all player contracts are in accordance with these caps, as well as consistent with the desires of the ownership and its ability to pay.

General managers are usually responsible for the selection of players in player drafts and work with the coaching staff and scouts to build a strong team. In sports with developmental or minor leagues, the general manager is usually the team executive with the overall responsibility for "sending down" and "calling up" players to and from these leagues, although the head coach may also have significant input into these decisions.

Some of the most successful sports general managers have been former players and coaches, while others have backgrounds in ownership and business management.

The term is not commonly used in Europe, especially in soccer, where the position of manager or coach is used instead to refer to the managing/coaching position. The position of director of football might be the most similar position on many European football clubs.

Homestay

Homestay is a form of tourism and/or study abroad program

that allows the visitor to rent a room from a local family to better learn the local lifestyle as well as improve their language ability. While homestays can occur in any destination worldwide, some countries do more to encourage homestay than others as a means of developing their tourism industry. Hosting a homestay participant also allows the local family to earn some additional, needed income. Having low profitability, as it is, homestay can not be regarded as strictly commercial activity, but more of cross cultural exchange. Students generally arrange a homestay with their school or educational institution, but can also informally arrange to stay with a family through social connections, and through a variety of private agencies. There are a number of online homestay agencies that connect students with hosts all over the world (usually for a nominal fee).

Types of Homestays

Homestay scenarios can range from a completely immersive family experience, to a very basic room rental.

In the immersive family experience a homestay student lives, eats, and shares the majority of their time in the host country with the hosts and their family. Family events such as dining out, amusement parks, camping, travel, etc. usually involve the host student who may or may not be expected to pay a portion for the participation (tickets, parking, gas, travel expenses, et al.) The student is invited to participate in Holiday festivities (Thanksgiving, Christmas, etc.) and family events (weddings, birthdays, etc.)

At the other end of the spectrum, students may simply be renting a room within a private home with minimal supervision from a host or family.

Additionally, there are a working homestay agreements where a student is expected to perform duties such as yard work, farm work, babysitting, maid services - usually in exchange for accommodation fees or as part of.

Besides homestays for students/ study abroad programmes they are an upcoming, unusual and interesting way of travel. Most property owners do this as a hobby simply because they enjoy hosting people. Homestays can be a very rewarding experience and leave you with memories that you would cherish forever.

People in several holiday destinations with large homes invite travellers to stay in their homes as their guests for the duration of their travel. What travellers can expect at a homestay is a comfortable homely stay, homemade food (definitely the best way to experience local cuisine), local culture (unlike typical hotel accommodations) while having your privacy as well.

Typical Contracts and Agreements

A clash of cultures can sometimes result between a homestay student and the host family. To mitigate any issues, most homestay arrangements involve a contract or written agreement between the host and student. A contract will outline what is expected of the homestay student and may include items such as;

- Chores to perform (cleaning, laundering)
- Curfews
- Use of the Internet, television
- Use of the telephone
- Guest visits
- Smoking/drinking rules

as well as the details of what is being provided by the host in terms of:

- Accommodations
- Furniture/facilities
- Meal provisions
- Transportation
- Communications (Internet, telephone)
- Entertainment (TV, radio)

Generally, a host must provide a private room for sleep and study that has a lock and a washroom must be available that is convenient for the student to use. Most other items are negotiable in terms of availability and price.

Risks for the Host

Typically, hosting a homestay student is a rich and rewarding experience that allows the sharing of cultures, information, and experience. However, studying abroad is often the first time the homestay student is away from the parents and home country. This may result in adjustment issues for the student. The host must be able to deal with separation issues, anxiety, and the like. Scams on the internet are becoming fairly commonplace - when engaging in financial transactions that may require international payments, cheques, and money orders being sent there is always the possibility of making oneself vulnerable to scams and fraud. The host family is best to educate themselves on the issues, and protect themselves adequately through the use of a good contract.

A recent and common example of a scam perpetrated on host families plays as follows;

- Parents of a student email the host family to request a room - usually claiming to be from Europe/Asia.
- The host replies with availability and costs etc.
- The parent agrees to the fees, and offers to pay the fees up front.
- Usually some sort of family crisis arises, and the transaction must be handled with urgency.
- The parent sends payment with an overage, and ask the host to refund the excess payment.
- The host family refunds the payment.
- The initial payment (cheque, money order, etc.) bounces or is fraudulent.
- The host family has lost the money it has sent as a refund.

This scam can happen in any situation any time payment is required in the form of cheque/money order/cashiers cheque, etc. In-depth discussion on frauds of this type is beyond the scope of this article, but the host family is encouraged to exercise caution when dealing with overseas payments and transactions.

Risks for the Student/guest

There are two basic motivations for a family to engage in the operation of a homestay:

1. The family is looking to assist students, inject culture, and better understand the world and its people through a mutual exchange of traditions, knowledge and culture.

2. The family is looking to augment their income.

Usually, a family bears a healthy mix of these two reasons in opening their home to students and international visitors.

Occasionally, however, there are instances where a family, or individual, is looking only to capitalize on the financial opportunity and has little or no concern for the interests of the student.

A student is encouraged to look at the history of students and guests that the family has hosted, and to ask for a reference from a student who has recently attended their homestay. If a family refuses to give a reference, a student is advised to stay away. Also, look for a contract that not only protects the interests of the homestay host, but also the interests of the student. There should be a clear listing of the obligations of both the student and host family.

3

Trends in the Hotel Property Industry

The hotel industry is facing some major challenges. In 2010, around 1 billion vacation travellers and an increasing number of business travellers will be in transit around the world. This prospect is resulting in the expansion of hotel services, particularly in tourist growth areas, and in heightened competition among hotels to gain customers. Hotel guests today travel around the world with a wealth of experience in their trunks. As a result, their expectations regarding service, comfort and environmental friendliness of hotels are also increasing.

A building's energy consumption is an important factor in its environmental friendliness. But this is not the only reason why hotel operators need to pay close attention to overall energy consumption. The increased cost of oil, gas and electricity around the world means that energy is becoming an increasingly significant expense for the hotel industry. As a result, hotel operators are finding themselves forced to cut their energy consumption, or to maintain it at a low level.

Savings from the Outset

A hotel's electrical fittings represent significant savings potential. Energy management systems and tools can be instrumental in cutting power costs, as can innovative building automation systems. However, the foundations for a cost-effective supply of electricity are laid right from the planning phase of a hotel, during the design of its electric distribution boards. It is at this point that decisions are taken as to the future power consumption of the electrical systems, and the components that will be required for these applications. Innovative software tools from Siemens support engineering consultants in calculating precise and therefore economically optimal dimensions. A design tailored to the hotel's specific requirements and a corresponding invitation to tender for the power distribution components are the key to keeping investment costs as low as possible in this area.

Focus on Energy Efficiency

Buildings account for around 40 % of current worldwide energy consumption. The European Union Directive 2002/91/EC of December 16, 2002 regarding the overall energy efficiency of buildings (effective as of January 4, 2003) was introduced in a bid to improve the energy efficiency of real estate. Some of the most important measures prescribed in the directive are the creation of energy certificates for buildings and the drawing up of minimum requirements for buildings. An energy certificate must be produced when buildings or parts of buildings are sold, leased, or rented.

This applies, for example, if a new hotel operator takes over the running of a hotel. The energy certificate contains clear information on a building's energy consumption, broken down into specific categories in a similar way to that in which energy information is displayed for large domestic appliances. In the case of buildings, the certificate contains information on the energy loss through the installations and the building shell, energy requirements per energy source, and CO_2 emissions.

Outside Europe, too, in the face of dwindling resources, rising energy prices, and goals of reducing carbon dioxide (CO2) emissions, many countries are placing more emphasis on the energy efficiency of buildings and are issuing country-specific regulations to this end. The "Green Building Council" in the United Arab Emirates, for example, stipulates that the energy consumption of buildings must be clearly indicated and that an energy consumption certificate must be provided for new buildings.

The Technology Platform: Totally Integrated Power

Totally Integrated Power™ (TIP) refers to integrated electrical power distribution in commercial and industrial buildings; from the medium voltage supply fed in by the utility company right up to the final electrical consumer.

Totally Integrated Power is underpinned by an array of helpful tools and support for accurate design, dimensioning and configuration of electrical power distribution within buildings. A coordinated product and systems portfolio for the construction of these systems is rounded off by standardized interfaces between the system components and the higher-level human-machine interface systems as well as for the connection to control and management systems.

In this way considerable savings can be made across the whole project cycle – from the planning stage, installation and start-up right through to operation – in both new buildings and renovations. The necessary investments in the hotel's electrical infrastructure can be optimized in line with demand and also with subsequent operating costs. This optimization potential represents significant added value for everyone involved in the project.

Optimum planning for cost- and time-effective solutions

An optimally dimensioned power distribution system is a key economic factor for hotels. Unused capacities cost money. The tried-and-tested TÜV-certified SIMARIS® design dimensioning software by Siemens provides electrical engineering consultants with an indispensable tool for planning the electrical network for a new or renovated hotel.

SIMARIS design brings many benefits, including simpler network calculation and selectivity verification. The software also recommends suitable coordinated devices from the integrated Siemens power distribution product portfolio. Electrical network upgrade reserves can be incorporated right from the planning stage to allow for later changes of use or hotel extensions.

Electrical engineering consultants can make time savings of up to 100 % by using SIMARIS design for the various network planning stages. Thereafter, SIMARIS configuration supports power distribution board manufacturers and installation contractors in the configuration of low-voltage power distribution boards. ALPHA SELECT, on the other hand, makes the selection of suitable distribution boards fast, safe and easy.

Simple Solutions for Complex Requirements

Hotels can be divided into three sectors, each with very specific requirements with regard to power supply.

General Guest Area

Whether in the reception area, the conference rooms, the spa area or the car park – in other words, all areas in which the hotel guests can move around without restriction during their stay – a reliable electricity supply that meets building conditions and regulations is required for the parts of the technical building equipment needed for evacuation and rescue in an emergency. Siemens offers an integrated and typetested system for reliable power distribution in this hotel sector. The individual components, such as SIVACON low-voltage power distribution board assemblies and busway systems, ALPHA distribution boards, and SENTRON and BETA protection devices, are optimally coordinated with each other – and satisfy the highest demands in terms of safe and cost-effective power distribution.

Personal Guest Area

About 30 % of a hotel's total energy demand is taken up by the guest rooms. Given the large surface area occupied by the personal guest sector in hotels, this represents a significant cost factor. With the right building automation and building management system, enormous savings can be made in this area – without sacrificing the guests' well-being in any way. Quite the reverse: the DESIGO™ INSIGHT building automation system fulfills the many and varied demands made of regulation, control and monitoring systems for heating, ventilation and air-conditioning facilities, room automation and other building services systems. The intelligent GAMMA building management system facilitates user-friendly lighting and shutter control in the hotel rooms. Whether in a modest single room or an upmarket suite, the individual room control and window monitoring system, combined with automatic shutter control, can bring about energy savings of up to 10 %.

Supply and Logistics Area

Logistics areas such as the reception and the reservation center, or supply areas such as the kitchen perform important functions in a hotel. Uninterrupted availability is absolutely essential in these areas. To guarantee operation even in the case of mains power failure, an uninterruptible power supply is necessary side by side with the normal power supply and the safety power supply required by building regulations. What is important here is that these processes internal to the hotel must be incorporated into the overall power distribution concept. The proven SIMARIS design dimensioning tool supports electrical engineering consultants in carrying out this task quickly and accurately.

Basic Network Operation Types

Normal Power Supply

For the areas of the hotel on the normal power supply, Siemens offers complete electrotechnical solutions with optimally coordinated products and systems: these range from the utility company's transfer point (generally a medium-voltage supply) right down to the consumer, light and power outlet circuits. This end-toend integration ensures optimum supply security and thereby reliable hotel operation. Optimum coordination of the individual system components also means an extremely cost-efficient solution. The normal power supply is tailored to the hotel's electrical equipment and configured in such a way that all electrical consumers have a reliable power source around the clock. This affects, for instance, the availability of electrical energy for the air-conditioning system around lunchtime and in the afternoon, particularly in holiday hotels.

Safety Power Supply (SPS)

If the normal supply fails due to external circumstances, the hotel's emergency power supply must be designed in such a way that operation is ensured without any interruptions. Technical problems should not affect the guests.

In line with a hotel's specific requirements, the design of the emergency power supply ensures that – where necessary – an uninterrupted power supply is also available via batteries and an emergency generator, for instance for the emergency lighting of escape and emergency routes, the PA system or for the reservation systems. In this way, a mains failure will have relatively little impact, and the hotel can continue to operate almost as normal.

Normal Supply and Emergency Generator

- The normal power supply system is fed in from the medium-voltage grid (20 kV) via distribution transformers.
- With the emergency generator, the choice of power sources is made on the basis of the admissible interruption time:
- Emergency generators for safety power supply (SPS) u Uninterruptible power supply (UPS) as static UPS, consisting of a rectifier and inverter unit and a battery

Power Distribution Design within the Hotel

With an integrated planning, instead of breaking down the hotel's requirements into the various installations and considering them separately, they are coordinated. Only when requirements are networked can an optimized solution be found. The electrical network structure is established on the basis of what the power is needed for. It is important to place the power sources as close as possible to the consumers, in order to avoid transmission losses.

To comply with the installation contractor's specifications and the building's use as well safety and comfort standards, the available electrical power must be divided between the normal power supply and the safety power supply. In order to achieve a high level of efficiency, the system components should work at approx. 70 %–80 % of their maximum capacity: undersizing often leads to malfunctions, oversizing to excessive costs. If redundancy is required, an additional reserve must be included in the design.

Safety Power Supply Design

Considerable demands are placed on the emergency power supply and its distribution network, such as continued functionality in the event of a fi re and a selective protection concept that ensures that only the network section affected by a fault is switched off. The safety power supply is provided via the emergency generator. The system parts that are always eligible for safety power are those that support or safeguard the required evacuation measures in the event of an emergency.

Here supply times of at least 30 to 90 minutes are generally necessary. Small consumers in these system parts are supplied by SPS sub-distribution boards, which in turn are supplied by fi reproof cable routes (red lines). Consumers that are typically connected include safety and emergency-exit lights. In addition, system parts of the building facilities that carry out safety functions are also allocated to the safety power supply. These consumers or their sub-distribution boards are also supplied with functional endurance via cables and wires (red lines).

Advantages in the event of an emergency: longer supply times together with lower fi re and smoke loads increase operational safety and reduce risks during evacuation.

Normal Power Supply Design

Consumers and/or distribution boards that are not connected to the safety power supply are powered from the normal power supply via transformers. Certain consumers powered by the normal power supply are often also assigned to the backup power supply due to operational requirements (e.g. heating/ air-conditioning, kitchens, administration). Here it is important that where the safety and backup supply systems are powered by a single generator, the safety power supply has absolute priority, something that must be assured through such measures as load shedding. A safer and more flexible option is to isolate these consumers from the safety power supply by providing energy via an additional safety generator. It is not necessary for such units to meet the same safety standards as for the safety power supply. The power supply to the guest rooms is provided via small distribution boards, which are supplied using radial cables via a centralized main distribution board for the normal power supply. The overall figures for the energy required, together with the distribution and structuring with regard to the different power sources, provide the basis for dimensioning the individual network components.

Fire Safety and Security Services

Hotels don't highlight fire safety like they do dining facilities and similar features. Apparently, this is out of concern that references to fire safety will accentuate the negative - the possibility of a fire. But fire safety is a bona fide concern. For one thing, individual travellers have concerns about their fire safety.

For another, people who arrange travel and meetings for employees or organizations may take on a liability if they neglect to confirm the level of fire safety equipment. This page attempts to address those needs. An overview of hotel fire safety.

The amount and type of fire safety equipment in a hotel varies by the size of the building, its height and age. Many high-rise hotels are protected with fire sprinklers, but one out of four still lack them. For all hotels and motels regardless of height, only 50 percent have fire sprinklers. Some hotel owners have corporate policies to retrofit older properties with fire sprinklers, but this is not the norm. And some hotels install state-of-the-art, well-maintained fire alarm systems that render false alarm problems nil, but other owners continue to tolerate the problem. As a result, many hotel guests ignore fire alarms.

The quality of fire protection also varies by region. In some areas, building and fire officials keep their safety codes current and diligently enforce them. But code advancement and enforcement are not uniform around the U. S. If these codes are not kept up to date and enforced by competent personnel, the quality of fire safety can suffer a great deal.

Fire Alarm System Required For Hotels/Motels

New hotels are more likely to have what we consider high-quality fire protection, that is, fire sprinklers in every guest room as well as detection and alarm systems. Older hotels may only have smoke alarms in guest rooms, if they have that.

Some fire safety equipment is obvious, even to people who are not trained in fire safety. Examples are fire sprinklers and smoke alarms. Other items may not be obvious because laymen do not associate them with fire safety. An example is passive protection like a solid-bonded 3-hinged corridor door with UL-listed hardware. Its role in fire safety is discussed below in the section on egress systems.

The components of a hotel fire safety system include the following items:

- Fire sprinklers.
- Smoke and fire detectors.
- Duct Smoke Detectors
- Automatic alarm systems.

- Connection between Air handling units and alarm systems
- Manual alarm systems (the pull-boxes you see near stairway doors and elevators).
- Fire department standpipes (the things that you see in stairways).
- Emergency lights.
- The emergency egress system.
- Fire Resistivity of Construction
- Exits & Exit signs.
- Pressurized stairways.
- Smoke control systems
- Portable fire extinguishers.
- Staff emergency response plans.
- Staff training.
- Gas Supply Shut-off Devices
- Fire Alarm System Required Hotels/Motels
- High Rise Buildings
- Place for a Helicopter to Land

Each of these items is described in a section below. You can get to a specific item by clicking on the hyperlinks at the top of the page, or you can scroll through the entire page. The description includes a discussion of each item's role and lists the questions that one should ask when inquiring about that item's presence and readiness.

All of the items discussed here are designed to work as part of an overall fire protection "system." This is important to remember because if one part of the system fails it increases the likelihood of other failures. Something as simple as a propped open stairway door can cause failure of the stairway pressurization, smoke control and emergency egress systems. Therefore, the hotel staff must be diligent in maintaining every fire protection device, and nothing can be overlooked because of the erroneous assumption that another safety device will compensate for it. But experience tells us that problems like this occur, and that is why we consider fire sprinklers as fundamental to hotel fire safety. They stop fires when they are small and reduce the dependence upon the other fire safety features.

What we don't cover here

This page does not contain guest instructions for response to fires. As a rule, hotels routinely provide this information, either in the security section of the hotel information left in each guest room or posted on guestroom doors. Our purpose is to inform you about the items that will keep a fire from becoming a threat in the first place. If they are effective, the need for emergency evacuation is unlikely

TIM

No, Tim isn't a code word that will get you a special deal on a room. It is an acronym for three important items: Testing, Inspection and Maintenance. Fire safety equipment that is present may be of no use if it is not regularly tested, inspected and maintained by qualified technicians. There are nationally recognized standards that dictate how often TIM should occur for sprinklers and other fire safety equipment. Hotels with high-quality fire protection will have records of TIM.

Fire investigations abound with reports of equipment that did not operate or was improperly adjusted, and that is why we refer to TIM throughout. Travellers may be fortunate enough to stay in a brand new hotel from time to time, but this is the exception to the rule. We are more likely to stay in buildings that are several generations old, with fire safety equipment that is as old as the building. The importance of TIM cannot be understated, and any hotel that does not adequately document TIM is neglecting its fire safety responsibilities.

What is a fire-safe hotel?

Fire safety is a relative term. If you define "fire-safe" as a zero chance of a fire, then one can never say that any hotel is fire-safe. However, we can describe hotels as relatively safer than others based on the fire protection equipment that is installed and the safety practices that they follow.

Fire Sprinklers

Fire sprinklers are fundamental to hotel fire safety. You must stay on a fully sprinklered hotel for your safety. We have a basic criterion for hotel fire safety - a fire sprinkler system with sprinklers in every room, installed in compliance with nationally recognized standards and then maintained by qualified technicians. Sprinklers are designed to stop a fire when it is small, and they have a superior track record in saving lives and property. In the U. S., the frequency of hotel fires is relatively low. But even though it is a low-probability event, it is a high-consequence event. Fires in residential settings can grow with amazing speed. In fact, most people drastically underestimate how quickly they can become deadly.

How fast can they grow? Fire tests confirm that a small fire in an average-sized room can ignite everything in the room in less than five minutes. The combustion products from that fire will start killing people in as little as two minutes. The fire investigation report for the Dupont Plaza Hotel fire that occurred in 1986 noted that 97 people died in a mere 12 minutes.

Another factor that increases the consequences of hotel fires is that hotels contain large numbers of people who are unfamiliar with the building and may be sleeping when a fire occurs. The history of hotel fires bears out the consequences of these factors.

You might be wondering how fast residential-type sprinklers work. In the same tests noted above, the sprinklers operated in just under one minute and stopped the fire long before the combustion products could reach lethal levels. Happily, hotels with fire sprinklers installed throughout are now routinely available, so we feel that sprinklers are a reasonable expectation. Many hotel and motel chains in the U. S. install them in all of their new buildings, and some have corporate policies to install them in all of their existing properties as well.

The Value of Fire Sprinklers

If a fire can be stopped before it grows, it cannot develop a lot of smoke, which is the biggest killer in fires. Smoke alarms are great and we look for them as well as sprinklers. But smoke alarms can only alert people to a fire, and fires can grow so quickly that they can kill before people can escape. A sprinkler will not only alert people to the fire (when a sprinkler opens, the water flowing through the system triggers an alarm), but it also opens very quickly and stops the fire. A fire that is quickly stopped cannot produce smoke and the carbon monoxide it carries.

Fire sprinklers are designed to operate when a fire is small and stop it before it grows to a stage known as flashover. At the flashover stage, the fire travels from the room of origin with a large burst of energy, pushing great amounts of heat and smoke to the rest of the building. Sprinklers are spaced so that they can stop a fire with a relatively small amount of water. In nearly all cases only one sprinkler opens. If you thought that all of the sprinklers in the room or building go off at the same time, you have been victimized by Hollywood gag writers looking for comic effect. Travellers need to be aware that some hotels have installed sprinklers in "common areas," such as corridors, restaurants, lobbies, etc., but not in the guest rooms. If a hotel does not have sprinklers in every room then it does not meet our criteria for hotel fire safety.

The reason for this is simple. If sprinklers are not installed in every room, a fire can grow to deadly proportions before the sprinklers outside the room stop its progress. A sprinkler located outside a burning room cannot stop the smoke that is being produced in the room, and this is a bigger threat to people than the flames.

Smoke Detection and Alarms

A system of interconnected smoke detectors should be installed, with units in every room including common areas and all non-guest rooms. If they are installed in compliance with nationally recognized standards, the alarm system will alert guests who are at risk. It is also important that the alarm system be monitored off-site by a qualified organization. An example is a Central Station Alarm company that has an Underwriters Laboratories certificate. Some alarm systems are connected directly to the fire department, which is even better.

When inquiring about the company that monitors the fire alarm system, ask for documentation that the company has standing orders to call the fire department without delay. There are instances where hotels have advised the alarm company to call the hotel so an employee can check for an actual fire before notifying the fire department. This is unacceptable and can lead to tragedy. Do not accept verbal statements about the specific policy between the hotel and alarm company. Any quality fire alarm company will have this in writing, so the documentation should be readily available.

In large hotels, the building codes now require a Fire Department Control Station. This is a protected area where the fire alarm panel is located. The fire officer in charge will use it to monitor all of the building controls and can manually operate some equipment, such as smoke control devices. The control station also has a communication system so the officer can send voice instructions throughout the hotel. Hotels may not have this item as part of the alarm system if they were built prior to the requirements being placed in the building code.

Equally important is documentation on TIM. Modern fire alarm systems can be very complex, especially in high-rise buildings. They need regular attention by qualified technicians.

Duct Smoke Detectors

All air handling duct system must be equipped with duct type some alarms.

Connection between Air handling units and alarm systems All the air handling units must be programmed due to fire alarm. They must be stopped whenever a fire alarm actuates. All the duct systems must include fire stopping dampers. Standpipes.

When you enter a hotel stairway and see a large pipe with a hose connection on it at each floor, you are looking at a fire department standpipe. They are installed in hotels, at least those higher than three stories, so that the firefighters can hook up their hose near the fire. This reduces the amount of hose that they need to carry up the stairs, which reduces the time it takes to set up and attack the fire.

TIM for standpipes is very important for two reasons. First, some of them are "dry," that is, there is no water in them. To get water to higher floors, the fire department hooks up its hoses to the standpipe connection on the outside of the building and pumps water into it. Dry standpipes can be clogged by debris placed there by vandals, so regular testing, inspection and maintenance is the only way to make sure that they will work as designed in a fire. "Wet" standpipes, those that have water present, are less prone to vandalism because the miscreant would get doused with water and set off an alarm.

The second reason primarily applies to to high-rise hotels. Standpipes in these buildings are connected to a fire pump that will start if water flow is detected in the standpipe or sprinkler system. The pumps must be powerful enough to supply adequate pressure at the highest floor, but this means that the pressure on the lower floors may be higher than firefighters can safely handle. To get an idea of the pressure, think about how your garden hose creates a pressure that pushes you backwards, then multiple that pressure by magnitudes.

When the pressure at an outlet is too high for safe use, a pressure-limiting valve will be installed at the outlet. These devices need to be regularly checked to make sure they are set at the correct pressure. If the setting is too high or too low for an effective fire stream, then the firefighters can be seriously delayed in attacking the fire.

Emergency Lighting

A fire may cause the building's electrical system to fail. Sometimes the fire originates in the electrical system. For this reason, the building should have emergency lights installed in all corridors and public rooms. Emergency lighting that complies with nationally recognized standards will be connected to a separate power supply that is backed up by an emergency generator. The lights will automatically go on when the system detects an electrical failure. Check for TIM.

Emergency Egress System

Every building should be built in compliance with a nationally recognized building code. These codes contain minimum standards for the emergency egress system, i.e., the pathways that provide evacuation routes from every part of the building to the outdoors at ground level. The building codes are based on the principle that the corridors and stairways are a vital part of the egress system, so they are required to have added protection that will theoretically last long enough to allow everyone to evacuate.

Have you ever noticed the metal labels on the edge of corridor doors and the doorways? They are there to document that the items comply with the additional protection requirements for egress paths. That is also why stairways are so spartan, with no decoration or carpeting. Because stairways are such a critical part of the egress path, they have stringent requirements that do not allow any combustible material at all - thus the lack of carpeting or even linoleum. And storage of anything, be it combustible or not, is forbidden in stairways. If you see these rules violated, it means that the hotel is not vigilant or is neglecting its fire safety responsibilities.

Along with the doors, the walls and ceilings of the egress paths are part of the added protection. These items combine to be the "compartmentation," the passive system of barriers that slows down the progress of a fire and smoke. That is why all doors should have self-closers, even the guest room doors.

Door wedges are a no-no. Doors that are propped open or ones that do not shut automatically and latch tightly are signs that the hotel is neglecting its fire safety responsibility. In large hotels, you may find doors across the corridor that divide the building into smaller fire compartments. These doors can be held open by approved devices. The devices are usually magnets that automatically release if the fire alarm panel activates.

We mention walls and ceilings because holes in walls or missing ceiling tiles defeat the required compartmentation. Any coverings on walls and ceilings should be limited to materials that will not contribute to the rapid spread of flames or development of a lot of smoke. When inspecting a hotel, visit all of the service areas as well. It is easier for the staff to neglect a hole or missing tile in areas were guests don't go. These are basic items, and their importance to the fire safety system is often overlooked (or worse, not understood). They should have records of TIM.

Exits &Exit Signs

Exit signs that comply with nationally recognized standards will be visible from any place in the corridor. Those that are not near an exit door will have an arrow showing the direction to the nearest exit. Again, TIM is important. It is very easy for exit lights to burn out over time, and just as easy to neglect replacing them. If the signs are being tested, inspected and maintained by qualified technicians, you have better assurance that they are accurate. A hotel employee may be tempted to replace a broken sign with one that has no direction arrow - or just as bad, with an arrow going the wrong way. They might make this mistake because they don't know what the installation standard requires. That is why we repeat the reminder that only qualified technicians should work on any fire safety system

Meeting Rooms

A general rule to keep in mind is that street-level meeting rooms are the easiest to evacuate. Rooms above the seventh floor are more hazardous because fire ladders may not reach that high. Hotel basement meeting rooms may not be a wise choice, because meeting participants must climb up stairs in the same direction smoke and flames will travel.

The meeting room should have adequate exits. A rule of thumb is that 50 to 300 persons require two exits. Three hundred to 1,000 need three exits and more than 1,000 persons should have four or more exits. The exits should be brightly lit, not blocked,by furniture or curtains and be easily opened. They should never be locked or chained. Seating or exhibit arrangements should allow enough aisle space for quick evacuation. You should familiarize yourself with exits and escape routes. Not only make sure that the hotel floor plan is visibly posted, but also walk the entire escape route. Hallways, exits and stairwells should be clear of obstructions. Stairs should have emergency lighting; elevators should be clearly marked to prevent use in a fire.

Stairway Pressurization

Hi-rise hotels should have pressurized stairways. An exception is a hotel where the stairways are open to the outside. In pressurized stairways, a fan operates when the fire alarm panel receives a signal from a fire detector or sprinkler. The air is blown in from the exterior, and this creates a positive pressure in the stairway, keeping smoke from creeping into the stairway and blocking the egress path. Ask about TIM. It is easy for these systems to go out of balance over time.

Smoke Control Systems

Very large buildings will have systems that automatically pressurize certain areas and depressurize others to contain smoke or exhaust it outside. This should definitely be present in buildings with atriums (where the rooms surround an open courtyard). Remember TIM.

Portable Fire Extinguishers

Portable extinguishers are designed to control or extinguish small fires. They are placed throughout a hotel to be readily available when someone finds a fire. Installers follow a nationally recognized standard that dictates what type (based on the type of fire expected at that location), their location, and size. Different locations will require different types, depending upon the type of fire expected. For example, the corridors will have units for extinguishing paper and other similar combustibles. A kitchen area will have units designed to put out grease fires.

Notice that the extinguishers are placed in wall cabinets or are hung on the wall at a height that makes it easy for an average-sized person to remove. If they are found on the floor, then they are not in the proper location. One reason for hanging them is to prevent items from being placed on top of them.

It is easy to use portable extinguishers. The instructions use icons to make them clear to someone who has not used one before. However, hotel employees should receive periodic hands-on training on how to use them. Extinguishers are more effective in the hands of experienced users, and periodic training increases expertise. But there is another reason why employees should be trained. The experience also teaches employees the limits of the extinguisher. Knowing when to use it and when to call the fire department without delay is a valuable lesson that all hotels should be teaching to every employee.

Have you ever noticed the paper tags hanging on each extinguisher? They indicate when the unit had its last TIM. The hotel should have a record of the periodic visits by an extinguisher technician, while the individual tags document when the last TIM was conducted. If it was over a year ago, then the hotel is not keeping up on its TIM responsibilities.

Fire Response Plan

A hotel with quality fire safety will have a written plan that describes every employee's responsibility in a fire or other emergency. The lack of a written plan or a refusal to show it are a cause for concern. Also be concerned if the instructions call for delaying the notification of guests or the fire department. Examples are orders to notify the manager before taking action, or orders to first investigate a fire alarm before calling the fire department or notifying guests.

Premature notification of guests due to false or nuisance alarms always concerns hotel management because they don't want to inconvenience guests. There are two things to consider here. First, if the hotel has replaced outmoded technology, and the fire alarm system was installed in compliance with nationally recognized standards (and TIM'd), false or nuisance alarms are rare. Modern smoke detectors are smart enough to quietly notify the monitoring company if they need servicing or are becoming too sensitive. That is why we stress the importance of TIM. There is no valid reason for a hotel to tolerate false or nuisance alarms.

Second, modern alarm systems have voice notification features that allow hotel employees to alert only those guests who are in immediate danger. For example, if a smoke detector on the 15th floor operates, the employee might be instructed to:

Notify the guests on the 14th, 15th and 16th floors to evacuate.

Alert guests on higher floors to prepare for an order to evacuate.

The specific evacuation message will vary by the type, size and layout of the building

Staff Training

Every employee should receive periodic formal training and practice on what to do in a fire emergency. A hotel with quality fire protection will have copies of their training plans and records of who attended each session. A verbal statement that "we give everyone regular training" should be suspect. The items covered in the plans should include such things as:

Each employee's responsibilities in a fire emergency.

Details about the building's fire equipment.

What the various fire alarm signals mean.

Who is responsible for notifying the fire department (this should always be done as a backup measure, even when the system is monitored). The records should document the orientation and continued training of every employee, including hands-on instruction on how to operate portable extinguishers

Place for a Helicopter to Land

Although there are building codes in some states, requiring new high-rise buildings to include a heli-pad, many of the older skyscrapers have a "forest" of antennas and other equipment on the roof.

In Conclusion

If you have read all of the above and concluded that a hotel's fire safety system is a complex set of critical items that are all interrelated, then we did an effective job. You will also appreciate the importance of testing, inspection and maintenance by qualified technicians, because the failure of one part of the system can effect the ability of the other parts to work effectively. As we said earlier, when a fire occurs it is too late to find the problems.

This brings us back to the very first item we talked about - fire sprinklers. We already mentioned their excellent track record for saving lives and property. In addition, studies show that they are the most reliable part of a building's fire safety system. This makes them extra insurance against the failure of another part of a hotel's fire safety system. It is for these reasons that we make sprinklers the fundamental criterion for a quality hotel fire safety system.

4

Fix Hotel Property

Fixed assets management is an accounting process that seeks to track fixed assets for the purposes of financial accounting, preventive maintenance, and theft deterrence.

Many organizations face a significant challenge to track the location, quantity, condition, maintenance and depreciation status of their fixed assets. A popular approach to tracking fixed assets utilizes serial numbered Asset Tags, often with bar codes for easy and accurate reading. Periodically, the owner of the assets can take inventory with a mobile barcode reader and then produce a report.

Off-the-shelf software packages for fixed asset management are marketed to businesses small and large. Some Enterprise Resource Planning systems are available with fixed assets modules.

Some tracking methods automate the process, such as by using fixed scanners to read bar codes on railway freight cars or by attaching a radio-frequency identification (RFID) tag to an asset.

Fixed Asset Tracking Software

Tracking assets is an important concern of every company, regardless of size. Fixed assets are defined as any 'permanent' object that a business uses internally including but not limited to computers, tools, software, or office equipment.

While employees may utilize a specific tool or tools, the asset ultimately belongs to the company and must be returned. And therefore without an accurate method of keeping track of these assets it would be very easy for a company to lose control of them.

With advancements in technology, asset tracking software is now available that will help any size business track valuable assets such as equipment and supplies. According to a study issued in December, 2005 by the ARC Advisory Group, the worldwide market for Enterprise Asset Management (EAM) was then at an estimated $2.2 billion and was expected to grow at about 5.0 percent per year reaching $2.8 billion in 2010.

Asset tracking software allows companies to track what assets it owns, where each is located, who has it, when it was checked out, when it is due for return, when it is scheduled for maintenance, and the cost and depreciation of each asset.

The reporting option that is built into most asset tracking solutions provides pre-built reports, including assets by category and department, check-in/check-out, net book value of assets, assets past due, audit history, and transactions.

All of this information is captured in one program and can be used on PCs as well as mobile devices. As a result, companies reduce expenses through loss prevention and improved equipment maintenance. They reduce new and unnecessary equipment purchases, and they can more accurately calculate taxes based on depreciation schedules.

The most commonly tracked assets are:

- Plant and equipment
- Buildings
- Fixtures and fittings.

Intangible Assets

Intangible assets are defined as identifiable non-monetary assets that cannot be seen, touched or physically measured, which are created through time and/or effort and that are identifiable as a separate asset. There are two primary forms of intangibles-legal intangibles (such as trade secrets (e.g., customer lists), copyrights, patents, and trademarks) and competitive intangibles (such as knowledge activities (know-how, knowledge), collaboration activities, leverage activities, and structural activities). Legal intangibles are known under the generic term intellectual property and generate legal property rights defensible in a court of law. Competitive intangibles, whilst legally non-ownable, directly impact effectiveness, productivity, wastage, and opportunity costs within an organization-and therefore costs, revenues, customer service, satisfaction, market value, and share price. Human capital is the primary source of competitive intangibles for organizations today. Competitive intangibles are the source from which competitive advantage flows, or is destroyed. The area of finance that deals with intangible assets is known as Intangible Asset Finance. The Uniform Commercial Code (Section 9-102(a)(42)) defines "general intangibles" as;

> *"any personal property...other than accounts, chattel paper, commercial tort claims, deposit accounts, documents, goods, instruments, investment property, letter of credit rights, letters of credit, money, and oil, gas, or other minerals before extraction. The term includes payment intangibles and software."*

Intangible assets lack of physical substance and usually are very hard to evaluate. They include patents, copyrights, franchises, goodwill, trademarks, trade names, etc. These assets are (according to US GAAP) amortized to expense over 5 to 40 years with the exception of goodwill. Websites are treated differently in different countries and may fall under either tangible or intangible assets.

Tangible Assets

Tangible assets are those that have a physical substance and can be touched, such as currencies, buildings, real estate, vehicles, inventories, equipment, and precious metals.

Other Related Meanings

Information Asset

In Information technology, chiefly in Information security, data needed to conduct the organization business and the technical equipment to manage (input, store, display, print) are called information asset. They can represent a large portion of intangible and tangible asset of an organization.

If these assets become unavailable, business operations can be disrupted. Confidential information disclosure can represent a huge liability.

While evaluating the potential loss tied to an asset or a group of assets, the value tied to the largest sum between the related asset and their value should be considered.

Property

Property is any physical or intangible entity that is owned by a person or jointly by a group of people. Depending on the nature of the property, an owner of property has the right to consume, sell, rent, mortgage, transfer, exchange or destroy it, or to exclude others from doing these things. Important widely recognized types of property include real property (the combination of land and any improvements to or on the land), personal property (physical possessions belonging to a person), private property (property owned by legal persons or business entities), public property (state owned or publicly owned and available possessions) and intellectual property (exclusive rights over artistic creations, inventions, etc.), although the latter is not always as widely recognized or enforced. A title, or a right of ownership, establishes the relation between the property and other persons, assuring the owner the right to dispose of the property as the owner sees fit. Some philosophers assert that property rights arise from social convention. Others find origins for them in morality or natural law.

Use of the Term

Various scholarly disciplines (such as law, economics, anthropology or sociology) may treat the concept more systematically, but definitions vary within and between fields. Scholars in the social sciences frequently conceive of property as a bundle of rights. They stress that property is not a relationship between people and things, but a relationship between people *with regard to* things. Property is usually thought of as being defined and protected by the local sovereignty. Ownership, however, does not necessarily equate with sovereignty. If ownership gave supreme authority, it would be sovereignty, not ownership. These are two different concepts.

Public property is any property that is controlled by a state or by a whole community. *Private property* is any property that is not public property. Private property may be under the control of a single person or by a group of persons jointly.

General Characteristics

Modern property rights are based on conceptions of owners and possession as belonging to legal persons, even if the legal person is not a natural person. In most countries, corporations, for example, have legal rights similar to those of citizens. Therefore, the corporation is a juristic person or artificial legal entity, under a concept that some refer to as "corporate personhood".

Traditional principles of property rights include:

1. control of the use of the property
2. the right to any benefit from the property (examples: mining rights and rent)
3. a right to transfer or sell the property
4. a right to exclude others from the property.

Traditional property rights do not include:

1. uses that unreasonably interfere with the property rights of another private party (the right of quiet enjoyment)
2. uses that unreasonably interfere with public property rights, including uses that interfere with public health, safety, peace or convenience.

Not every person or entity with an interest in a given piece of property may be able to exercise all possible property rights. For example, as a lessee of a particular piece of property, you may not sell the property, because a tenant is only in possession and does not have title to transfer. Similarly, while you are a lessee, the owner cannot use their right to exclude to keep you from the property, or, if they do, you may be entitled to stop paying rent or sue for access.

Further, property may be held in a number of forms, such as through joint ownership, community property, sole ownership or lease. These different types of ownership may complicate an owner's ability to exercise property rights unilaterally. For example, if two people own a single piece of land as joint tenants then, depending on the law in the jurisdiction, each may have limited recourse for the actions of the other. For example, one of the owners might sell their interest in the property to a stranger whom the other owner does not particularly like.

Legal systems have evolved to cover transactions and disputes that arise over the possession, use, transfer, and disposal of property, most particularly involving contracts. Positive law defines such rights, and the judiciary is used to adjudicate and to enforce property rights.

According to Adam Smith, the expectation of profit from "improving one's stock of capital" rests on private property rights. It is an assumption central to capitalism that property rights encourage their holders to develop the property, generate wealth, and efficiently allocate resources based on the operation of markets. From this has evolved the modern conception of property as a right enforced by positive law, in the expectation that this will produce more wealth and better standards of living.

In his text *The Common Law*, Oliver Wendell Holmes describes property as having two fundamental aspects. The first is possession, which can be defined as control over a resource based on the practical inability of another to contradict the ends of the possessor. The second is title, which is the expectation that others will recognize rights to control resource, even when it is not in possession. He elaborates the differences between these two concepts, and proposes a history of how they came to be attached to persons, as opposed to families or entities such as the church.

Classical Liberals, Objectivists, and Related Traditions

Most thinkers from these traditions subscribe to the labor theory of property. They hold that you own your own life, and it follows that you must own the products of that life, and that those products can be traded in free exchange with others.

> *"Every man has a property in his own person. This nobody has a right to, but himself." (John Locke, Second Treatise on Civil Government)*
>
> *"The reason why men enter into society is the preservation of their property." (John Locke, Second Treatise on Civil Government)*
>
> *"Life, liberty, and property do not exist because men have made laws. On the contrary, it was the fact that life, liberty, and property existed beforehand that caused*

men to make laws in the first place." (*Frédéric Bastiat, The Law*)

- Socialism's fundamental principles are centered on a critique of this concept, stating, among other things, that the cost of defending property is higher than the returns from private property ownership, and that, even when property rights encourage their holders to develop their property or generate wealth, they do so only for their own benefit, which may not coincide with benefit to other people or to society at large.
- Libertarian socialism generally accepts property rights, but with a short abandonment period. In other words, a person must make (more or less) continuous use of the item or else lose ownership rights. This is usually referred to as "possession property" or "usufruct". Thus, in this usufruct system, absentee ownership is illegitimate and workers own the machines or other equipment that they work with.
- Communism argues that only collective ownership of the means of production through a polity (though not necessarily a state) will assure the minimization of unequal or unjust outcomes and the maximization of benefits, and that therefore private ownership of capital should be abolished.

Both communism and some kinds of socialism have also upheld the notion that private ownership of capital is inherently illegitimate. This argument centers mainly on the idea that private ownership of capital always benefits one class over another, giving rise to domination through the use of this privately owned capital. Communists are not opposed to personal property that is "hard-won, self-acquired, self-earned" (Communist Manifesto) by members of the proletariat. Both socialism and communism are careful to make the distinction between private ownership of capital (land, factories, resources, etc...) and private property (homes, material objects, and so forth).

Theories of Property

There exist many theories. One is the relatively rare first possession theory of property, where ownership of something is seen as justified simply by someone seizing something before someone else does. Perhaps one of the most popular, is the natural rights definition of property rights as advanced by John Locke. Locke advanced the theory that when one mixes one's labor with nature, one gains a relationship with that part of nature with which the labor is mixed, subject to the limitation that there should be "enough, and as good, left in common for others."

From the Rerum Novarum, Pope Leo XIII wrote "It is surely undeniable that, when a man engages in remunerative labor, the impelling reason and motive of his work is to obtain property, and thereafter to hold it as his very own."

Anthropology studies the diverse systems of ownership, rights of use and transfer, and possession under the term "theories of property." Western legal theory is based, as mentioned, on the owner of property being a legal person. However, not all property systems are founded on this basis.

In every culture studied ownership and possession are the subject of custom and regulation, and "law" where the term can meaningfully be applied. Many tribal cultures balance individual ownership with the laws of collective groups: tribes, families, associations and nations. For example the 1839 Cherokee Constitution frames the issue in these terms: The lands of the Cherokee Nation shall remain common property; but the improvements made thereon, and in the possession of the citizens respectively who made, or may rightfully be in possession of them: Provided, that the citizens of the Nation possessing exclusive and indefeasible right to their improvements, as expressed in this article, shall possess no right or power to dispose of their improvements, in any manner whatever, to the United States, individual States, or to individual citizens thereof; and that, whenever any citizen shall remove with his effects out of the limits of this Nation, and become a citizen of any other government, all his rights and privileges as a citizen of this Nation shall cease: Provided, nevertheless, That the National Council shall have power to re-admit, by law, to all the rights of citizenship, any such person or persons who may, at any time, desire to return to the Nation, on memorializing the National Council for such readmission.

Communal property systems describe ownership as belonging to the entire social and political unit. Such arrangements can under certain conditions erode to open access resources. This development has been critiqued by the tragedy of the commons.

Corporate systems describe ownership as being attached to an identifiable group with an identifiable responsible individual. The Roman property law was based on such a corporate system.

Different societies may have different theories of property for differing types of ownership. Pauline Peters argued that property systems are not isolable from the social fabric, and notions of property may not be stated as such, but instead may be framed in negative terms: for example the taboo system among Polynesian peoples.

Property in Philosophy

In medieval and Renaissance Europe the term "property" essentially referred to land. Much rethinking has come to be regarded as only a special case of the property genus. This rethinking was inspired by at least three broad features of early modern Europe: the surge of commerce, the breakdown of efforts to prohibit interest (then called "usury"), and the development of centralized national monarchies.

Ancient Philosophy

Urukagina, the king of the Sumerian city-state Lagash, established the first laws that forbade compelling the sale of property.

The Ten Commandments shown in Exodus 20:2-17 and Deuteronomy 5:6-21 stated that the Israelites were not to steal, a blanket early protection of private property.

Aristotle, in *Politics,* advocates "private property" He argues that self-interest leads to neglect of the commons. "[T]hat which is common to the greatest number has the least care bestowed upon it. Every one thinks chiefly of his own, hardly at all of the common interest; and only when he is himself concerned as an individual."

In addition he says that when property is common, there are natural problems that arise due to differences in labor: "If they do not share equally enjoyments and toils, those who labor much and get little will necessarily complain of those who labor little and receive or consume much. But indeed there is always a difficulty in men living together and having all human relations in common, but especially in their having common property."

Pre-industrial English Philosophy

Thomas Hobbes (17th Century)

The principal writings of Thomas Hobbes appeared between 1640 and 1651—during and immediately following the war between forces loyal to King Charles I and those loyal to Parliament. In his own words, Hobbes' reflection began with the idea of "giving to every man his own," a phrase he drew from the writings of Cicero. But he wondered: How can anybody call anything his own? He concluded: My own can only truly be mine if there is one unambiguously strongest power in the realm, and that power treats it as mine, protecting its status as such.

James Harrington (17th century)

A contemporary of Hobbes, James Harrington, reacted differently to the same tumult; he considered property natural but not inevitable. The author of 'Oceana', he may have been the first political theorist to postulate that political power is a consequence, not the cause, of the distribution of property. He said that the worst possible situation is one in which the commoners have half a nation's property, with crown and nobility holding the other half—a circumstance fraught with instability and violence. A much better situation (a stable republic) will exist once the commoners own most property, he suggested.

In later years, the ranks of Harrington's admirers included American revolutionary and founder John Adams.

Robert Filmer (17th Century)

Another member of the Hobbes/Harrington generation, Sir Robert Filmer, reached conclusions much like Hobbes', but through Biblical exegesis. Filmer said that the institution of kingship is analogous to that of fatherhood, that subjects are but children, whether obedient or unruly, and that property rights are akin to the household goods that a father may dole out among his children—his to take back and dispose of according to his pleasure.

John Locke (17th Century)

In the following generation, John Locke sought to answer Filmer, creating a rationale for a balanced constitution in which the monarch had a part to play, but not an overwhelming part. Since Filmer's views essentially require that the Stuart family be uniquely descended from the patriarchs of the Bible, and since even in the late 17th century that was a difficult view to uphold, Locke attacked Filmer's views in his First Treatise on Government, freeing him to set out his own views in the Second Treatise on Civil Government. Therein, Locke imagined a pre-social world, the unhappy residents of which create a social contract. They would, he allowed, create a monarchy, but its task would be to execute the will of an elected legislature.

"To this end" he wrote, meaning the end of their own long life and peace, "it is that men give up all their natural power to the society they enter into, and the community put the legislative power into such hands as they think fit, with this trust, that they shall be governed by declared laws, or else their peace, quiet, and property will still be at the same uncertainty as it was in the state of nature." Even when it keeps to proper legislative form, though, Locke held that there are limits to what a government established by such a contract might rightly do.

"It cannot be supposed that [the hypothetical contractors] they should intend, had they a power so to do, to give any one or more an absolute arbitrary power over their persons and estates, and put a force into the magistrate's hand to execute his unlimited will arbitrarily upon them; this were to put themselves into a worse condition than the state of nature, wherein they had a liberty to defend their right against the injuries of others, and were upon equal terms of force to maintain it, whether invaded by a single man or many in combination. Whereas by supposing they have given up themselves to the absolute arbitrary power and will of a legislator, they have disarmed themselves, and armed him to make a prey of them when he pleases..." Note that both "persons *and* estates" are to be protected from the arbitrary power of any magistrate, inclusive of the "power and will of a legislator." In Lockean terms, depredations against an estate are just as plausible a justification for resistance and revolution as are those against persons. In neither case are subjects required to allow themselves to become prey. To explain the ownership of property Locke advanced a labor theory of property.

William Blackstone (18th Century)

In the 1760s, William Blackstone sought to codify the English common law. In his famous *Commentaries on the Laws of England* he wrote that "every wanton and causeless restraint of the will of the subject, whether produced by a monarch, a nobility, or a popular assembly is a degree of tyranny."

How should such tyranny be prevented or resisted? Through property rights, Blackstone thought, which is why he emphasized that indemnification must be awarded a non-consenting owner whose property is taken by eminent domain, and that a property owner is protected against physical invasion of his property by the laws of trespass and nuisance. Indeed, he wrote that a landowner is free to kill any stranger on his property between dusk and dawn, even an agent of the King, since it isn't reasonable to expect him to recognize the King's agents in the dark.

David Hume (18th Century)

In contrast to the figures discussed in this section thus far, David Hume lived a relatively quiet life that had settled down to a relatively stable social and political structure. He lived the life of a solitary writer until 1763 when, at 52 years of age, he went off to Paris to work at the British embassy.

In contrast, one might think, to his outrage-generating works on religion and his skeptical views in epistemology, Hume's views on law and property were quite conservative.

He did not believe in hypothetical contracts, or in the love of mankind in general, and sought to ground politics upon actual human beings as one knows them. "In general," he wrote, "it may be affirmed that there is no such passion in human mind, as the love of mankind, merely as such, independent of personal qualities, or services, or of relation to ourselves." Existing customs should not lightly be disregarded, because they have come to be what they are as a result of human nature. With this endorsement of custom comes an endorsement of existing governments, because he conceived of the two as complementary: "A regard for liberty, though a laudable passion, ought commonly to be subordinate to a reverence for established government."

These views led to a view on property rights that might today be described as legal positivism. There are property rights because of and to the extent that the existing law, supported by social customs, secure them. He offered some practical home-spun advice on the general subject, though, as when he referred to avarice as "the spur of industry," and expressed concern about excessive levels of taxation, which "destroy industry, by engendering despair."

Critique and Response

> *"Civil government, so far as it is instituted for the security of property, is, in reality, instituted for the defence of the rich against the poor, or of those who have property against those who have none at all."*
>
> — Adam Smith, *The Wealth of Nations*, 1776

By the mid 19th century, the industrial revolution had transformed England and had begun in France. The established conception of what constitutes property expanded beyond land to encompass scarce goods in general. In France, the revolution of the 1790s had led to large-scale confiscation of land formerly owned by church and king. The restoration of the monarchy led to claims by those dispossessed to have their former lands returned. Furthermore, the labor theory of value popularized by classical economists such as Adam Smith and David Ricardo were utilized by a new ideology called socialism to critique the relations of property to other economic issues, such as profit, rent, interest, and wage-labor. Thus, property was no longer an esoteric philosophical question, but a political issue of substantial concern.

Charles Comte – Legitimate Origin of Property

Charles Comte, in *Traité de la propriété* (1834), attempted to justify the legitimacy of private property in response to the Bourbon Restoration. According to David Hart, Comte had three main points: "firstly, that interference by the state over the centuries in property ownership has had dire consequences for justice as well as for economic productivity; secondly, that property is legitimate when it emerges in such a way as not to harm anyone; and thirdly, that historically some, but by no means all, property which has evolved has done so legitimately, with the implication that the present distribution of property is a complex mixture of legitimately and illegitimately held titles." (*The Radical Liberalism of Charles Comte and Charles Dunoyer*

Comte, as Proudhon later did, rejected Roman legal tradition with its toleration of slavery. He posited a communal "national" property consisting of non-scarce goods, such as land in ancient hunter-gatherer societies. Since agriculture was so much more efficient than hunting and gathering, private property appropriated by someone for farming left remaining hunter-gatherers with more land per person, and hence did not harm them. Thus this type of land appropriation did not violate the Lockean proviso – there was "still enough, and as good left." Comte's analysis would be used by later theorists in response to the socialist critique on property.

Pierre Proudhon – Property is Theft

In his 1849 treatise *What is Property?*, Pierre Proudhon answers with "Property is theft!" In natural resources, he sees two types of property, *de jure* property (legal title) and *de facto* property (physical possession), and argues that the former is illegitimate. Proudhon's conclusion is that "property, to be just and possible, must necessarily have equality for its condition." His analysis of the product of labor upon natural resources as property (usufruct) is more nuanced. He asserts that land itself cannot be property, yet it should be held by individual possessors as stewards of mankind with the product of labor being the property of the producer. Proudhon reasoned that any wealth gained without labor was stolen from those who labored to create that wealth. Even a voluntary contract to surrender the product of labor to an employer was theft, according to Proudhon, since the controller of natural resources had no moral right to charge others for the use of that which he did not labor to create and therefore did not own. Proudhon's theory of property greatly influenced the budding socialist movement, inspiring anarchist theorists such as Mikhail Bakunin who modified Proudhon's ideas, as well as antagonizing theorists like Karl Marx.

Frédéric Bastiat – Property is Value

In a radical departure from traditional property theory, he defines property not as a physical object, but rather as a relationship between people with respect to an object. Thus, saying one owns a glass of water is merely verbal shorthand for *I may justly gift or trade this water to another person*. In essence, what one owns is not the object but the value of the object. By "value," Bastiat apparently means *market value*; he emphasizes that this is quite different from utility. *"In our relations with one another, we are not owners of the utility of things, but of their value, and value is the appraisal made of reciprocal services."*

Strongly disputing Proudhon's equality-based argument, Bastiat theorizes that, as a result of technological progress and the division of labor, the stock of communal wealth increases over time; that the hours of work an unskilled laborer expends to buy e.g. 100 liters of wheat decreases over time, thus amounting to "gratis" satisfaction. Thus, private property continually destroys itself, becoming transformed into communal wealth. The increasing proportion of communal wealth to private property results in a tendency toward equality of mankind. *"Since the human race started from the point of greatest poverty, that is, from the point where there were the most obstacles to be overcome, it is clear that all that has been gained from one era to the next has been due to the spirit of property."*

This transformation of private property into the communal domain, Bastiat points out, does not imply that private property will ever totally disappear. This is because man, as he progresses, continually invents new and more sophisticated needs and desires.

Contemporary Views

Among contemporary political thinkers who believe that natural persons enjoy rights to own property and to enter into contracts, there are two views about John Locke. On the one hand there are ardent Locke admirers, such as W.H. Hutt (1956), who praised Locke for laying down the "quintessence of individualism." On the other hand, there are those such as Richard Pipes who think that Locke's arguments are weak, and that undue reliance thereon has weakened the cause of individualism in recent times. Pipes has written that Locke's work "marked a regression because it rested on the concept of Natural Law" rather than upon Harrington's sociological framework. Hernando de Soto has argued that an important characteristic of capitalist market economy is the functioning state protection of property rights in a formal property system where ownership and transactions are clearly recorded. These property rights and the whole formal system of property make possible:

- Greater independence for individuals from local community arrangements to protect their assets;
- Clear, provable, and protectable ownership;
- The standardization and integration of property rules and property information in the country as a whole;
- Increased trust arising from a greater certainty of punishment for cheating in economic transactions;
- More formal and complex written statements of ownership that permit the easier assumption of shared risk and ownership in companies, and insurance against risk;
- Greater availability of loans for new projects, since more things could be used as collateral for the loans;
- Easier access to and more reliable information regarding such things as credit history and the worth of assets;
- Increased fungibility, standardization and transferability of statements documenting the ownership of property, which paves the way for structures such as national markets for companies and the easy transportation of property through complex networks of individuals and other entities;
- Greater protection of biodiversity due to minimizing of shifting agriculture practices.

All of the above enhance economic growth.

Types of Property

Most legal systems distinguish different types (immovable property, estate in land, real estate, real property) of property, especially between land and all other forms of property—goods and chattels, movable property or personal property. They often distinguish tangible and intangible property. One categorization scheme specifies three species of property: land, improvements (immovable man-made things), and personal property (movable man-made things).

In common law, real property (immovable property) is the combination of interests in land and improvements thereto, and personal property is interest in movable property.

Real property rights are rights relating to the land. These rights include ownership and usage. Owners can grant rights to persons and entities in the form of leases, licenses and easements.

Later, with the development of more complex forms of non-tangible property, personal property was divided into tangible property (such as cars and clothing) and intangible property (such as financial instruments, including stocks and bonds, and intellectual property, including patents, copyrights, and trademarks).

What can be Property?

The two major justifications given for original property, or homesteading, are effort and scarcity. John Locke emphasized effort, "mixing your labor" with an object, or clearing and cultivating virgin land. Benjamin Tucker preferred to look at the telos of property, i.e. What is the purpose of property? His answer: to solve the scarcity problem. Only when items are relatively scarce with respect to people's desires do they become property. For example, hunter-gatherers did not consider land to be property, since there was no shortage of land. Agrarian societies later made arable land property, as it was scarce. For something to be economically scarce, it must necessarily have the *exclusivity property*-that use by one person excludes others from using it. These two justifications lead to different conclusions on what can be property. Intellectual property-non-corporeal things like ideas, plans, orderings and arrangements (musical compositions, novels, computer programs)-are generally considered valid property to those who support an effort justification, but invalid to those who support a scarcity justification, since they don't have the exclusivity property (however they may still support other 'intellectual property'-laws such as Copyright, as long as these are a subject of contract instead of government arbitration). Thus even ardent propertarians may disagree about IP. By either standard, one's body is one's property.

From some anarchist points of view, the validity of property depends on whether the "property right" requires enforcement by the state. Different forms of "property" require different amounts of enforcement: intellectual property requires a great deal of state intervention to enforce, ownership of distant physical property requires quite a lot, ownership of carried objects requires very little, while ownership of one's own body requires absolutely no state intervention.

Many things have existed that did not have an owner, sometimes called the commons. The term "commons," however, is also often used to mean something quite different: "general collective ownership"-i.e. common ownership. Also, the same term is sometimes used by statists to mean government-owned property that the general public is allowed to access (public property). Law in all societies has tended to develop towards reducing the number of things not having clear owners. Supporters of property rights argue that this enables better protection of scarce resources, due to the tragedy of the commons, while critics argue that it leads to the 'exploitation' of those resources for personal gain and that it hinders taking advantage of potential network effects. These arguments have differing validity for different types of "property"—things that are not scarce are, for instance, not subject to the tragedy of the commons. Some apparent critics advocate general collective ownership rather than ownerlessness.

Things that do not have owners include: ideas (except for intellectual property), seawater (which is, however, protected by anti-pollution laws), parts of the seafloor, gases in Earth's atmosphere, animals in the wild (though there may be restrictions on hunting etc. — and in some legal systems, such as that of New York, they are actually treated as government property), celestial bodies and outer space, and land in Antarctica.

The nature of children under the age of majority is another contested issue here. In ancient societies children were generally considered the property of their parents. Children in most modern societies theoretically own their own bodies but are not considered competent to exercise their rights, and their parents or guardians are given most of the actual rights of control over them.

Questions regarding the nature of ownership of the body also come up in the issue of abortion, drugs and euthanasia.

In many ancient legal systems (e.g. early Roman law), religious sites (e.g. temples) were considered property of the God or gods they were devoted to. However, religious pluralism makes it more convenient to have religious sites owned by the religious body that runs them.

Intellectual property and air (airspace, no-fly zone, pollution laws, which can include tradeable emissions rights) can be property in some senses of the word.

Rights of use as Property

Ownership of land can be held separately from the ownership of rights over that land, including sporting rights, mineral rights, development rights, air rights, and such other rights as may be worth segregating from simple land ownership.

Who can be an Owner?

Ownership is the state or fact of exclusive rights and control over property, which may be an object, land/real estate or intellectual property. Ownership involves multiple rights, collectively referred to as title, which may be separated and held by different parties. The concept of ownership has existed for thousands of years and in all cultures. Over the millennia, however, and across cultures what is considered eligible to be property and how that property is regarded culturally is very different. Ownership is the basis for many other concepts that form the foundations of ancient and modern societies such as money, trade, debt, bankruptcy, the criminality of theft and private vs. public property. Ownership is the key building block in the development of the capitalist socio-economic system.

The process and mechanics of ownership are fairly complex since one can gain, transfer and lose ownership of property in a number of ways. To acquire property one can purchase it with money, trade it for other property, receive it as a gift, steal it, find it, make it or homestead it. One can transfer or lose ownership of property by selling it for money, exchanging it for other property, giving it as a gift, being robbed of it, misplacing it, or having it stripped from one's ownership through legal means such as eviction, foreclosure, seizure or taking. Ownership is self-propagating in that the owner of any property will also own the economic benefits of that property.

Types of Owners

In Person

Individuals may own property directly. In some societies only adult men may own property; in other societies (such as the Haudenosaunee), property is matrilinear and passed on from mother to the son. In most societies both men and women can own property with no restrictions and limitations at all.

Structured Ownership Entities

Throughout history, nations (or governments) and religious organizations have owned property. These entities exist primarily for other purposes than to own or operate property, hence they may have no clear rules regarding the disposition of their property.

To own and operate property, structures (often known today as legal entities) have been created in many societies throughout history. The differences in how they deal with members' rights is a key factor in determining their type. Each type has advantages and disadvantages derived from their means of recognizing or disregarding (rewarding or not), contributions of financial capital or personal effort.

Cooperatives, corporations, trusts, partnerships, condominium associations are only some of the many varied types of structured ownership; each type has many subtypes. Legal advantages or restrictions on various types of structured ownership have existed in many societies past and present. To govern how assets are to be used, shared or treated, rules and regulations may be legally imposed or internally adopted or decreed.

Liability for the Group or for Others in the Group

Ownership implies responsibility, for actions regarding the property. A "legal shield" is said to exist if the entity's legal liabilities do not get redistributed among the entity's owners or members. An application of this, to limit ownership risks, is to form a new entity to purchase, own and operate each property. Since the entity is separate and distinct from others, if a problem occurs which leads to a massive liability, the individual is protected from losing more than the value of that one property. Many other properties are protected, when owned by other distinct entities.

In the loosest sense of group ownership, a lack of legal framework, rules and regulations may mean that group ownership of property places every member in a position of responsibility (liability) for the actions of each other member. A structured group duly constituted as an entity under law may still not protect members from being personally liable for each others' actions. Court decisions against the entity itself may give rise to unlimited personal liability for each and every member. An example of this situation is a professional partnership (e.g. law practice) in some jurisdictions. Thus, being a partner or owner in a group may give little advantage in terms of share ownership while producing a lot of risk to the partner, owner or participant.

Sharing Gains

At the end of each financial year, accounting rules determine a surplus or profit, which may be retained inside the entity or distributed among owners according to the initial setup intent when the entity was created.

Entities *with a member focus* will give financial surplus back to members according to the volume of financial activity that the participating member generated for the entity. Examples of this are producer cooperatives, buyer cooperatives and participating whole life policyholders in both mutual and share-capital insurance companies.

Entities *with share voting rights that depend on financial capital* distribute surplus among shareholders without regard to any other contribution to the entity. Depending on internal rules and regulations, certain classes of shares have the right to receive increases in financial "dividends" while other classes do not. After many years the increase over time is substantial if the business is profitable. Examples of this are common shares and preferred shares in private or publicly listed share capital corporations.

Entities *with a focus on providing service in perpetuam* do not distribute financial surplus; they must retain it. It will then serve as a cushion against losses or as a means to finance growth activities. Examples of this are not-for-profit entities: they are allowed to make profits, but are not permitted to give any of it back to members except by way of discounts in the future on new transactions.

Depending on the charter at the foundation of the entity, and depending on the legal framework under which the entity was created, the form of ownership is determined once and for all time. To change it requires significant work in terms of communicating with stakeholders (member-owners, governments, etc.) and acquiring their approval. Whatever structural constraints or disadvantages exist at the creation thus remain an integral part of the entity. Common in for instance New York City, Hamburg and Berlin in Germany is a form of real estate ownership known as a cooperative (also co-operative or co-op, in German Wohnungsgenossenschaft-apartment co-operative) which relies heavily on internal rules of operation instead of the legal framework governing condominium associations. These "co-ops", owning the building for the mutual benefit of its members, can ultimately perform most of the functions of a legally constituted condominium, i.e. restricting use appropriately and containing financial liabilities to within tolerable levels. To change their structure now that they are up and operating would require significant effort to achieve acceptance among members and various levels of government.

Sharing Use

The owning entity makes rules governing use of property; each property may comprise areas that are made available to any and every member of the group to use. When the group is the entire nation, the same principle is in effect whether the property is small (e.g. picnic rest stops along highways) or large such as national parks, highways, ports, and publicly owned buildings. Smaller examples of shared use include common areas such as lobbies, entrance hallways and passages to adjacent buildings. One disadvantage of communal ownership, known as the Tragedy of the Commons, occurs where unlimited unrestricted and unregulated access to a resource (e.g. pasture land) destroys the resource because of over-exploitation. The benefits of exploitation accrue to individuals immediately, while the costs of policing or enforcing appropriate use, and the losses dues to over exploitation, are distributed among many, and are only visible to these gradually.

In an ideal communist nation the means of production of goods would be owned communally by all people of that nation; the original thinkers did not specify rules and regulations.

Ownership Models

State ownership-Assets that a state or certain state agency has jurisdiction over in terms of use.

Government ownership-Assets belonging to a body of government.

Public property-Assets owned by a government or state that are available for public use to all their constituents.

Personal ownership-Assets and property belonging to an individual, also known as individual ownership.

Common ownership-Assets and property that are held in common by all members of society (or non-ownership).

Communal ownership-Property held in common by a commune.

- Collective ownership-Assets and property that belong to a collective body of people who control their use and collect the proceeds of their operation.
  - o Private ownership-A subset of collective property whereby a collective group of owners (such as shareholders) own productive property that is used by employees, usually for the purpose of generating a profit.
  - o Cooperative ownership-Property that is owned by those who operate and use it. Also referred to as social ownership.

Types of Property

Personal Property

Personal property is a type of property. In the common law systems personal property may also be called chattels. It is distinguished from real property, or real estate. In the civil law systems personal property is often called movable property or movables-any property that can be moved from one location or another. This term is used to distinguish property that different from immovable property or immovables, such as land and buildings.

Personal property may be classified in a variety of ways, such as goods, money, negotiable instruments, securities, and intangible assets including choses in action.

Land Ownership

Real estate or immovable property is a legal term (in some jurisdictions) that encompasses land along with anything permanently affixed to the land, such as buildings. Real estate (immovable property) is often considered synonymous with real property, in contrast from personal property (also sometimes called *chattel* or *personalty*). However, for technical purposes, some people prefer to distinguish real estate, referring to the land and fixtures themselves, from real property, referring to ownership rights over real estate. The terms *real estate* and *real property* are used primarily in common law, while civil law jurisdictions refer instead to immovable property.

In law, the word *real* means relating to a thing (from Latin *reâlis,* ultimately from *rçs,* 'matter' or 'thing'), as distinguished from a person. Thus the law broadly distinguishes between *real property* (land and anything affixed to it) and *personal property* (everything else, e.g., clothing, furniture, money). The conceptual difference is between immovable property, which would transfer title along with the land, and movable property, which a person would retain title to. (Incidentally, the word *real* in *real estate* is not derived from the notion of land having historically been "royal" property. The word *royal*—and its Spanish cognate, *real*—come from the unrelated Latin word *rçgâlis* 'kingly,' which is a derivative of *rçx,* meaning 'king.')

With the development of private property ownership, real estate has become a major area of business.

Corporations and Legal Entities

An individual or group of individuals can own corporations and other legal entities. A legal entity is a legal construct through which the law allows a group of natural persons to act as if it were an individual for certain purposes. Some companies and entities are owned privately by the individuals who registered them with the government while other companies are owned publicly. Some duly incorporated entities may not be owned by individuals nor by other entities; they exist without being owned once they are created. Not being owned, they cannot be bought and sold. Mutual life insurance companies, credit unions, and cooperatives are examples of this. No person can purchase the company, as their ownership is not legally available for sale, neither as shares nor as a single whole.

A publicly listed company, known as a public company, is owned by any member of the public who wishes to purchase stock in that company rather than by a relatively few individuals. A company that is owned by stockholders who are members of the general public and trade shares publicly, often through a listing on a stock exchange. Ownership is open to anyone who has the money and inclination to buy shares in the company. Owners, however, are generally classified in three groups. Those with 5% Ownerships of the stock usually hold significant sway over the company. Mutual Funds and regular institutions can also own the stock; if they own enough, can are considered as part of the 5% ownership category. Public companies usually are differentiated from privately held companies where the shares are held by a small group of individuals often members of one or a small group of families or otherwise related individuals (or other companies). For a discussion of the British and Irish variant of this type of company.

Intellectual Property

Intellectual (IP) property refers to a legal entitlement which sometimes attaches to the expressed form of an idea, or to some other intangible subject matter. This legal entitlement generally enables its holder to exercise exclusive rights of use in relation to the subject matter of the IP. The term *intellectual property* reflects the idea that this subject matter is the product of the mind or the intellect, and that IP rights may be protected at law in the same way as any other form of property.

Intellectual property laws confer a bundle of exclusive rights in relation to the particular form or manner in which ideas or information are expressed or manifested, and not in relation to the ideas or concepts themselves. It is therefore important to note that the term "intellectual property" denotes the specific legal rights which authors, inventors and other IP holders may hold and exercise, and not the intellectual work itself. Intellectual property laws are designed to protect different forms of intangible subject matter, although in some cases there is a degree of overlap.

- copyright may subsist in creative and artistic works (e.g. books, movies, music, paintings, photographs and software), giving a copyright holder the exclusive right to control reproduction or adaptation of such works for a certain period of time.
- A patent may be granted in relation to an invention that is new, useful and not simply an obvious advancement over what existed when the application was filed. A patent gives the holder an exclusive right to commercially exploit the invention for a certain period of time (typically 20 years from the filing date of a patent application).
- A trademark is a distinctive sign which is used to distinguish the products or services of one business from those of another business.
- An industrial design right protects the form of appearance, style or design of an industrial object (e.g. spare parts, furniture or textiles).
- A trade secret (also known as "confidential information") is an item of confidential information concerning the commercial practices or proprietary knowledge of a business.

Patents, trademarks and designs fall into a particular subset of intellectual property known as industrial property.

Like other forms of property, intellectual property (or rather the exclusive rights which subsist in the IP) can be transferred (with or without consideration) or licensed to third parties. In some jurisdictions it may also be possible to use intellectual property as security for a loan. The basic public policy rationale for the protection of intellectual property is that IP laws facilitate and encourage disclosure of innovation into the public domain for the common good, by granting authors and inventors exclusive rights to exploit their works and invention for a limitěd period.

However, various schools of thought are critical of the very concept of intellectual property, and some characterise IP as *intellectual protectionism*. There is ongoing debate as to whether IP laws truly operate to confer the stated public benefits, and whether the protection they are said to provide is appropriate in the context of innovation derived from such things as traditional knowledge and folklore, and patents for software and business methods. Manifestations of this controversy can be seen in the way different jurisdictions decide whether to grant intellectual property protection in relation to subject matter of this kind, and the North-South divide on issues of the role and scope of intellectual property laws.

Ownership laws may vary widely among countries depending on the nature of the property of interest (e.g. firearms, real property, personal property, animals). Persons can own property directly. In most societies legal entities, such as corporations, trusts and nations (or governments) own property.

In the Inca empire, the dead emperors, who were considered gods, still controlled property after death.

Whether and to what Extent the State may Interfere with Property

Under United States law the principal limitations on whether and the extent to which the State may interfere with property rights are set by the Constitution. The "Takings" clause requires that the government (whether state or federal—for the 14th Amendment's due process clause imposes the 5th Amendment's takings clause on state governments) may take private property only for a public purpose, after exercising due process of law, and upon making "just compensation." If an interest is not deemed a "property" right, or the conduct is merely an intentional tort, these limitations do not apply and the doctrine of sovereign immunity precludes relief. Moreover, if the interference does not almost completely make the property valueless, the interference will not be deemed a taking but instead a mere regulation of use. On the other hand, some governmental regulations of property use have been deemed so severe that they have been considered "regulatory takings." Moreover, conduct sometimes deemed only a nuisance or other tort has been held a taking of property where the conduct was sufficiently persistent and severe.

SARA Hospitality (Hotel/Resort/Property Management System)

At one time, a hotel was just a place for temporary stay. Now hotels are also used for entertainment, marketing communication, business development, cultural programs, product launches, wining and dining, socializing, etc. To tap all these opportunities, today's hotels have to use IT to efficiently deliver all the services that a customer requires while simultaneously ensuring customer delight in each and every interaction. SARA Hospitality covers reservation, check-in and check-out, services and facilities, guest details, kitchen and restaurant management, automatic billing, finance and administration, procurement, inventory control, payroll, employee data, and human resources management. The system is suitable for managing Hotels, Resorts and Properties.

Modules of SARA Hospitality Management System:

- Guest Reservation and Registration
- Guest Care
- Facilities Management and Scheduling
- Guest Record History
- Guest Billing
- Kitchen and Restaurant Management
- Finance and Administration
- Purchase Management
- Payroll
- Human Resources Management.

Asset Management

Asset management, broadly defined, refers to any system whereby things that are of value to an entity or group are monitored and maintained. It may apply to both tangible assets and to intangible concepts such as intellectual property and goodwill.

Asset Management is a systematic process of operating, maintaining, and upgrading assets cost-effectively, (American Associate of State Highway and Transportation Officials).

Alternative views of Asset Management in the engineering environment are:

- The practice of managing assets so that the greatest return is achieved (this concept is particularly useful for productive assets such as plant and equipment)
- the process by which built systems of facilities are monitored and maintained, with the objective of providing the best possible service to users (appropriate for public infrastructure assets).

Historical Background of Asset Management

Civilisation has always relied on its technological assets to support key functions like transport, public health, business and commerce.

There is a clear link between the provision and sophistication of technological assets and our modern lifestyle. Romans built a strong empire through their construction of roads, aqueducts and other assets. Similar storys are found when examining Asia, Africa, Europe and America.

Financial Asset Management

- Investment management-the sector of the financial services industry that manages collective investment schemes and segregated client accounts.
- Global assets under management
- List of asset management firms.

Enterprise Asset Management

Enterprise asset management is the business processes and enabling information systems that support management of an organization's assets, both physical (such as buildings, equipment, infrastructure etc.) and non-physical such as:

- Physical asset management-the practice of managing the whole life cycle (design, construction, commissioning, operating, maintaining, repairing, modifying, replacing and decommissioning/disposal) of physical and infrastructure assets such as structures, production and service plant, power, water and waste treatment facilities, distribution networks, transport systems, buildings and other physical assets. Infrastructure asset management expands on this theme in relation primarily to public sector, utilities, property and transport systems.

- Fixed assets management-an accounting process that seeks to track fixed assets for the purposes of financial accounting.
- IT asset management-the set of business practices that join financial, contractual and inventory functions to support life cycle management and strategic decision making for the IT environment. This is also one of the processes defined within IT service management.
- Digital asset management – a form of electronic media content management that includes digital assets.

Public Asset Management

Public asset management expands the definition of Enterprise Asset Management (EAM) by incorporating the management of all things which are of value to a municipal jurisdiction and its citizens' expectations.

An EAM requires an asset registry (inventory of assets and their attributes) combined with a computerized maintenance management system. All public assets are interconnected and share proximity, and this connectivity is possible through the use of GIS.

GIS-centric public asset management standardizes data and allows interoperability, providing users the capability to reuse, coordinate, and share information in an efficient and effective manner by making the GIS geo-database the asset registry. A GIS-centric public asset management which standardizes data and allows interoperability, providing users the capability to reuse, coordinate, and share information in an efficient and effective manner.

In the United States the defacto GIS standard is the Esri GIS for utilities and municipalities. An Esri GIS platform combined with the overall public asset management umbrella of both physical "hard" assets and "soft" assets helps remove the traditional silos of structured municipal functions. While the hard assets are the typical physical assets or infrastructure assets, the soft assets of a municipality includes permits, license, code enforcement, right-of-ways and other land-focused work activities.

This definition of "public asset management" was coined and defined by Brian L. Haslam, President and CEO of a leading international GIS-centric Computerized Maintenance Management System (CMMS) company which software is certified by the National Association of GIS-Centric Solutions (NAGCS). GIS-centric public asset management is a system design approach for managing public assets that leverages the investment local governments continue to make in GIS and provides a common framework for sharing useful data from disparate systems. Permits, licenses, code enforcement, right-of-way, and other land-focused work activities are examples of land-focused public assets managed by local government. These public assets occupy location just as in-the-ground or above-ground public assets do.

Land-use development and planning is another area which is interconnected to other local government assets and work activities. Public Asset Management is the term that encompasses this subset of land-focused asset management, considering the importance that public assets affect other public assets and work activities and are important sources of revenue and are various points of citizen interaction.

Enterprise Asset Management

Enterprise asset management (EAM) means the whole life optimal management of the physical assets of an organization to maximize value. It covers such things as the design, construction, commissioning, operations, maintenance and decommissioning/replacement of plant, equipment and facilities. "Enterprise" refers to the management of the assets across departments, locations, facilities and, in some cases, business units. By managing assets across the facility, organizations can improve utilization and performance, reduce capital costs, reduce asset-related operating costs, extend asset life and subsequently improve ROA (return on assets). The functions of asset management are taking a fundamental turn where organizations are moving from historical reactive (run-to-failure) models and beginning to embrace whole life planning, life cycle costing, planned and proactive maintenance and other industry best practices. Some companies still regard physical asset management as just a more business-focused term for maintenance management-until they begin to realize the organization-wide impact and interdependencies with operations, design, asset performance, personnel productivity and lifecycle costs. This shift in focus exemplifies the progression from maintenance management to Enterprise Asset Management and is embodied in the British Standards specification PAS 55 (Requirements specification for the optimal management of physical infrastructure assets).

What is Enterprise Asset Management?

In capital-intensive industries such as·utilities, process/ discrete manufacturing, healthcare as well as real estate, physical assets (buildings, infrastructure and equipment) form a significant proportion of the total assets of the organization. These industries face the harsh realities of operating in highly competitive markets and dealing with high value assets and equipment where each failure is disruptive and costly. At the same time, they must also adhere to stringent occupational and environmental safety regulations.

It is thus important for organizations to maximize the return on investment from their asset base. Life Cycle Asset Management (LCAM) and EAM are paradigms employed to achieve that goal. Given a physical asset, the objective of LCAM is to extract maximum productivity from the asset and minimize the total costs involved in its acquisition, operations as well as maintenance. Quantitatively, the objective of asset management is to strike an optimal balance between maximizing Overall Asset Productivity (OAP) and minimizing Total Cost of Ownership (TCO). Furthermore, LCAM provides guidance on whether it is more cost-effective to continue to maintain, overhaul or replace a failing asset.

When the entire asset portfolio of the organization is considered, EAM takes over. As business and market requirements are dynamic, the output specifications for the organization's assets change constantly (e.g., increase in output capacity due to new customers). EAM provides the framework for capital and labor allocation decision processes across the competing categories of equipment addition/reduction, replacement, over-hauling, redundancy setup and maintenance budgets in order to meet business needs. Correspondingly, it merges the collective LCAM efforts and re-evaluates decisions based on long and short-term economic considerations at the enterprise lével.

Public asset management expands the definition of Enterprise Asset Management (EAM) by incorporating the management of all things which are of value to a municipal jurisdiction and its citizen's expectations. An EAM requires an asset registry (inventory of assets and their attributes) combined with a computerized maintenance management system. Public Asset Management is the term that considers the importance that public assets affect other public assets and work activities which are important sources of revenue for municipal governments and has various points of citizen interaction. The versatility and functionality of a GIS system allows for the control and management of all assets and land-focused activities. All public assets are interconnected and share proximity, and this connectivity is possible through the use of GIS. GIS-centric public asset management standardizes data and allows interoperability, providing users the capability to reuse, coordinate, and share information in an efficient and effective manner by making the GIS geo-database the asset registry.

In the United States the defacto GIS standard is the ESRI GIS for utilities and municipalities. An ESRI GIS platform combined with the overall public asset management umbrella of both physical "hard" assets and "soft" assets helps remove the traditional silos of structured municipal functions which serves the citizens. While the hard assets are the typical physical assets or infrastructure assets, the soft assets of a municipality includes permits, license, code enforcement, right-of-ways and other land-focused work activities.

This definition of "public asset management" was coined and defined by Brian L. Haslam, President and CEO of a leading International ESRI GIS-centric Computerized Maintenance Management System (CMMS) company located in Utah whose software is certified by the National Association of GIS-Centric Solutions (NAGCS). GIS-centric public asset management is a system design approach for managing public assets that leverages the investment local governments continue to make in GIS and provides a common framework for sharing useful data from disparate systems.

Permits, licenses, code enforcement, right-of-way, and other land-focused work activities are examples of land-focused public assets managed by municipal governments. These public assets occupy location just as in-the-ground or above-ground public assets do. Land-use development and planning is another area which is interconnected to other local government assets and work activities.

Professional Bodies

Investment Recovery Association;

- Institute of Asset Management
- National Property Management Association (NPMA)
- Asset Management Council
- Plant Engineering and Maintenance Association of Canada
- American Water Works Association AWWA
- National Association of GIS-Centric Solutions NAGS.

Information Technology Enterprise Asset Management

ITEAM differs from EAM only in its focus on IT assets. This focus is important for a number of key reasons:

1. Organizational dependence on these assets
2. High cost, particularly of datacenter assets
3. Rapid pace of change/turn-over for assets.

ITEAM focuses on both hardware and software asset management, ensuring that the organization has the ability to manage these assets throughout their life. In the case of software, there is the added component of ensuring license compliance.

Why is EAM Important?

Competitive pressures force organizations to minimize asset total cost of ownership and streamline their asset management operations (these typically involve myriad activities ranging from inventory, parts and labor management to contracts and vendor management for new works). As downtimes become increasingly expensive, both in terms of lost production capacity and unfavorable publicity, organizations are compelled to maximize their asset productive life cycles via optimal maintenance programs. When EAM is used in collaboration with all other forms of service-based operations to achieve better customer retention, it is, called Service Lifecycle Management (SLM).

In the event of asset failure, quick response time is critical. In recent years, stringent industry-specific environmental health and occupational safety regulations are being enforced by government oversight agencies, with industrial owners and operators responsible for compliance. Asset registers, risk registers, work planning and scheduling, life cycle costing and systematic methods for problem identification, root cause analysis and continuous improvement are increasingly seen as prerequesites for a robust asset management system.

By providing a platform for connecting people, processes, assets, industry-based knowledge and decision support capabilities based on quality information,EAM provides a holistic view of an organization's asset base, enabling managers to control and optimize their operations for quality and efficiency.

EAM System Challenges

EAM systems need a lot of high quality data to track and analyze the execution of business processes. Capturing data in the field using traditional paper forms and manually inputting it into the EAM system often turns out to be too expensive to be practical. This often slows adoption and erodes the ROI of many EAM deployments.

EAM systems are often not integrated with the rest of the company's enterprise systems (including purchasing, HR, inventory, etc.), which increases management overhead and prevents the organization from realizing the system's full potential.

Mobility

Role of Mobility Technology in EAM

Enterprises use mobility to improve their EAM system in a number of ways. First, mobility can be leveraged to improve dispatch processes. Traditionally, work order dispatch relies on an antiquated, paper-based system. This process is cumbersome because technicians are required travel back-and-forth between work sites and the dispatch center for new assignments. With mobility, technicians can receive their assignments in the field, spend more time working, and create work orders right on their devices.

Also, companies have been using mobility to allow their technicians to access EAM information while on-site. Mobile technology lets technicians view more EAM relevant data. As a result of this increased access, technicians are better prepared to service assets when they require maintenance, service, or inspection.

Finally, with mobile technology, field technicians have the ability to capture more, and better quality, EAM data. Improved data capturing processes allow for better analysis and evaluation; as a result, companies are quickly embracing mobile solutions. With the many uses for mobility, the EAM solution market has seen steady growth over the last few years. Commonly sought providers have solutions that enterprises deploy based upon factors, such as: ease of configurability, integration with back-end systems, cost, features, availability of support, etc. As companies continue to mobilize their EAM processes, the market is expected to continue expanding.

Healthcare Enterprise Asset Management

Healthcare enterprise asset management (HEAM) presents complexities not found in most other industries. Specifically, healthcare environments have a large number of relatively small, mobile, expensive and sophisticated pieces of equipment. Further, the availability, maintenance and cleanliness of these assets directly impacts the "environment of care" and patient safety, as well as the bottom line. Finally, hospitals are highly regulated and assets must be maintained in a manner that complies with JCAHO and U.S. Food and Drug Administration (FDA) requirements. HEAM can include the following components related to assets:

1. Inventory and depreciation
2. Scheduling of repair and maintenance

3. Location and logistics (RFID or barcode powered)
4. Availability and utilization
5. Safety monitoring and incident tracking
6. Total Lifecycle Cost
7. Performance management
8. Capital planning support.

HEAM provides complete visibility of the asset base across the health system, enabling active control of the planning, acquisition, tracking, maintenance and retirement of capital assets.

Real Estate

Real estate is a legal term (in some jurisdictions, such as the United Kingdom, Canada, Australia, USA, Dubai, Trinidad and Tobago and The Bahamas) that encompasses land along with improvements to the land, such as buildings, fences, wells and other site improvements that are fixed in location—immovable. Real estate law is the body of regulations and legal codes which pertain to such matters under a particular jurisdiction and include things such as commercial and residential real property transactions. Real estate is often considered synonymous with real property (sometimes called *realty*), in contrast with personal property (sometimes called *chattel* or *personalty* under *chattel law* or *personal property law*).

However, in some situations the term "real estate" refers to the land and fixtures together, as distinguished from "real property", referring to ownership of land and appurtenances, including anything of a permanent nature such as structures, trees, minerals, and the interest, benefits, and inherent rights thereof. Real property is typically considered to be immovable property. The terms *real estate* and *real property* are used primarily in common law, while civil law jurisdictions refer instead to immovable property.

Etymology

In law, the word *real* means relating to a thing (*res/rei*, thing, from O.Fr. *reel*, from L.L. *realis* "actual," from Latin. *res*, "matter, thing"), as distinguished from a person. Thus the law broadly distinguishes between "real" property (land and anything affixed to it) and "personal" property (everything else, *e.g.*, clothing, furniture, money). The conceptual difference was between immovable property, which would transfer title along with the land, and movable property, which a person would retain title to. The oldest use of the term "Real Estate" that has been preserved in historical records was in 1666.

This use of "real" also reflects the ancient and feudal preference for land, and the ownership (and owners) thereof. Some people have claimed that the word *real* in this sense is descended (like French *royal* and Spanish *real*) from the Latin word for 'king'.

In the feudal system (which has left many traces in the common law) the king was the owner of all land, and everyone who occupied land paid him rent directly or indirectly (through lords who in turn paid the king), in cash, goods or services (including military service). Property tax, paid to the state, can be seen as a relic of that system, as is the term fee simple. However, this derivation of *real* is a misconception.

Real Estate Terminology and Practice Outside the United States (Around the World)

Real Estate as "Real Property" in the U.K.

In British usage, "real property", often shortened to just "property", generally refers to land and fixtures, while the term "real estate" is used mostly in the context of probate law, and means all interests in land held by a deceased person at death, excluding interests in money arising under a trust for sale of or charged on land. In English Common Law, real property, real estate, realty, or immovable property is any subset of land that has been legally defined and the improvements to it made by human efforts: any buildings, machinery, wells, dams, ponds, mines, canals, roads, various property rights, and so forth. *Real property* and *personal property* are the two main subunits of property in *English Common Law*.

In countries with personal ownership of real property, civil law protects the status of real property in real-estate markets, where licensed agents, realtors, work in the market of buying and selling real estate. Scottish civil law calls real property *"heritable property"*, and in French-based law, it is called *immobilier*.

Identification of Real Property

To be of any value a claim to any property must be accompanied by a verifiable and legal property description. Such a description usually makes use of natural or manmade boundaries such as seacoasts, rivers, streams, the crests of ridges, lakeshores, highways, roads, and railroad tracks, and/or purpose-built artificial markers such as cairns, surveyor's posts, fences, official government surveying marks (such as ones affixed by the U.S. Geodetic Survey (USGS)), and so forth.

Estates and Ownership Interests Defined

The law recognizes different sorts of interests, called estates, in real property. The type of estate is generally determined by the language of the deed, lease, bill of sale, will, land grant, etc., through which the estate was acquired. Estates are distinguished by the varying property rights that vest in each, and that determine the duration and transferability of the various estates. A party enjoying an estate is called a "tenant."

Some important types of estates in land include:

- Fee simple: An estate of indefinite duration, that can be freely transferred. The most common and perhaps most absolute type of estate, under which the tenant enjoys the greatest discretion over the disposition of the property.
- Conditional Fee simple: An estate lasting forever as long as one or more conditions stipulated by the deed's grantor does not occur. If such a condition does occur, the property reverts to the grantor, or a remainder interest is passed on to a third party.
- Fee tail: An estate which, upon the death of the tenant, is transferred to his or her heirs.
- Life estate: An estate lasting for the natural life of the grantee, called a "life tenant." If a life estate can be sold, a sale does not change its duration, which is limited by the natural life of the original grantee.
    - A life estate *pur autre vie* is held by one person for the natural life of another person. Such an estate may arise if the original life tenant sells her life estate to another, or if the life estate is originally granted *pur autre vie*.

- Leasehold: An estate of limited duration, as set out in a contract, called a lease, between the party granted the leasehold, called the lessee, and another party, called the lessor, having a longer lived estate in the property. For example, an apartment-dweller with a one year lease has a leasehold estate in her apartment. Lessees typically agree to pay a stated rent to the lessor.

A tenant enjoying an undivided estate in some property after the termination of some estate of limited duration, is said to have a "future interest." Two important types of future interests are:

- Reversion: A reversion arises when a tenant grants an estate of lesser maximum duration than his own. Ownership of the land returns to the original tenant when the grantee's estate expires. The original tenant's future interest is a reversion.
- Remainder: A remainder arises when a tenant with a fee simple grants someone a life estate or conditional fee simple, and specifies a third party to whom the land goes when the life estate ends or the condition occurs. The third party is said to have a remainder. The third party may have a legal right to limit the life tenant's use of the land.

Estates may be held jointly as joint tenants with rights of survivorship or as tenants in common. The difference in these two types of joint ownership of an estate in land is basically the inheritability of the estate and the shares of interest that each tenant owns.

In a joint tenancy with rights of survivorship deed, or JTWROS, the death of one tenant means that the surviving tenant(s) become the sole owner(s) of the estate. Nothing passes to the heirs of the deceased tenant. In some jurisdictions, the specific words "with right of survivorship" must be used, or the tenancy will assumed to be tenants in common without rights of survivorship. The co-owners always take a JTWROS deed in equal shares, so each tenant must own an equal share of the property regardless of his/her contribution to purchase price. If the property is someday sold or subdivided, the proceeds must be distributed equally with no credits given for any excess than any one co-owner may have contributed to purchase the property.

The death of a co-owner of a tenants in common (TIC) deed will have a heritable portion of the estate in proportion to his ownership interest which is presumed to be equal among all tenants unless otherwise stated in the transfer deed. However, if TIC property is sold or subdivided, in some States, Provinces, etc., a credit can be automatically made for unequal contributions to the purchase price (unlike a partition of a JTWROS deed). However, do not forget that these considerations

Real property may be owned jointly with several tenants, through devices such as the condominium, housing cooperative, and building cooperative.

Jurisdictional Peculiarities

In the law of almost every country, the state is the ultimate owner of all land under its jurisdiction, because it is the sovereign, or supreme lawmaking authority. Physical and corporate persons do not have allodial title; they do not "own" land but only enjoy estates in the land, also known as "equitable interests."

England and Wales

In the United Kingdom, The Crown is held to be the ultimate owner of all real property in the realm. This fact is material when, for example, property has been disclaimed by its erstwhile owner, in which case the law of escheat applies. In some other jurisdictions (not including the United States), real property is held absolutely. English law has retained the common law distinction between real property and personal property, whereas the civil law distinguishes between "movable" and "immovable" property. In English law, real property is not confined to the ownership of property and the buildings sited thereon – often referred to as "land." Real property also includes many legal relationships between individuals or owners of land that are purely conceptual. One such relationship is the easement, where the owner of one property may enjoy the right to pass over a neighboring property. Another is the various "incorporeal hereditaments," such as profits a prendre, where an individual may have the right to take crops from land that is part of another's estate. English law retains a number of forms of property which are largely unknown in other common law jurisdictions such as the advowson, chancel repair liability and lordships of the manor. These are all classified as real property, as they would have been protected by real actions in the early common law.

USA

Each U.S. State except Louisiana has its own laws governing real property and the estates therein, grounded in the common law. In Arizona, real property is generally defined as land and the things permanently attached to the land. Things that are permanently attached to the land, which also can be referred to as improvements, include homes, garages, and buildings. Manufactured homes can obtain an affidavit of affixture.

Economic Aspects of Real Property

Land use, land valuation, and the determination of the incomes of landowners, are among the oldest questions in economic theory. Land is an essential input (factor of production) for agriculture, and agriculture is by far the most important economic activity in preindustrial societies. With the advent of industrialization, important new uses for land emerge, as sites for factories, warehouses, offices, and urban agglomerations. Also, the value of real property taking the form of man-made structures and machinery increases relative to the value of land alone. The concept of real property eventually comes to encompass effectively all forms of tangible fixed capital. with the rise of extractive industries, real property comes to encompass natural capital. With the rise of tourism and leisure, real property comes to include scenic and other amenity values.

Starting in the 1960s, as part of the emerging field of law and economics, economists and legal scholars began to study the property rights enjoyed by tenants under the various estates, and the economic benefits and costs of the various estates. This resulted in a much improved understanding of the:

- Property rights enjoyed by tenants under the various estates. These include the right to:
    - o Decide how a piece of real property is used;
    - o Exclude others from enjoying the property;

  - o Transfer (alienate) some or all of these rights to others on mutually agreeable terms;
- Nature and consequences of transaction costs when changing and transferring estates.

For an introduction to the economic analysis of property law, see Shavell (2004), and Cooter and Ulen (2003). For a collection of related scholarly articles, see Epstein (2007). Ellickson (1993) broadens the economic analysis of real property with a variety of facts drawn from history and ethnography.

Historical Background

The word "real" ultimately derives from Latin *res* "thing" and was used to Middle English to mean "relating to things, especially real property".

In common law, real property was property that could be protected by some form of real action, in contrast to personal property, where a plaintiff would have to resort to another form of action. As a result of this formalist approach, some things the common law deems to be land would not be classified as such by most modern legal systems, for example an advowson (the right to present to the living of a church) was real property. By contrast the rights of a leaseholder originate in personal actions and so the common law originally treated a leasehold as part of personal property.

The law now broadly distinguishes between real property (land and anything affixed to it) and personal property (everything else, *e.g.*, clothing, furniture, money). The conceptual difference was between immovable property, which would transfer title along with the land, and movable property, which a person would retain title to. In modern legal systems derived from English common law, classification of property as *real* or *personal* may vary somewhat according to jurisdiction or, even within jurisdictions, according to purpose, as in defining whether and how the property may be taxed. Bethell (1998) contains much historical information on the historical evolution of real property and property rights.

Real Estate in Mexico and Central America

The real estate businesses in Mexico, Canada, Guam and Central America are different from the way that they are conducted in the United States. Some similarities include a variety of legal formalities (with professionals such as real estate agents generally employed to assist the buyer); taxes need to be paid (but typically less than those in U.S.); legal paperwork will ensure title; and a neutral party such as a title company will handle documentation and money to make the smooth exchange between the parties. Increasingly, U.S. title companies are doing work for U.S. buyers in Mexico and Central America.

Prices are often much cheaper than most areas of the U.S., but in many locations, prices of houses and lots are as expensive as the U.S., one example being Mexico City. U.S. banks have begun to give home loans for properties in Mexico, but, so far, not for other Latin American countries.

One important difference from the United States is that each country has rules regarding where foreigners can buy. For example, in Mexico, foreigners cannot buy land or homes within 50 km (31 mi) of the coast or 100 km (62 mi) from a border unless they hold title in a Mexican Corporation or a Fideicomiso (a Mexican trust). In Honduras, however, they may buy beach front property directly in their name. There are different rules regarding certain types of property: *ejidal land* – communally held farm property – can only be sold after a lengthy entitlement process, but that does not prevent them from being offered for sale.

In Costa Rica, real estate agents do not need a license to operate, but the transfer of property requires a lawyer. In Mexico, real estate agents do not need a license to operate, but the transfer of property requires a notary public.

Business Sector

With the development of private property ownership, real estate has become a major area of business, commonly referred to as commercial real estate. Purchasing real estate requires a significant investment, and each parcel of land has unique characteristics, so the real estate industry has evolved into several distinct fields. Specialists are often called on to valuate real estate and facilitate transactions. Some kinds of real estate businesses include:

- Appraisal: Professional valuation services

- Brokerages: A mediator who charges a fee to facilitate a real estate transaction between the two parties.
- Development: Improving land for use by adding or replacing buildings
- Net leasing
- Property management: Managing a property for its owner(s)
- Real estate marketing: Managing the sales side of the property business
- Real estate investing: Managing the investment of real estate
- Relocation services: Relocating people or business to a different country
- Corporate Real Estate: Managing the real estate held by a corporation to support its core business—unlike managing the real estate held by an investor to generate income.

Within each field, a business may specialize in a particular type of real estate, such as residential, commercial, or industrial property. In addition, almost all construction business effectively has a connection to real estate.

Professional university-level education in real estate is primarily focused at the graduate level. Focus in towards the commercial real estate sector, primarily real estate development or investment rather than residential real estate sales conducted by a REALTOR.

"Internet real estate" is a term coined by the internet investment community relating to ownership of domain names and the similarities between high quality internet domain names and real-world, prime real estate.

Residential Real Estate

The legal arrangement for the right to occupy a dwelling in some countries is known as the housing tenure. Types of housing tenure include owner occupancy, Tenancy, housing cooperative, condominiums (individually parceled properties in a single building), public housing, squatting, and cohousing. The occupants of a residence constitute a household.

Residences can be classified by, if, and how they are connected to neighboring residences and land. Different types of housing tenure can be used for the same physical type. For example, connected residents might be owned by a single entity and leased out, or owned separately with an agreement covering the relationship between units and common areas and concerns.

- Attached/multi-unit dwellings
  - o Apartment-An individual unit in a multi-unit building. The boundaries of the apartment are generally defined by a perimeter of locked or lockable doors. Often seen in multi-story apartment buildings.
  - o Multi-family house-Often seen in multi-story detached buildings, where each floor is a separate apartment or unit.
  - o Terraced house (a.k.a. *townhouse* or *rowhouse*)-A number of single or multi-unit buildings in a continuous row with shared walls and no intervening space.
  - o Condominium-Building or complex, similar to apartments, owned by individuals. Common grounds and common areas within the complex are owned and shared jointly. There are *townhouse* or *rowhouse* style condominiums as well.
  - o Cooperative (a.k.a. "co-op)-A type of multiple ownership in which the residents of a multi-unit housing complex own shares in the cooperative corporation that owns the property, giving each resident the right to occupy a specific apartment or unit.
- Semi-detached dwellings
  - o Duplex-Two units with one shared wall.
- Single-family detached home
- Portable dwellings
  - o Mobile homes-Potentially a full-time residence which can be (might not in practice be) movable on wheels.
  - o Houseboats-A floating home
  - o Tents-Usually very temporary, with roof and walls consisting only of fabric-like material.

The size of an apartment or house can be described in square feet or meters. In the United States, this includes the area of "living space", excluding the garage and other non-living spaces. The "square meters" figure of a house in Europe may report the total area of the walls enclosing the home, thus including any attached garage and non-living spaces, which makes it important to inquire what kind of surface definition has been used.

It can be described more roughly by the number of rooms. A studio apartment has a single bedroom with no living room (possibly a separate kitchen). A one-bedroom apartment has a living or dining room separate from the bedroom. Two bedroom, three bedroom, and larger units are common. (A bedroom is defined as a room with a closet for clothes storage.)

Major categories in India and the Asian Subcontinent;

- Housing Societies (CGHS)
- Condominiums
- Builder flats
- Chawls
- Havelis
- Lal Dora-Where people carry out commercial and residential activities both.

The size is measured in Gaz (square yards), Quila, Marla, Beegha, and acre.

Market Sector Value

According to *The Economist*, "developed economies'" assets at the end of 2002 were the following:

- Residential property: $48 trillion;
- Commercial property: $14 trillion;
- Equities: $20 trillion;
- Government bonds: $20 trillion;
- Corporate bonds: $13 trillion;
- Total: $115 trillion.

That makes real estate assets 54% and financial assets 46% of total stocks, bonds, and real estate assets. Assets not counted here are bank deposits, insurance "reserve" assets, natural resources, and human assets. It is not clear if all debt and equity investments are counted in the categories equities and bond.

Mortgages in Real Estate

In recent years, many economists have recognized that the lack of effective real estate laws can be a significant barrier to investment in many developing countries. In most societies, rich and poor, a significant fraction of the total wealth is in the form of land and buildings.

In most advanced economies, the main source of capital used by individuals and small companies to purchase and improve land and buildings is mortgage loans (or other instruments). These are loans for which the real property itself constitutes collateral. Banks are willing to make such loans at favorable rates in large part because, if the borrower does not make payments, the lender can foreclose by filing a court action which allows them to take back the property and sell it to get their money back. For investors, profitability can be enhanced by using an off plan or pre-construction strategy to purchase at a lower price which is often the case in the pre-construction phase of development.

But in many developing countries there is no effective means by which a lender could foreclose, so the mortgage loan industry, as such, either does not exist at all or is only available to members of privileged social classes.

5

Movable Property

Elevator Air Conditioning

Concept

Elevator air conditioning is fast becoming a popular concept around the world. The primary reason for installing an elevator air conditioner is the comfort that it provides while travelling in the elevator. It stabilizes the condition of the air inside the lift car. Some elevator air conditioners can be used in countries with cold climates if a thermostat is used to reverse the refrigeration cycle to warm the lift car.

Health

One of the benefits of installing an elevator air conditioner is the clean air it provides. Air was typically drawn from the elevator shaft or hoistway into the car using a motorized fan. This air could contain dust mites, germs and bacteria. With an elevator air conditioner, the air is much cleaner because it is recirculated within the car itself and is usually filtered to remove contaminants. A poorly maintained air-conditioning system may promote the growth and spread of microorganisms, but as long as the air conditioner is kept clean, these health hazards can be avoided.

Drawbacks

Heat generated from the cooling process is rejected into the hoistway. The elevator cab (or car) is not air-tight, and some of this heat will reenter the car and reduce the overall cooling effect, which may be less than ideal.

Energy

The air from the lobby constantly leaks into the elevator shaft due to elevator movements as well as elevator shaft ventilation requirements. Using this conditioned air in the elevator does not increase energy costs. However, by using an independent elevator air conditioner to achieve better temperature control inside the car, more energy will be used.

Condensation

Air conditioning poses a problem to elevators because of the condensation that occurs. The condensed water produced has to be disposed of; otherwise, it would create flooding in the elevator car and hoistway.

Ways to Remove Condensed Water

There are at least four ways to remove condensed water from the air conditioner. However, each solution has its pros and cons.

Atomizing

Atomizing, also known as misting the condensed water, is another way to dispose of the condensed water. Spraying ultra-fine water droplets onto the hot coils of the air conditioner ensures that the condensed water evaporates quickly. Though this is one of the best methods to dispose of the condensed water, it is also one of the costliest because the nozzle that atomizes the water easily gets choked. The majority of the cost goes to maintaining the entire atomizing system.

Boiling

Disposing of condensed water works by firstly collecting the condensed water and then heating it to above boiling point. The condensed water is eventually evaporated, thereby disposing of it. Consumers are reluctant to employ this system because of the high rate of energy used just to dispose of this water.

Cascading

The cascading method works by flowing the condensed water directly onto the hot coils of the air conditioner. This eventually evaporates the condensed water. The downside of this technology is that the coils have to be at extremely high temperature for the condensed water to be evaporated. There is a chance that the water might not evaporate entirely and that would cause water to overflow onto the exterior of the car.

Drainage System

Drainage system works by creating a sump to collect the condensed water and using a pump to dispose it through a drainage system. It is an efficient method, but it comes at a heavy price because the cost of building the sump. Moreover, maintaining the pump to make sure it operates is very expensive. Furthermore, the pipes used for drainage would look ugly on the exterior. This system also cannot be implemented on a built project.

Controlling Elevators

General Controls

A typical modern passenger elevator will have:

- Space to stand in, guardrails, seating cushion (luxury)
- Overload sensor—prevents the elevator from moving until excess load has been removed. It may trigger a voice prompt or buzzer alarm. This may also trigger a "full car" indicator, indicating the car's inability to accept more passengers until some are unloaded.
- Electric fans or air conditioning units to enhance circulation and comfort.
- Call buttons to choose a floor. Some of these may be key switches (to control access). In some elevators, certain floors are inaccessible unless one swipes a security card or enters a passcode (or both). In the United States and other countries, call button text and icons are raised to allow blind users to operate the elevator; many have Braille text besides.
- A set of doors kept locked on each floor to prevent unintentional access into the elevator shaft by the unsuspecting individual. The door is unlocked and opened by a machine sitting on the roof of the car, which also drives the doors that travel with the car. Door controls are provided to close immediately or reopen the doors. Objects in the path of the moving doors will

either be detected by sensors or physically activate a switch that reopens the doors. Otherwise, the doors will close after a preset time.

- A stop switch (not allowed under British regulations) to halt the elevator while in motion and often used to hold an elevator open while freight is loaded. Keeping an elevator stopped for too long may trigger an alarm. Unless local codes require otherwise, this will most likely be a key switch.
- An alarm button or switch, which passengers can use to signal that they have been trapped in the elevator.

Some elevators may have one or more of the following:

- An elevator telephone, which can be used (in addition to the alarm) by a trapped passenger to call for help.
- Hold button: This button delays the door closing timer, useful for loading freight and hospital beds.
- Call cancellation: A destination floor may be deselected by double clicking.
- Access restriction by key switches, RFID reader, code keypad, hotel room card, etc..
- One or more additional sets of doors that can serve different floor plans. For example, in an elevated crosswalk setup, the front doors may open on the street level, and the rear doors open on the crosswalk level.
- Security camera
- Plain walls or mirrored walls giving the illusion of larger area
- Glass windowpane providing a view of the building interior or onto the streets.

Other controls, which are generally inaccessible to the public (either because they are key switches, or because they are kept behind a locked panel), include:

- Fireman's service, phase II key switch
- Switch to enable or disable the elevator.
- An *inspector's* switch, which places the elevator in inspection mode (this may be situated on top of the elevator)

- Manual up/down controls for elevator technicians, to be used in inspection mode, for example.
- An *independent service/exclusive mode* will prevent the car from answering to hall calls and only arrive at floors selected via the panel. The door should stay open while parked on a floor. This mode may be used for temporarily transporting goods.
- Attendant service mode.

Controls in Early Elevators

- Some older freight elevators are controlled by switches operated by pulling on adjacent ropes. Safety interlocks ensure that the inner and outer doors are closed before the elevator is allowed to move.
- Early elevators had no automatic landing positioning. Elevators were operated by elevator operators using a motor controller. The controller was contained within a cylindrical container about the size and shape of a cake container and this was operated via a projecting handle. This allowed some control over the energy supplied to the motor (located at the top of the elevator shaft or beside the bottom of the elevator shaft) and so enabled the elevator to be accurately positioned — if the operator was sufficiently skilled. More typically the operator would have to "jog" the control to get the elevator reasonably close to the landing point and then direct the outgoing and incoming passengers to "watch the step". After stopping at the landing the operator would open the door/doors. Some slightly later lifts though, had door(s) that could be operated by the same control (so when the lever is moved in the desired direction, between the idle and motion points there is a trigger to close the doors. When the handle is moved to idle, the doors open again.) This sort of arrangement was used sometimes in subway stations. Manually operated elevators were generally refitted or the cabs replaced by automatic equipment by the 1950s. The major exception is freight elevators which today are just as commonly operated manually as automatically, and even when equipped with automatic controls, are often operated by an attendant to ensure efficiency.

- Early automatic elevators used relays as logic gates to control them, which began to be replaced by microprocessors in the late 1980s.
- Large buildings with multiple elevators of this type also had an *elevator dispatcher* stationed in the lobby to direct passengers and to signal the operator to leave with the use of a mechanical "cricket" noisemaker.
- Some elevators still in operation have pushbutton manual controls.

External Controls

Elevators are typically controlled from the outside by up and down buttons at each stop. When pressed at a certain floor, the elevator arrives to pick up more passengers. If the particular elevator is currently serving traffic in a certain direction, it will only answer hall calls in the same direction unless there are no more calls beyond that floor.

In a group of two or more elevators, the call buttons may be linked to a central dispatch computer, such that they illuminate and cancel together. This is done to ensure that only one car is called at one time.

Key switches may be installed on the ground floor so that the elevator can be remotely switched on or off from the outside.

In sky lobby elevator systems, one selects the intended destination floor (in lieu of pressing "up") and is then notified which elevator will serve their request.

Floor Numbering

The Elevator Algorithm

The elevator algorithm, a simple algorithm by which a single elevator can decide where to stop, is summarized as follows:

- Continue travelling in the same direction while there are remaining requests in that same direction.
- If there are no further requests in that direction, then stop and become idle, or change direction if there are requests in the opposite direction.

The elevator algorithm has found an application in computer operating systems as an algorithm for scheduling hard disk requests. Modern elevators use more complex heuristic algorithms to decide which request to service next. An introduction to these algorithms can be found in the "Elevator traffic handbook: theory and practice" given in the references below.

Destination Control System

Some skyscraper buildings and other types of installation feature a destination operating panel where a passenger registers their floor calls before entering the car. The system lets them know which car to wait for, instead of everyone boarding the next car. In this way, travel time is reduced as the elevator makes fewer stops for individual passengers, and the computer distributes adjacent stops to different cars in the bank. Although travel time is reduced passenger waiting times may be longer as they will not necessarily be allocated the next car to depart. During the down peak period the benefit of destination control will be limited as passengers have a common destination.

It can also improve accessibility, as a mobility-impaired passenger can move to his or her designated car in advance.

Inside the elevator there is no call button to push, or the buttons are there but they cannot be pushed-except door opening and alarm button – they only indicate stopping floors.

The idea of destination control was originally conceived by Leo Port from Sydney in 1961 but at that time lift controllers were implemented in relays and were unable to optimise the performance of destination control allocations.

The system was first pioneered by Schindler Elevator in 1992 as the Miconic 10. Manufacturers of such systems claim that average travelling time can be reduced by up to 30%.

However, performance enhancements cannot be generalized as the benefits and limitations of the system are dependent on many factors. One problem is that the system is subject to gaming. Sometimes, one person enters the destination for a large group of people going to the same floor. The dispatching algorithm is usually unable to completely cater for the variation, and latecomers may find the elevator they are assigned to is already full. Also, occasionally, one person may press the floor multiple times. This is common with up/down buttons when people believe this to be an effective way to hurry elevators. However, this will make the computer think multiple people are waiting and will allocate empty cars to serve this one person.

To prevent this problem, in one implementation of destination control, every user gets an RFID card to identify himself so the system knows every user call and can cancel the first call if the passenger decides to travel to another destination to prevent empty calls. The newest invention knows even where people are located and how many on which floor because of their identification, either for the purposes of evacuating the building or for security reasons.

The same destination scheduling concept can also be applied to public transit such as in group rapid transit.

Special Operating Modes

Anti-Crime Protection (ACP)

Anti-Crime Protection will force each car to stop at a pre-defined landing and open its doors. This allows a security guard or a receptionist at the landing to visually inspect the passengers. The car stops at this landing as it passes to serve further demand.

Up Peak (MIT)

During Up Peak mode (also called Moderate Incoming Traffic), elevator cars in a group are recalled to the lobby to provide expeditious service to passengers arriving at the building, most typically in the morning as people arrive for work or at the conclusion of a lunch-time period. Elevators are dispatched one-by-one when they reach a pre-determined passenger load, or when they have had their doors opened for a certain period of time. The next elevator to be dispatched usually has its hall lantern or a "this car leaving next" sign illuminated to encourage passengers to make maximum use of the available elevator system capacity. The commencement of Up Peak may be triggered by a time clock, by the departure of a certain number of fully loaded cars leaving the lobby within a given time period, or by a switch manually operated by a building attendant.

Down Peak

During Down Peak mode, elevator cars in a group are sent away from the lobby towards the highest floor served, after which they commence running down the floors in response to hall calls placed by passengers wishing to leave the building. This allows the elevator system to provide maximum passenger handling capacity for people leaving the building.

The commencement of Down Peak may be triggered by a time clock, by the arrival of a certain number of fully loaded cars at the lobby within a given time period, or by a switch manually operated by a building attendant.

Sabbath Service (SHO)

In areas with large populations of observant Jews or in facilities catering to Jews, one may find a "Sabbath elevator". In this mode, an elevator will stop automatically at every floor, allowing people to step on and off without having to press any buttons. This prevents violation of the Sabbath prohibition against operating electrical devices when Sabbath is in effect for those who observe this ritual. However, Sabbath mode has the side effect of wasting considerable amounts of energy, running the elevator car sequentially up and down every floor of a building, repeatedly servicing floors where it is not needed. For a tall building with many floors, the car must move on a frequent enough basis so as to not cause undue delay for potential users that will not touch the controls as it opens the doors on every floor up the building.

Independent Service (ISC)

Independent service is a special service mode found on most elevators. It is activated by a key switch either inside the elevator itself or on a centralized control panel in the lobby. When an elevator is placed on independent service, it will no longer respond to hall calls. (In a bank of elevators, traffic is rerouted to the other elevators, while in a single elevator, the hall buttons are disabled). The elevator will remain parked on a floor with its doors open until a floor is selected and the door close button is held until the elevator starts to travel. Independent service is useful when transporting large goods or moving groups of people between certain floors.

Inspection Service (INS)

Inspection service is designed to provide access to the hoistway and car top for inspection and maintenance purposes by qualified elevator mechanics. It is first activated by a key switch on the car operating panel usually labeled 'Inspection', 'Car Top', 'Access Enable' or 'HWENAB'. When this switch is activated the elevator will come to a stop if moving, car calls will be cancelled (and the buttons disabled), and hall calls will be assigned to other elevator cars in the group (or cancelled in a single elevator configuration). The elevator can now only be moved by the corresponding 'Access' key switches, usually located at the top-most (to access the top of the car) and bottom-most (to access the elevator pit) landings. The access key switches will bypass the door lock circuit for the floor it is located on and allow the car to move at reduced inspection speed with the hoistway door open. This speed can range from anywhere up to 60% of normal operating speed on most controllers, and is usually defined by local safety codes.

Elevators have a car top inspection station that allows the car to be operated by a mechanic in order to move it through the hoistway. Generally, there are three buttons-UP, RUN, and DOWN. Both the RUN and a direction button must be held to move the car in that direction, and the elevator will stop moving as soon as the buttons are released. Most other elevators have an up/down toggle switch and a RUN button. The inspection panel also has standard power outlets for work lamps and powered tools.

Fire Service Mode (EFS)

Depending on the location of the elevator, fire service code will vary state to state and country to country. Fire service is usually split up into two modes: Phase One and Phase Two. These are separate modes that the elevator can go into.

Phase one mode is activated by a corresponding smoke sensor or heat sensor in the building. Once an alarm has been activated, the elevator will automatically go into phase one. The elevator will wait an amount of time, then proceed to go into nudging mode to tell everyone the elevator is leaving the floor. Once the elevator has left the floor, depending on where the alarm was set off, the elevator will go to the Fire Recall Floor. However, if the alarm was activated on the fire recall floor the elevator will have an alternate floor to recall to. When the elevator is recalled, it proceeds to the recall floor and stops with its doors open. The elevator will no longer respond to calls or move in any direction. Located on the fire recall floor is a fire service key switch. The fire service key switch has the ability to turn fire service off, turn fire service on or to bypass fire service. The only way to return the elevator to normal service is to switch it to bypass after the alarms have reset.

Phase two mode can only be activated by a key switch located inside the elevator on the centralized control panel. This mode was created for firefighters so that they may rescue people from a burning building. The phase two key switch located on the COP has three positions: off, on, and hold. By turning phase two on, the firefighter enables the car to move. However, like independent service mode, the car will not respond to a car call unless the firefighter manually pushes and holds the door close button. Once the elevator gets to the desired floor it will not open its doors unless the firefighter holds the door open button. This is in case the floor is burning and the firefighter can feel the heat and knows not to open the door. The firefighter must hold door open until the door is completely opened. If for any reason the firefighter wishes to leave the elevator, they will use the hold position on the key switch to make sure the elevator remains at that floor. If the firefighter wishes to return to the recall floor, they simply turn the key off and close the doors.

Fire Service is for emergency use only, although fire service keys can be purchased on eBay, and other websites. Only trained responders should use this feature, and it is by no means a safe way to escape from a burning building.

Medical Emergency/'Code Blue' Service (EHS)

Commonly found in hospitals, Code Blue service allows an elevator to be summoned to any floor for use in an emergency situation. Each floor will have a 'Code Blue' recall key switch, and when activated, the elevator system will immediately select the elevator car that can respond the fastest, regardless of direction of travel and passenger load. Passengers inside the elevator will be notified with an alarm and indicator light to exit the elevator when the doors open.

Once the elevator arrives at the floor, it will park with its doors open and the car buttons will be disabled to prevent a passenger from taking control of the elevator. Medical personnel must then activate the Code Blue key switch inside the car, select their floor and close the doors with the door close button. The elevator will then travel non-stop to the selected floor, and will remain in Code Blue service until switched off in the car. Some hospital elevators will feature a 'hold' position on the Code Blue key switch (similar to fire service) which allows the elevator to remain at a floor locked out of service until Code Blue is deactivated.

Emergency Power Operation (EPR)

Many elevator installations now feature emergency power systems which allow elevator use in blackout situations and prevent people from becoming trapped in elevators.

Traction Elevators

When power is lost in a traction elevator system, all elevators will initially come to a halt. One by one, each car in the group will return to the lobby floor, open its doors and shut down. People in the remaining elevators may see an indicator light or hear a voice announcement informing them that the elevator will return to the lobby shortly. Once all cars have successfully returned, the system will then automatically select one or more cars to be used for normal operations and these cars will return to service. The car(s) selected to run under emergency power can be manually overridden by a key or strip switch in the lobby. In order to help prevent entrapment, when the system detects that it is running low on power, it will bring the running cars to the lobby or nearest floor, open the doors and shut down.

Hydraulic Elevators

In hydraulic elevator systems, emergency power will lower the elevators to the lowest landing and open the doors to allow passengers to exit. The doors then close after an adjustable time period and the car remains unusable until reset, usually by cycling the elevator main power switch. Typically, due to the high current draw when starting the pump motor, hydraulic elevators aren't run using standard emergency power systems. Buildings like hospitals and nursing homes usually size their emergency generators to accommodate this draw. However, the increasing use of current limiting motor starters, commonly known as "Soft-Start" contactors, avoid much of this problem and the current draw of the pump motor is less of a limiting concern.

Elevator Convenience Features

Elevators may feature talking devices as an accessibility aid for the blind. In addition to floor arrival notifications, the computer announces the direction of travel, and notifies the passengers before the doors are to close.

In addition to the call buttons, elevators usually have floor indicators (often illuminated by LED) and direction lanterns. The former are almost universal in cab interiors with more than two stops and may be found outside the elevators as well on one or more of the floors. Floor indicators can consist of a dial with a rotating needle, but the most common types are those with successively illuminated floor indications or LCDs. Likewise, a change of floors or an arrival at a floor is indicated by a sound, depending on the elevator.

Direction lanterns are also found both inside and outside elevator cars, but they should always be visible from outside because their primary purpose is to help people decide whether or not to get on the elevator. If somebody waiting for the elevator wants to go up, but a car comes first that indicates that it is going down, then the person may decide not to get on the elevator. If the person waits, then one will still stop going up. Direction indicators are sometimes etched with arrows or shaped like arrows and/or use the convention that one that lights up red means "down" and green means "up". Since the colour convention is often undermined or overridden by systems that do not invoke it, it is usually used only in conjunction with other differentiating factors. An example of a place whose elevators use only the colour convention to differentiate between directions is the Museum of Contemporary Art in Chicago, where a single circle can be made to light up green for "up" and red for "down". Sometimes directions must be inferred by the position of the indicators relative to one another.

In addition to lanterns, most elevators have a chime to indicate if the elevator is going up or down either before or after the doors open, usually in conjunction with the lanterns lighting up. Universally, one chime is for up, two is for down, and none indicates an elevator that is 'free'. Observatory service elevators often convey other facts of interest, including elevator speed, stopwatch, and current position (altitude), as with the case for Taipei 101's service elevators.

Standards

The mechanical and electrical design of elevators is dictated according to various standards (aka elevator codes), which may be international, national, state, regional or city based. Whereas once many standards were prescriptive, specifying exact criteria which must be complied with, there has recently been a shift towards more performance-based standards where the onus falls on the designer to ensure that the elevator meets or exceeds the standard.

Some of the national elevator standards include:

- Australia – AS1735
- Canada – CAN/CSA B44
- Europe – EN 81 series (EN 81-1, EN 81-2, EN 81-28, EN 81-70, EN 12015, EN 12016, EN 13015, etc.)
- USA – ASME A17.

Because an elevator is part of a building, it must also comply with standards relating to earthquake resilience, fire standards, electrical wiring rules and so forth.

The American National Elevator Standards Group (ANESG) sets an elevator weight standard to be 2200 lbs.

Additional requirements relating to access by disabled persons, may be mandated by laws or regulations such as the Americans with Disabilities Act.

US and Canadian Elevator Standard Specifics

In most US and Canadian jurisdictions, passenger elevators are required to conform to the American Society of Mechanical Engineers' Standard A17.1, Safety Code for Elevators and Escalators. In Canada the document is the CAN/CSA B44 Safety Standard, which was harmonized with the US version in the 2000 edition. In addition, passenger elevators may be required to conform to the requirements of A17.3 for existing elevators where referenced by the local jurisdiction. Passenger elevators are tested using the ASME A17.2 Standard. The frequency of these tests is mandated by the local jurisdiction, which may be a town, city, state or provincial standard.

Passenger elevators must also conform to many ancillary building codes including the Local or State building code, National Fire Protection Association standards for Electrical, Fire Sprinklers and Fire Alarms, Plumbing codes, and HVAC codes. Also, passenger elevators are required to conform to the Americans with Disabilities Act and other State and Federal civil rights legislation regarding accessibility.

Residential elevators are required to conform to ASME A17.1. Platform and Wheelchair lifts are required to comply with ASME A18.1 in most US jurisdictions.

Most elevators have a location in which the permit for the building owner to operate the elevator is displayed. While some jurisdictions require the permit to be displayed in the elevator cab, other jurisdictions allow for the operating permit to be kept on file elsewhere – such as the maintenance office – and to be made available for inspection on demand. In such cases instead of the permit being displayed in the elevator cab, often a notice is posted in its place informing riders of where the actual permits are kept.

Unique Elevator Installations

World statistics

Country	*Number of elevators installed*
Italy	900,000
United States	700,000
People's Republic of China	610,000

As of January 2008, Italy is the nation with the most elevators installed in the world, with 850,000 elevators installed that run more than one hundred million lifts every day, followed by United States with 700,000 elevators installed and People's Republic of China with 610,000 elevators installed since 1949. In Brazil, it is estimated that there are approximately 300,000 elevators currently in operation. The world's largest market for elevators is Italy with more than 1,629 million euros of sales and 1,224 million euros of internal market.

Eiffel Tower

The Eiffel Tower has Otis double-deck elevators built into the legs of the tower, serving the ground level to the first and second levels. Even though the shaft runs diagonally upwards with the contour of the tower, both the upper and lower cars remain horizontally level. The offset distance of the two cars changes throughout the journey.

There are four elevator cars of the traditional design that run from the second level to the third level. The cars are connected to their opposite pairs (opposite in the elevator landing/hall) and use each other as the counterweight. As one car ascends from level 2, the other descends from level 3. The operations of these elevators are synchronized by a light signal in the car.

Taipei 101

Double deck elevators are used in the Taipei 101 office tower. Tenants of even-numbered floors first take an escalator (or an elevator from the parking garage) to the 2nd level, where they will enter the upper deck and arrive at their floors. The lower deck is turned off during low-volume hours, and the upper deck can act as a single-level elevator stopping at all adjacent floors. For example, the 85th floor restaurants can be accessed from the 60th floor sky-lobby. Restaurant customers must clear their reservations at the reception counter on the 2nd floor. A bank of express elevators stop only on the sky lobby levels (36 and 60, upper deck car), where tenants can transfer to "local" elevators.

The high speed observation deck elevators accelerate to a world-record certified speed of 1010 meters per minute (60.6 km/h) in 16 seconds, and then it slows down for arrival with subtle air pressure sensations. The door opens after 37 seconds from the 5th floor. Special features include aerodynamic car and counterweights, and cabin pressure control to help passengers adapt smoothly to pressure changes. The downwards journey is completed at a reduced speed of 600 meters per minute, with the doors opening at the 52nd second.

The Gateway Arch

The Gateway Arch in St. Louis, Missouri has a unique elevator system which carries passengers from the visitors' center underneath the Arch to the observation deck at the top of the structure.

Called a *tram* or *tramway*, people enter this unique tramway much as one would enter an ordinary elevator, through double doors. Passing through the doors the passengers in small groups enter a horizontal cylindrical compartment containing seats on each side and a flat floor. A number of these compartments are linked to form a train. These compartments each individually retain an appropriate level orientation by tilting while the entire train follows curved tracks up one leg of the arch.

There are two tramways within the Arch, one at the north end, and the other at the south end. The entry doors have windows, so people travelling within the Arch are able to see the interior structure of the Arch during the ride to and from the observation deck. At the beginning of the trip the cars hang from the drive cables, but as the angle of the shaft changes, they end up beside and then on top of the cables.

New City Hall, Hanover, Germany

The elevator in the New City Hall in Hanover, Germany is a technical rarity, and unique in Europe, as the elevator starts straight up but then changes its angle by 15 degrees to follow the contour of the dome of the hall. The cabin therefore tilts 15 degrees during the ride. The elevator travels a height of 43 meters. The new city hall was built in 1913. The elevator was destroyed in 1943 and rebuilt in 1954.

Luxor Inclinator Elevator

In Las Vegas, Nevada, at the Luxor Hotel, is the Inclinator. The shape of this casino is a pyramid. Therefore, the elevator travels up the side of the pyramid at a 39 degree angle. Although people refer to this "inclined elevator" as an inclinator, this is incorrect.

Twilight Zone Tower of Terror

The Twilight Zone Tower of Terror is the common name for a series of elevator attractions at the Disney's Hollywood Studios park in Orlando, the Disney's California Adventure park in Anaheim, the Walt Disney Studios Park in Paris and the Tokyo DisneySea park in Tokyo. The central element of this attraction is a simulated free-fall achieved through the use of a high-speed elevator system. For safety reasons, passengers are seated and secured in their seats rather than standing. Unlike most traction elevators, the elevator car and counterweight are joined using a rail system in a continuous loop running through both the top and the bottom of the drop shaft. This allows the drive motor to pull down on the elevator car from underneath, resulting in downward acceleration greater than that of normal gravity. The high-speed drive motor is used to rapidly lift the elevator as well.

The passenger cabs are mechanically separated from the lift mechanism, thus allowing the elevator shafts to be used continuously while passengers board and embark from the cabs. Multiple elevator shafts are used to further improve passenger throughput. The doorways of the top few "floors" of the attraction are open to the outdoor environment, thus allowing passengers to look out from the top of the structure.

"Top of the Rock" elevators

Guests ascending to the 67th, 69th, and 70th level observation decks (dubbed "Top of the Rock") atop the GE Building at Rockefeller Center in New York City ride a high-speed glass-top elevator. When entering the cab, it appears to be any normal elevator ride. However, once the cab begins moving, the interior lights turn off and a special blue light above the cab turns on. This lights the entire shaft, so riders can see the moving cab through its glass ceiling as it rises and lowers through the shaft. Music plays and various animations are also displayed on the ceiling. The entire ride takes about 60 seconds.

Disneyland, Anaheim, California

Part of the Haunted Mansion attraction at Disneyland in Anaheim, California, takes place on an elevator. The "stretching room" on the ride is actually an elevator that travels downwards, giving access to a short underground tunnel which leads to the rest of the attraction. The elevator has no ceiling and its shaft is decorated to look like walls of a mansion. Because there is no roof, passengers are able to see the walls of the shaft by looking up, which gives the illusion of the room stretching. The Haunted Mansion attraction at Disney World does not feature this, rather it gives you the illusion it is moving while it remains stationary.

Elevators for Urban Transport

In some towns where terrain is difficult to navigate, elevators are used as part of urban transport systems. Examples:

- Almada, Portugal: *Elevador da Boca do Vento*
- Asansor, Izmir, Turkey
- Ascensores de Valparaíso, urban funicular in Valparaíso, Chile
- Bad Schandau Elevator in Bad Schandau, Germany
- Barcelona, Spain-Elevator and cableway line connecting the port terminal to Montjuic hill
- Bilbao-Casco Viejo Bilbao Metro station (fare-paying elevator connecting upper and lower neighbourhoods, as well as the station)
- Brussels-Marolles, Belgium: "Ascenseur des Marolles", links the upper part of the city to the lower one, from Place Poelaert to Breughel square.
- Coimbra, Portugal: *Elevador do Mercado*
- East Hill Cliff Railway, Hastings, UK
- Genoa, Italy-eleven public elevators
- Hammetschwand Elevator in Bürgenstock, Switzerland
- Jersey City, New Jersey elevator at Bergen Hudson Light Rail station at 9th Street and Palisade Avenue.
- Katarina Elevator in Stockholm, Sweden
- Lisbon, Portugal: *Elevador de Santa Justa, Castelo* (planned), *Chiado* (closed), *Município/Biblioteca* (demolished)
- Luxembourg
- Lynchburg, Virginia-Outdoor Public elevator.
- Marburg, Germany-some parts of the historic city core built on higher ground (Uppertown, "Oberstadt" in German) are accessible from the lower street level by elevators. These elevators are unique in servicing also various buildings partially embedded in the steep-sloping terrain.
- Monaco, seven elevators

- Naples, Italy-three public elevators
- Oporto, Portugal: *Elevador da Ribeira*
- Oregon City Municipal Elevator in Oregon City, Oregon, United States
- Salvador, Bahia, Brazil: *Elevador Lacerda*
- Santa Justa Lift in Lisbon, Portugal
- Savannah, Georgia: Public elevators with access to River Street.
- Shanklin Cliff Lift in Shanklin, Isle of Wight
- Skyway in Nagasaki, Japan
- Yalta, Ukraine.

Escalator

An escalator is a moving staircase – a conveyor transport device for carrying people between floors of a building. The device consists of a motor-driven chain of individual, linked steps that move up or down on tracks, allowing the step treads to remain horizontal.

Escalators are used around the world to move pedestrian traffic in places where elevators would be impractical. Principal areas of usage include department stores, shopping malls, airports, transit systems, convention centers, hotels, and public buildings.

The benefits of escalators are many. They have the capacity to move large numbers of people, and they can be placed in the same physical space as one might install a staircase. They have no waiting interval (except during very heavy traffic), they can be used to guide people toward main exits or special exhibits, and they may be weatherproofed for outdoor use.

Design, Components, and Operation

Operation and Layout

Escalators, like moving walkways, are powered by constant-speed alternating current motors and move at approximately 1–2 feet (0.30–0.61 m) per second. The typical angle of inclination of an escalator to the horizontal floor level is 30 degrees with a standard rise up to about 60 feet (18 m). Modern escalators have single-piece aluminum or steel steps that move on a system of tracks in a continuous loop.

Escalators have three typical configuration options: parallel (up and down escalators "side by side or separated by a distance", seen often in metro stations and multilevel motion picture theaters), crisscross (minimizes structural space requirements by "stacking" escalators that go in one direction, frequently used in department stores or shopping centers), and multiple parallel (two or more escalators together that travel in one direction next to one or two escalators in the same bank that travel in the other direction).

Escalators are required to have moving handrails that keep pace with the movement of the steps. The direction of movement (up or down) can be permanently the same, or be controlled by personnel according to the time of day, or automatically be controlled by whoever arrives first, whether at the bottom or at the top (the system is programmed so that the direction is not reversed while a passenger is on the escalator).

Design and Layout Considerations

A number of factors affect escalator design, including physical requirements, location, traffic patterns, safety considerations, and aesthetic preferences. Foremost, physical factors like the vertical and horizontal distance to be spanned must be considered. These factors will determine the pitch of the escalator and its actual length. The ability of the building infrastructure to support the heavy components is also a critical physical concern. Location is important because escalators should be situated where they can be easily seen by the general public. In department stores, customers should be able to view the merchandise easily. Furthermore, up and down escalator traffic should be physically separated and should not lead into confined spaces.

Traffic patterns must also be anticipated in escalator design. In some buildings, the objective is simply to move people from one floor to another, but in others there may be a more specific requirement, such as funneling visitors towards a main exit or exhibit. The number of passengers is important because escalators are designed to carry a certain maximum number of people. For example, a single-width escalator travelling at about

1.5 feet (0.46 m) per second can move an estimated 170 persons per five-minute period. The carrying capacity of an escalator system must match the expected peak traffic demand, presuming that passengers ride single file. This is crucial for applications in which there are sudden increases in the number of riders. For example, escalators at stations must be designed to cater for the peak traffic flow discharged from a train, without causing excessive bunching at the escalator entrance.

In this regard, escalators help in controlling traffic flow of people. For example, an escalator to an exit effectively discourages most people from using it as an entrance, and may reduce security concerns. Similarly, escalators often are used as the exit of airport security checkpoints. Such an egress point would generally be staffed to prevent its use as an entrance, as well.

It is preferred that staircases be located adjacent to the escalator if the escalator is the primary means of transport between floors. It may also be necessary to provide an elevator lift adjacent to an escalator for wheelchairs and disabled persons. Finally, consideration should be given to the aesthetics of the escalator. The architects and designers can choose from a wide range of styles and colours for the handrails and balustrades.

Components

Landing Platforms

These two platforms house the curved sections of the tracks, as well as the gears and motors that drive the stairs. The top platform contains the motor assembly and the main drive gear, while the bottom holds the step return idler sprockets. These sections also anchor the ends of the escalator truss. In addition, the platforms contain a floor plate and a combplate. The floor plate provides a place for the passengers to stand before they step onto the moving stairs. This plate is flush with the finished floor and is either hinged or removable to allow easy access to the machinery below. The combplate is the piece between the stationary floor plate and the moving step. It is so named because its edge has a series of cleats that resemble the teeth of a comb. These teeth mesh with matching cleats on the edges of the steps. This design is necessary to minimize the gap between the stair and the landing, which helps prevent objects from getting caught in the gap.

Truss

The truss is a hollow metal structure that bridges the lower and upper landings. It is composed of two side sections joined together with cross braces across the bottom and just below the top. The ends of the truss are attached to the top and bottom landing platforms via steel or concrete supports. The truss carries all the straight track sections connecting the upper and lower sections.

Tracks

The track system is built into the truss to guide the step chain, which continuously pulls the steps from the bottom platform and back to the top in an endless loop. There are actually two tracks: one for the front wheels of the steps (called the step-wheel track) and one for the back wheels of the steps (called the trailer-wheel track). The relative positions of these tracks cause the steps to form a staircase as they move out from under the combplate. Along the straight section of the truss the tracks are at their maximum distance apart. This configuration forces the back of one step to be at a 90-degree angle relative to the step behind it. This right angle bends the steps into a shape resembling a staircase. At the top and bottom of the escalator, the two tracks converge so that the front and back wheels of the steps are almost in a straight line. This causes the stairs to lay in a flat sheetlike arrangement, one after another, so they can easily travel around the bend in the curved section of track. The tracks carry the steps down along the underside of the truss until they reach the bottom landing, where they pass through another curved section of track before exiting the bottom landing. At this point the tracks separate and the steps once again assume a staircase configuration. This cycle is repeated continually as the steps are pulled from bottom to top and back to the bottom again.

Steps

The steps themselves are solid, one piece, die-cast aluminum or steel. Yellow demarcation lines may be added to clearly indicate their edges. In most escalator models manufactured after 1950, both the riser and the tread of each step is cleated (given a ribbed appearance) with comblike protrusions that mesh with the combplates on the top and bottom platforms and the succeeding steps in the chain. Seeberger-or "step-type" escalators featured flat treads and smooth risers; other escalator models have cleated treads and smooth risers. The steps are linked by a continuous metal chain that forms a closed loop. The front and back edges of the steps are each connected to two wheels. The rear wheels are set further apart to fit into the back track and the front wheels have shorter axles to fit into the narrower front track. As described above, the position of the tracks controls the orientation of the steps.

Handrail

The handrail provides a convenient handhold for passengers while they are riding the escalator. In an escalator, the handrail is pulled along its track by a chain that is connected to the main drive gear by a series of pulleys. It is constructed of four distinct sections. At the center of the handrail is a "slider", also known as a "glider ply", which is a layer of a cotton or synthetic textile. The purpose of the slider layer is to allow the handrail to move smoothly along its track. The next layer, known as the "tension member", consists of either steel cable or flat steel tape, and provides the handrail with tensile strength and flexibility. On top of tension member are the inner construction components, which are made of chemically treated rubber designed to prevent the layers from separating. Finally, the outer layer—the only part that passengers actually see—is the cover, which is a blend of synthetic polymers and rubber. This cover is designed to resist degradation from environmental conditions, mechanical wear and tear, and human vandalism.

In the factory, handrails are constructed by feeding rubber through a computer-controlled extrusion machine to produce layers of the required size and type in order to match specific orders. The component layers of fabric, rubber, and steel are shaped by skilled workers before being fed into the presses, where they are fused together.

In the mid-twentieth century, some handrail designs consisted of a rubber bellows, with rings of smooth metal cladding called "bracelets" placed between each coil. This gave the handrail a rigid yet flexible feel. Additionally, each bellows section was no more than a few feet long, so if part of the handrail was damaged, only the bad segment needed to be replaced. These forms of handrail have largely been replaced with conventional fabric-and-rubber railings.

Safety

Safety is also major concern in escalator design. In India where women wear saris, there are heavy chances of getting the *pallu* entangled in the escalator. As a result, a special *sari guard* is built in to most escalators.

There is a risk of feet injuries for children wearing footwear such as Crocs and flip-flops that might get caught in escalator mechanisms. This was due to the softness of the shoe's material combined with the smaller size of children's feet.

Fire protection of an escalator floor opening may be provided by adding automatic sprinklers or fireproof shutters to the opening, or by installing the escalator in an enclosed fire-protected hall. To limit the danger of overheating, ventilation for the spaces that contain the motors and gears must be provided.

Accidents and Litigation

Accidents

There have been reports of people falling off a moving escalator or getting their shoe stuck in part of the escalator; shoe laces are a hazard when loose. Some accidents are caused by improper or unsafe use such as riding the hand rails or by escalator spinning. A few fatal accidents are:

- Eight people died and 30 more were injured on Wednesday, February 17, 1982, when an escalator collapsed on the Moscow Metro. Wrongly set up service brakes were later blamed for the accident.
- 31 people died after a fire, begun in the undercarriage of an MH-type Otis escalator, exploded into the ticketing hall at King's Cross St. Pancras station in 1987.
- On Monday, December 13, 1999, 8-year-old Jyotsna Jethani was killed at New Delhi's international airport. Jethani fell into a gaping hole that resulted from improper maintenance.
- On Saturday, June 15, 2002, Andrea Albright, a 24-year-old J.C. Penney employee in Columbia, Maryland, was critically injured while riding the store's escalator from

the first to the second level, and died from her injuries 10 days later. She somehow got her head caught between the escalator rail and a low ceiling. In 2005, her parents sued the property manager, two design firms, and the escalator company for $5 million.

- On New Year's Eve, 2004, escalators at the Taipei City Hall Station kept moving commuters onto the overcrowded island platform. A woman whose hair got caught in the escalator received 20 stitches to the scalp.
- Francisco Portillo, a Salvadoran sushi chef, died after being strangled when his sweatshirt got caught in an escalator at the Porter Square MBTA station in Cambridge, Massachusetts on February 21, 2005. He was allegedly drunk at the time.
- On Saturday, September 13, 2008, an 11-year old boy died after falling off an escalator in Lyngdal, Norway. On Monday, April 20, 2009, a teenage boy died after getting very serious skull injuries after falling off an escalator in Falun, Sweden. On Friday, June 26, 2009, a man died after falling off an escalator in Helsingborg, Sweden. All three were riding the handrail.
- On Tuesday, July 6, 2011, a 13-year old boy has been killed and dozens of people were injured when they were thrown off an escalator that suddenly changed direction in a busy Beijing subway station. In response to concerns regarding China's safety standards, officials have identified the manufacturers of the escalator as a possible reason for the accident. The escalator was built by Otis and was still in its guarantee period.

Lessons of the King's Cross Fire

The King's Cross fire of 1987 illustrated the demanding nature of escalator upkeep and the devices' propensity to collect "fluff" when not properly maintained.

Since the station was part of a public institution (the London Underground) and there was a substantial casualty rate, the incident yielded vociferous public outcry as riders and victims' families demanded the removal of all wooden escalators systemwide. In the official inquiry that followed, the Fennell

Report, it was determined that the fire started slowly, smoldered virtually undetected for a time, then exploded into the ticketing hall above in a phenomenon known as the "trench effect." This slow-burning fire, Fennell found, was allegedly kindled by a discarded unextinguished cigarette, which was shown in laboratory tests to be a more powerful ignition source than a lit match. In the escalators' undercarriage, approximately 8,800 kilograms (19,000 lb) of accumulated detritus acted as a wick to a neglected buildup of interior lubricants; wood veneers, paper and plastic advertisements, solvent-based paint, plywood in the ticket hall, and melamine combustion added to the impact of the calamity. Taking this particular situation as an example, one could easily speculate that any accretion of flammable fuels, cloth, or scrâps (the "fluff" denoted by Fennell) could likewise lead to a devastating fire.

Consequentially, older wooden escalators were removed from service in the London Underground, though at least one set remains in operation, at Greenford Station. Additionally, sections of the London Underground that were actually below ground were made nonsmoking; eventually the whole system became a smoke-free zone.

Litigation

In the 1930s, at least one suit was filed against a department store, alleging that its escalators posed an attractive nuisance, responsible for a child's injury. These cases were almost always dismissed. Moreover, continual updating of escalator safety codes facilitated increased levels of consumer safety as well as a reduction in court cases.

Legislation and Escalators

United States

Despite their considerable scope, two Congressional Acts, the Rehabilitation Act of 1973 and the Americans with Disabilities Act of 1990 (ADA), did not directly affect escalators or their public installations. Since Section 504 of the Rehabilitation Act included public transportation systems, for a few years, the United States Department of Transportation considered designs to retrofit existing escalators for wheelchair access. Nonetheless, Foster-Miller Associates' 1980 plan, *Escalator Modification for the*

Handicapped was ultimately ignored in favour of increased elevator installations in subway systems. Likewise, the ADA provided more accessibility options, but expressly excluded escalators as "accessible means of egress," advocating neither their removal nor retention in public structures.

Codes and Regulation

In the United States and Canada, new escalators must abide by ASME A17.1 standards, and old/historic escalators must conform to the safety guidelines of ASME A17.3. In Europe, the escalator safety code is EN115.

Key Safety Features Developed Over Time

To enhance passenger safety, newer models of escalators are equipped with one or more of the following safety implementations, as per ASME A17.1 code:

- Antislide devices: Raised circular objects that often stud the escalator balustrade. Sometimes informally called "hockey pucks" due to their appearance, their purpose is to prevent objects (and people) from precipitously sliding down the otherwise smooth metallic surface.
- Combplate impact switches: Stop the escalator if a foreign object gets caught between the steps and the combplate on either end.
- Deflector brush: A long continuous brush made of stiff bristles running up the sides of the escalator just above the step level. This helps deflect garments, shoes, and other items away from the gap between the moving steps and the skirt board.
- Emergency stop button: At each end of the escalator (in some models, also on the balustrade), a large red button can be pressed to stop the device in the event of an emergency. Typically, an alarmed transparent plastic guardplate covers the button; restarting requires turning a key.
- Extended balustrades: Allows riders to grasp the handrail before setting foot on an escalator, to ease customer comfort and stability/equilibrium. (The effect is similar to the flat steps described below.)

- Flat steps: Like a moving walkway, the first two or three steps at either end of the escalator are flat. This gives the passenger extra time to orient him/herself when boarding, and more time to maintain balance when exiting. Longer escalators often have four or more flat steps.
- Handrail inlet switches:. Sensors located at the bottom and top of the unit that guard the handrail termini. If something gets caught in these locations, a hard fault is generated in the controller, and the escalator shuts down automatically.
- Handrail speed sensors: These sensors are usually optical, and monitor how fast the handrail moves. If the sensor notices a speed difference between the handrail and the steps, it sounds an alarm, pauses, and then automatically stops the escalator. In these situations, the escalator must be serviced by authorized personnel before returning to an operable state.
- Missing step detectors: Depending on the manufacturer and model, this sensor is either optical or physical. When a missing step is detected, the escalator automatically shuts down.
- Raised step edges: In some models, a difference in tread height is utilized to keep passengers' feet from the skirt board.
- Safety instructions: A sign, typically posted on both escalator newels at the entrance landing platform. In some situations, safety precautions are posted on walls near the escalator, included on freestanding signs, or—as in some models—printed on the riser surface itself.
- Sensor switch: In automatic-start/stop escalators, this sensor automatically engages the escalator motion when a rider is detected on the first step of the entrance landing platform, and stops the escalator when there are no riders on the unit.
- Step demarcation lights: Either fluorescent or LED lights (traditionally green in colour) located inside the truss. The illumination between the steps improves the

passengers' awareness of the step divisions.

- Step demarcation lines: In order to clearly delineate the edges of each individual step, manufacturers offer steps trimmed in yellow, either painted or with plastic inserts.

Safe Riding: Official Safety Foundation Guidelines

While some escalator accidents are caused by a mechanical failure, most can be avoided by following some simple safety precautions. The Elevator Escalator Safety Foundation is a major advocate for safe riding in the United States and Canada, sponsors National Elevator Escalator Safety Week each year, and publishes its own suggestions for safe riding.

History

Inventors and Manufacturers

Nathan Ames: Nathan Ames, a patent solicitor from Saugus, Massachusetts, is credited with patenting the first "escalator" in 1859, despite the fact that no working model of his design was ever built. His invention, the "revolving stairs", is largely speculative and the patent specifications indicate that he had no preference for materials or potential use (he noted that steps could be upholstered or made of wood, and suggested that the units might benefit the infirm within a household use), though the mechanization was suggested to run either by manual or hydraulic power.

Leamon Souder: In 1889, Leamon Souder successfully patented the "stairway", an escalator-type device that featured a "series of steps and links jointed to each other". No model was ever built. This was the first of at least four escalator-style patents issued to Souder, including two for spiral designs (U. S. Patent Nos. 723,325 and 792,623).

Jesse Wilford Reno, George A. Wheeler, and Charles Seeberger

In 1892, Jesse W. Reno patented the "Endless Conveyor or Elevator." A few months after Reno's patent was approved, George A. Wheeler patented his ideas for a more recognizable moving staircase, though it was never built. Wheeler's patents were bought by Charles Seeberger; some features of Wheeler's designs were incorporated in Seeberger's prototype built by the Otis Elevator Company in 1899.

Reno, a graduate of Lehigh University, produced the first working escalator (he actually called it the "inclined elevator") and installed it alongside the Old Iron Pier at Coney Island, New York in 1896. This particular device was little more than an inclined belt with cast-iron slats or cleats on the surface for traction, and traveled along a 25° incline. A few months later, the same prototype was used for a monthlong trial period on the Manhattan side of the Brooklyn Bridge. Reno eventually joined forces with Otis Elevator Company, and retired once his patents were purchased outright. Some Reno-type escalators were still being used in the Boston subway until construction for the Big Dig precipitated their removal. The Smithsonian Institution considered re-assembling one of these historic units from 1914 in their collection of Americana, but "logistics and reassembly costs won out over nostalgia", and the project was discarded.

Around May 1895, Charles Seeberger began drawings on a form of escalator similar to those patented by Wheeler in 1892. This device actually consisted of flat, moving stairs, not unlike the escalators of today, except for one important detail: the step surface was smooth, with no comb effect to safely guide the rider's feet off at the ends. Instead, the passenger had to step off sideways. To facilitate this, at the top or bottom of the escalator the steps continued moving horizontally beyond the end of the handrail (like a miniature moving sidewalk) until they disappeared under a triangular "divider" which guided the passenger to either side. Seeberger teamed with Otis Elevator Company in 1899, and together they produced the first commercial escalator which won the first prize at the Paris 1900 *Exposition Universelle* in France. Also on display at the *Exposition* were Reno's inclined elevator, a similar model by James M. Dodge and the Link Belt Machinery Co., and two different devices by French manufacturers Hallé and Piat.

Early European Manufacturers: Hallé, Hocquardt, and Piat

Piat installed its "stepless" escalator in Harrods Knightsbridge store on Wednesday, November 16, 1898, though the company relinquished its patent rights to the department store. Noted by Bill Lancaster in *The Department Store: a Social History*, "customers unnerved by the experience were revived by shopmen dispensing free smelling salts and cognac." The Harrods unit was a continuous leather belt made of "224 pieces... strongly linked together travelling in an upward direction," and was the first "moving staircase" in England.

Hocquardt received European patent rights for the *Fahrtreppe* in 1906. After the *Exposition*, Hallé continued to sell its escalator device in Europe, but was eventually eclipsed in sales by other major manufacturers.

Major Competitors and Product Nomenclature

In the first half of the twentieth century, several manufacturers developed their own escalator products, though they had to market their devices under different names, due to Otis' hold on the trademark rights to the word "escalator." New York-based Peelle Company called their models the *Motorstair*, and Westinghouse called their model an *Électric Stairway*. The Toledo-based Haughton Elevator company referred to their product as simply *Moving Stairs*.

Manufacturing Mergers and Buyouts: The Playing Field Narrows

Kone and Schindler introduced their first escalator models several decades after the Otis Elevator Co., but grew to dominance in the field over time. Today, they, Mitsubishi, and ThyssenKrupp are Otis' primary rivals. Schindler now stands as the largest maker of escalators and second largest maker of elevators in the world, though their first escalator installation did not occur until 1936. In 1979, the company entered the United States market by purchasing Haughton Elevator; nine years later, Schindler assumed control of the North American escalator/elevator operations of Westinghouse. Kone expanded internationally by acquisition in the 1970s, buying out Swedish elevator manufacturer Asea-Graham, and purchasing other minor French, German, and Austrian elevator makers before assuming control of Westinghouse's European elevator business. As the last "big four" manufacturers held on to the escalator market, KONE first acquired Montgomery Elevator Company, then took control of Germany's Orenstein & Koppel *Rolltreppen*.

Model Development and Design Types

"Cleat-type" Escalators

Jesse Reno's escalators did not resemble modern escalators

too closely. Passengers' feet tilted upward at an angle, and the treads consisted of cleated metal (initially) or wood (later models). Reno worked on his own for several years, gaining success with installations from Toronto to Cape Town, South Africa. Similar units of the day by other manufacturers resembled conveyor belts more than moving staircases. For a time, Otis Elevator sold Reno's escalators as their own "cleat-type" escalators.

"Step-type" Escalators

Seeberger's model, bought by Otis, clearly became the first "step-type" escalator, so called after its visual likeness to steps on a regular staircase. The company later combined the best aspects of both inventions (guiding slats and flat steps) and in 1921 produced an escalator similar to the type used today: they called it the "L-type" escalator. It was succeeded by the "M-type", the "O-type", and current models by Otis such as the "NCE-type" escalator.

Spiral Escalators: From Reno to Mitsubishi

Reno, in addition to his notoriety for the first "practical" escalator in public use, also bears the unique distinction of designing the very first escalators installed in any underground subway system – a single spiral escalator at Holloway Road tube station in London in 1906. The experimental device never saw public use, and was forgotten for several decades. The remains of this are now in the London Transport Museum's depot in Acton. Also the first fully operational spiral escalator, Reno's design was nonetheless only one in a series of several similar proposed contraptions. Souder patented two spiral designs, Wheeler drafted spiral stairway plans in 1905, Seeberger devised at least two different spiral units between 1906 and 1911 (including an unrealized arrangement for the London Underground), and Gilbert Luna obtained West German, Japanese, and United States patents for his version of a spiral escalator by 1973. When interviewed for the *Los Angeles Times* that year, Luna was in the process of soliciting "major firms" for acquisition of his patents and company, but statistics are unclear on the outcome of his endeavors in that regard.

The Mitsubishi Electric Corporation was most successful in its development of "spiral" (more "curve" than true spiral) escalators, and has sold them exclusively since the mid-1980s.

The world's first "practical" spiral escalator—a Mitsubishi model—was installed in Osaka, Japan, in 1985.

In use, a major planning advantage presented by spiral escalators is that they take up much less horizontal floor space than traditional units, which frequently house large machine rooms underneath the truss.

Etymology

Several authors and historians have contributed their own differing interpretations of the source of the word "escalator", and some degree of misinformation has heretofore proliferated on the Internet. For reference, contradictory citations by seven separate individuals, including the Otis Elevator Company itself, are provided below.

Name Development and Original Intentions

Charles Seeberger trademarked the word "escalator" in 1900, to coincide with his device's debut at the *Exposition Universelle*. According to his own account, in 1895, his legal counsel advised him to name his new invention, and he then set out to devise a title for it on his own. As evidenced in Seeberger's own handwritten documents, archived at the Otis Elevator Company headquarters in Farmington, Connecticut, the inventor consulted "a Latin lexicon" and "adopted as the root of the new word, 'Scala'; as a prefix, 'E' and as a suffix, 'Tor.'" His own rough translation of the word thus created was "means of traversing from", and he intended for the word to be pronounced, (es-CAL-a-tor).

"Escalator" was not a combination of other French or Greek words, and was never a derivative of "elevator" in the original sense, which means "one who raises up, a deliverer" in Latin. Similarly, the root word "*scala*" does not mean "a flight of steps", but is defined by Lewis and Short's *A Latin Dictionary* as the singular form of the plural noun "*scalae*", which denotes any of the following: "a flight of steps or stairs, a staircase; a ladder, [or] a scaling-ladder."

The alleged intended capitalization of "escalator" is likewise a topic of debate. Seeberger's trademark application lists the word not only with the "E" but also with all of the letters capitalized (in two different instances), and he specifies that, "any other form and character of type may be employed... without altering in any essential manner the character of [the] trade-mark." That his initial specifications are ostensibly inconsistent, and since Otis Elevator Co. advertisements so frequently capitalized all of the letters in the word, suppositions about the "capital 'e'" are difficult to formulate.

Derivatives of 'Escalator'

The verb "escalate" originated in 1922, and has two uses, the primary: "to climb or reach by means of an escalator" or "to travel on an escalator", and the secondary: "to increase or develop by successive stages; *spec.* to develop from 'conventional' warfare into nuclear warfare." The latter definition was first printed in the *Manchester Guardian* in 1959, but grew to prominent use during the late 1960s and early 1970s.

Loss of Trademark Rights

In 1950, the landmark case *Haughton Elevator Co. v. Seeberger* precipitated the end of Otis' reign over exclusive use of the word "escalator", and simultaneously created a cautionary study for companies and individuals interested in trademark retention. Confirming the contention of the Examiner of Trademark Interferences, Assistant Commissioner of Patents Murphy's decision rejected the Otis Elevator Company's appeal to keep their trademark intact, and noted that "the term 'escalator' is recognized by the general public as the name for a moving stairway and not the source thereof", observing that the Otis Elevator Co. had "used the term as a generic descriptive term...in a number of patents which [had] been issued to them and...in their advertising matter." All trademark protections were removed from the word "escalator", the term was officially genericized, and it fell into the public domain.

Primary uses and Application

Department Stores/Shopping

As noted above, a few escalator types were installed in major department stores (including Harrods) before the *Expo*. Escalators proved instrumental in the layout and design of shopping venues in the twentieth century. By 1898, the first of Reno's "inclined elevators" were incorporated into the

Bloomingdale Bros. store at Third Avenue and 59th Street. This was the first retail application of the devices in the US, and no small coincidence, considering that Reno's primary financier was Lyman Bloomingdale, co-owner of the department store with brother Joseph Bloomingdale.

Public Transportation

The first "standard" escalator installed on the London Underground was a Seeberger model at Earls Court. Noted above, London's Underground installed a rare spiral escalator designed by Reno, William Henry Aston and Scott Kietzman for the Holloway Road Underground station in 1906; it was run for a short time but was taken out of service the same day it debuted. The older lines of the London Underground had many escalators with wooden treads (ca. 1930s) until they were rapidly replaced following the King's Cross fire, noted above.

Other Applications

Factories and other Industrial Production Environments

In 1905, the American Woolen Company's Wood Mill in Lawrence, Massachusetts (then "the largest single worsted mill in the world") utilized Otis' Seeberger-type "reversible" escalators to carry its workers between floors four times a day. The machines did not run all day: rather, escalators ran solely to transport employees to/from midday meals and in/out of the mill.

In its advertising, Otis Elevator Company hailed this unconventional use for its unique benefits to both workers and owners: "The profitable and practicable feature of the Escalator, from the viewpoint of the owner, is the increased efficiency of each operator due to the elimination of stair climbing."

Military use

In San Francisco, an escalator at Hunters Point Naval Shipyard was used to convey personnel between the first and third floors. At the time of its construction in 1948, it was touted thus: "[it has the] highest lift of any industrial building in the world. It rises 42 feet." Escalators were also utilized on aircraft carriers such as the USS *Hornet* (CV-12), to transport pilots from "ready rooms" to the flight deck.

Extant Historic Escalator Models

A few notable examples of historic escalators still in operation are:

Australia

- Town Hall Railway Station, Sydney, Australia
- Wynyard Railway Station, Sydney, Australia.

Europe

- St. Anna Pedestrian Tunnel underneath the Schelde in Antwerp, Belgium. This tunnel was opened in 1933.
- Tyne Cyclist and Pedestrian Tunnel, Tyne and Wear, England.

-These escalators, manufactured by Waygood Otis in 1951, were "believed to be the longest single lift escalators in the world", at the time of installation. Presumably the first escalators in Britain designed specifically for cyclists, they are also "thought to be still" the longest escalators in the United Kingdom. At most, they may be the longest extant wooden escalators in operation in the world.

- Greenford Station in Greenford, England contains the oldest escalator still in use on the London Underground service. This was the first above ground station to install an escalator to its high levels and one of the only (if not the only) wooden escalators not to be replaced after the fire at Kings Cross station.

North America

- Macy's Herald Square department store, Otis L-type units with wood treads and replacement metal treads, New York, New York
- Kaufmann's department store (now Macy's), two 16-inch (400 mm) Otis L-type units with original floorplates, several 40-inch (1000 mm) Otis escalators ca. 1950s, Pittsburgh, Pennsylvania
- Westfield San Francisco Centre (formerly The Emporium), chrome-and-glass escalator by Eleanor LeMaire for Otis, San Francisco, California.

Escalators: Superlatives

Longest Systems

- Central-Mid-Levels escalator: in Hong Kong, tens of thousands of commuters travel each work day between Central, the central business district, and the Mid-levels, a residential district hundreds of feet uphill, using this long distance system of escalators and moving walkways. It is the world's longest outdoor escalator *system* (not a single escalator span), at a total length of 2,600 feet (790 m). It goes only one way at a time; the direction reverses depending on rush hour traffic direction.
- Ocean Park, Hong Kong: a long escalator system connecting two parts of the Park, with an overall length of 730 feet (220 m).

Longest Individual Escalators

Asia and Europe

Several "metro" or "subway" systems in Central and Eastern Europe feature very long escalators.

- In the Park Pobedy station of the Moscow Metro, opened in 2003, the escalators are 126.8 m (63.4 m high), or 740 steps, long, and take nearly three minutes to transit. Deep underground stations in St. Petersburg have escalators up to approximately 142 m long (71 m high).
- The Kiev Metro Kreschatik station's lower-level second exit escalator (a type ËÒ-2, circa 1965), lifts riders 216 feet (66 m), or 743 steps, up a 432-foot (132 m)-long incline.
- The longest escalator in Prague is at the Námìstí Míru station at 290 feet (88 m).
- The longest escalator of a European shopping mall is at MyZeil, Frankfurt, Germany, with a length of 150 feet (46 m).
- The tallest escalator on the London Underground system is at Angel station with a length of 197 feet (60 m), and a vertical rise of 90 feet (27 m).

- The longest wooden escalators in the United Kingdom are at the Tyne Tunnel, with a length of 200 feet (61 m).
- The longest escalator on the Stockholm Metro, and in Western Europe, is at Västra skogen with a length of 220 feet (67 m) and in Helsinki Metro at Kamppi station with a length of 210 feet (64 m).
- The largest "single truss escalator" is in the Bentall Centre in Kingston upon Thames in Greater London, UK. It connects the ground floor with the second floor with only top and bottom supports.

North and South America

- The longest set of single-span uninterrupted escalators in the Western Hemisphere is at the Wheaton station of the Washington Metro system. They are 230 feet (70 m) long with a vertical rise of 115 feet (35 m), and take what is variously described as 2 minutes and 45 seconds or nearly three-and-a-half minutes, to ascend or descend without walking.
- The longest *freestanding* (supported only at the ends) escalator in the world is inside CNN Center's atrium in Atlanta, Georgia. It rises 8 stories and is 205 feet (62 m) long. Originally built as the entrance to the amusement park The World of Sid and Marty Krofft, the escalator is now used for CNN studio tours.

Shortest Examples

Asia

According to Guinness, the shortest escalator in the world is in the Okadaya Mores shopping mall in Kawasaki, Japan. Its vertical rise is only 32.8 inches (83 cm).

North America

The shortest escalator in the United States is a Schindler unit at the entrance to the JCPenney Department Store in Westfield Garden State Plaza in Paramus, New Jersey.

Notable Spiral Escalator Installations

Asia

- Wheelock Place, Singapore

- Jeddah Hilton, Saudi Arabia
- Landmark Tower, Japan
- Times Square shopping mall, Causeway Bay, Hong Kong
- Langham Place, Mongkok, Hong Kong
- Lotte World, South Korea
- The Venetian hotel and casino, Cotai, Macau
- WTC Mangga Dua, Jakarta, Indonesia (the only one in Indonesia)
- Taipei, Taiwan.

North America

- Wynn Las Vegas, Las Vegas, Nevada, United States
- The Forum Shops at Caesars, Las Vegas, Nevada, United States
- Westfield San Francisco Centre, San Francisco, California, United States—the first such installation in the Western Hemisphere.
- River Rock Casino Resort, Richmond, British Columbia, Canada-the first in Canada.

Moving Walkway

A moving walkway (British English) or moving sidewalk (American English) (colloquially sometimes travelator, horizontal escalator, walkalator, autowalk, movator, people mover) is a slow moving conveyor mechanism that transports people, across a horizontal or inclined plane, over a short to medium distance. Moving walkways can be used by standing or walking on them. They are often installed in pairs, one for each direction.

History

The first moving walkway debuted at the World's Columbian Exposition of 1893, in Chicago, Illinois. It had two different divisions: one where passengers were seated, and one where riders could stand or walk. It ran in a loop down the length of a lakefront pier to a casino. Six years later a moving walkway was also presented to the public at the Paris *Exposition Universelle* in 1900. The walkway consisted of three elevated platforms, the first was stationary, the second moved at a moderate speed, and the third at about six miles an hour. These demonstrations likely served as inspiration for some of H. G. Wells' settings mentioned in the "Science Fiction" section below.

The Beeler Organization, a New York City consulting firm, proposed a Continuous Transit System with Sub-Surface Moving Platforms for Atlanta in 1924, with a design roughly similar to the Paris Exposition system. The proposed drive system used a linear induction motor. The system was not constructed.

The first commercial moving walkway in the United States was installed in 1954 in Jersey City, NJ, inside the Hudson & Manhattan Railroad Erie station) at the Pavonia Terminal. Named the "Speedwalk" and built by Goodyear, it was 277 ft (84.5 m) long and moved up a 10 percent grade at a speed of 1.5 mph (2.4 km/h).

The walkway was removed a few years later when traffic patterns at the station changed.

The first moving walkway in an airport was installed in 1958 at Love Field in Dallas, Texas. On Jan 1, 1960 Tina Marie Brandon, age 3, was killed on the moving sidewalk.

Designs

Moving walkways are built in one of two basic styles:

- Pallet type — a continuous series of flat metal plates join together to form a walkway. Most have a metal surface, though some models have a rubber surface for extra traction.
- Moving belt — these are generally built with mesh metal belts or rubber walking surfaces over metal rollers. The walking surface may have a solid feel or a "bouncy" feel.

Both types of moving walkway have a grooved surface to mesh with combplates at the ends. Also, nearly all moving walkways are built with moving handrails similar to those on escalators.

Pallet-types consists of one-piece, die-cast aluminium pallets. Example dimensions are: widths (between balustrades): between 32 inches (800 mm) and 56 inches (1200 mm), with a speed of 100 feet per minute (.5 metres per second), powered by an AC induction motor.

High-speed Walkways

In the 1970s Dunlop developed the *Speedaway* system. It was in fact an invention by Gabriel Bouladon and Paul Zuppiger of the Battelle Memorial Institute in Geneva (Switzerland). A prototype was built and demonstrated at the Battelle Institute in Geneva in the early 1970s, as can be attested by a (French-speaking) Swiss television program entitled Un Jour une Heure aired in October 1974. The great advantage of the Speedaway, as compared to the then existing systems, was that the embarking/disembarking zone was both wide and slow moving (up to 4 passengers could embark simultaneously, allowing for a large number of passengers, up to 10,000 per hour), whereas the transportation zone was narrower and fast moving.

The entrance to the system was like a very wide escalator, with broad metal tread plates of a parallelogram shape. After a short distance the tread plates were accelerated to one side, sliding past one another to form progressively into a narrower but faster moving track which travelled at almost a right-angle to the entry section. The passenger was accelerated through a parabolic path to a maximum design speed of 15 km/h (9 mph). The experience was unfamiliar to passengers, who needed to understand how to use the system to be able to do so safely. Developing a moving hand-rail for the system presented a challenge, also solved by the Battelle team. The Speedaway was intended to be used as a stand alone system over short distances or to form acceleration and deceleration units providing entry and exit means for a parallel conventional (but fast running) *Starglide* walkway which covered longer distances. The system was still in development in 1975 but never went into commercial production.

Another attempt at an accelerated walkway in the 1980s was the TRAX (*Trottoir Roulant Accéléré*), which was developed by Dassault and RATP and whose prototype was installed in the Paris Invalides metro station. The speed at entry and exit was 3 km/h (2 mph), while the maximum speed was 15 km/h (9 mph). It was a technical failure due to its complexity, and was never commercially exploited.

In the mid 1990s the Loderway Moving Walkway company patented and licenced a design to a number of larger moving walkway manufacturers. Trial systems were installed at Flinders

Street Station in Melbourne and Brisbane Airport Australia. These met with a positive response from the public, but no permanent installations were made. This system is of the belt type, with a sequence of belts moving at different speeds to accelerate and decelerate riders. A sequence of different speed handrails is also used. A video of the trials systems can be found at the following link.

In 2002, the first successful high-speed walkway was installed in the Montparnasse—Bienvenüe Métro station in Paris. At first it operated at 12 km/h (7 mph) but due to people losing their balance, the speed was reduced to 9 km/h (6 mph). It has been estimated that commuters using a walkway such as this twice a day would save 15 minutes per week and 10 hours a year.

Using the high-speed walkway is like using any other moving walkway, except that for safety there are special procedures to follow when joining or leaving. When this walkway was introduced, staff (seen here in yellow jackets) determined who could and who could not use it. As riders must have at least one hand free to hold the handrail, those carrying bags, shopping, etc., or who are infirm, must use the ordinary walkway nearby.

On entering, there is a 10-metre acceleration zone where the 'ground' is a series of metal rollers. Riders stand still with both feet on these rollers and use one hand to hold the handrail and let it pull them so that they glide over the rollers. The idea is to accelerate the riders so that they will be travelling fast enough to step onto the moving walkway belt. Riders who try to walk on these rollers are at significant risk of falling over.

Once on the walkway, riders can stand or walk. Owing to Newton's laws of motion, there is no special sensation of travelling at speed, except for headwind.

At the exit, the same technique is used to decelerate the riders. Users step on to a series of rollers which decelerate them slowly, rather than the abrupt halt which would otherwise take place.

In 2007, a similar high-speed walkway was opened in the newly opened Pier F of Pearson International Airport in Toronto, Canada. This walkway is of the pallet type rather than the belt type. The pallets "intermesh" with a comb and slot arrangement. They expand out of each other when speeding up, and compress into each other when slowing down. The handrailings work in a similar manner. The walkway moves at roughly 2 km/h when riders step onto it, speeds up to approximately 7 km/h for the bulk of the length, and slows to 2 km/h again at the end.

In May 2009 it was announced that because of its unreliability and the number of users having accidents, in 2011 the Parisian high-speed moving walkway will be replaced with a standard moving walkway.

Inclined Moving Walkways

An inclined moving walkway is used in airports and supermarkets to move people to another floor with the convenience of an elevator (namely, that people can take along their suitcase trolley or shopping cart, or baby carriage) and the capacity of an escalator.

The carts have either a brake that is automatically applied when the cart handle is released, strong magnets in the wheels to stay adhered to the floor, or specially designed wheels that secure the cart within the grooves of the ramp, so that wheeled items travel alongside the riders and do not slip away.

The Central-Mid-levels escalator system on Hong Kong Island, Hong Kong also has several inclined moving sidewalks. In Carlton, Victoria, Australia, another inclined moving sidewalk can be found at Lygon Court.

Some department stores instead use Vermaport or Cartveyors—conveying systems that move shopping carts in a similar fashion to an escalator—to transport passengers and their carts between store levels simultaneously. Inclined moving walkways can also be found at the National Aquarium in Baltimore, Maryland; the international arrivals area of Pierre Elliott Trudeau International Airport in Montreal, Quebec, Canada; Piccadilly Station in Manchester, UK and Ikea in Bristol, UK. Slightly inclined ones can be found at Logan Airport, in Boston, MA.

Applications

Moving walkways are frequently found in the following locations:

Airports

They are popular there because most larger airports require passengers – often with heavy luggage in tow – to walk considerable distances. Moving walkways may be utilized:

- in passageways between concourses and the terminal
- within particularly long concourses
- as a connector between terminals, or
- as access to a parking facility or a ground transport station.

Of particular note is the Charles de Gaulle International Airport in Paris, which has several moving walkways inside a series of futuristic suspended tubes.

Museum Exhibits

Moving sidewalks may be used:

- to ensure that a museum exhibit is viewed in a certain sequence
- to provide a particular aesthetic effect
- to make sure the crowd moves through at a reliable pace.

The 1975-76 American Freedom Train did this; they had a moving walkway inside each successive railroad car, thus maximizing the number of people who could view the interior exhibits in the limited time the train was stopped in each town.

The National Gallery of Art in Washington, DC uses a moving walkway to connect the two main galleries.

The Tower of London in London, UK, uses a moving walkway where visitors are passing the cabinets which contain the Crown Jewels.

Zoos

Similar to museums, some zoological park exhibits have a moving walkway to ease guests through an animal display or habitat. An aquarium at the Mall of America does this with a moving walkway made up of specially rounded pallets that enable it to change directions en route. And the San Diego Zoo uses moving ramps not for an exhibit per se, but to help guests ascend steep grades.

Theme Parks

Some amusement park rides, such as continuous-motion dark rides like Disney's Haunted Mansion, make use of a moving sidewalk to assist passengers in boarding and disembarking rides and attractions. Some examples include:

- the Ultra Twister, a roller coaster at the now closed Astroworld in Houston, Texas. (It had a moving walkway with no handrail for passengers to step on prior to boarding their car. The walkway would move at the same speed as the approaching cars, allowing passengers completing the ride to step off and for boarding passengers to enter the car. A loudspeaker announced "Moving conveyor, please watch your step" to warn of the moving walkway.)
- the exit from the Space Mountain attraction at Walt Disney World has a long moving walkway which changes inclination multiple times.
- the exit from the Pirates of the Caribbean attraction at Walt Disney World has an inclined moving walkway leading towards a gift shop.

Theatre

Andrew Lloyd Weber's The Phantom of the Opera (1986 musical) utilizes a travelator for the number 'The Phantom of the Opera' (Act one, scene six), to give the illusion the Phantom and Christine are travelling the catacombs below the Paris Opera House a great distance to the Phantom's lair on the subterranean lake.

Public Transport

Moving walkways are useful for remote platforms in underground subway/metro stations, or assisting with lengthier connections between lines, for example Waterloo Underground Station in London, United Kingdom, and between Central and Hong Kong stations on Hong Kong Island, Hong Kong, as well as between Tsim Sha Tsui and East Tsim Sha Tsui stations in Kowloon, Hong Kong.

Similar walkways exist in Singapore's Bugis MRT Station, Dhoby Ghaut MRT Station and Serangoon MRT Station. In

Glasgow's Buchanan Street subway station a moving walkway is used to connect the Subway station with Glasgow Queen Street Station. A moving walkway existed between Spadina station on the Bloor-Danforth subway line and Spadina station on the Yonge–University–Spadina line. Installed in 1978, the series of moving walkways has since been removed (2004) and patrons are now required to walk between the stations.

Urban Areas

Hong Kong is one of the world's most heavily populated cities, and has public escalators that connect many streets.

Paternoster

A paternoster or paternoster lift is a passenger elevator which consists of a chain of open compartments (each usually designed for two persons) that move slowly in a loop up and down inside a building without stopping. Passengers can step on or off at any floor they like. The same technique is also used for filing cabinets to store great amounts of (paper) documents or for small spare parts.

History

First built in 1884 by Londoner J. E. Hall as the Cyclic Elevator, the name *paternoster* ("Our Father", the first two words of the Lord's Prayer in Latin) was originally applied to the device because the elevator is in the form of a loop and is thus similar to rosary beads used as an aid in reciting prayers. In another alternative, the word origin could be derived from Czech words *pater* meaning "floors" and *nosit* meaning "to carry".

Paternosters were popular throughout the first half of the 20th century as they could carry more passengers than ordinary elevators. They were more common in continental Europe, especially in public buildings, than in the United Kingdom. They are rather slow elevators, typically travelling at about 0.3 metres per second, thus improving the chances of getting on and off successfully. Today, in many countries the construction of new paternosters is no longer allowed because of the high risk of accidents (people tripping or falling over when trying to enter or alight). Five people were killed by paternosters from 1970 to 1993. The elderly, the handicapped and children are the most in danger of being crushed. In 1989, the paternoster in Newcastle

University's Claremont Tower was taken out of service after a passenger undertaking an up-and-over journey became caught in the drive chain, necessitating a rescue by the Fire Service. A conventional elevator was subsequently installed in its place. This accident led to an 18-month close-down of all UK paternosters for a safety review, during which additional safety devices were fitted.

In April 2006, Hitachi announced plans for a modern paternoster-style elevator with computer-controlled cars and normal elevator doors to alleviate safety concerns.

Popular Culture

- The movie *Night People,* a 1954 cold war thriller set in post-war Berlin uses a paternoster for comic relief in a scene with Gregory Peck and Buddy Ebsen.
- In the novelization of *Metropolis,* worker 11811 operates the machine controlling a paternoster in the New Tower of Babel; inspired by the machine's name, he continuously mutters a disturbed version of the Lord's Prayer. In the actual film, a paternoster is seen in the scene at the place where Josaphat lives (this scene is only in the 2010 version as it occurs in part of the "lost footage" that was discovered in 2008).
- In German writer Boris Meyn's mystery novel, Die rote Stadt (Rowohlt Taschenbuch Verlag, 7th ed, 2007), lawyer Soren Bischop begins his detective career with the discovery of a bloody corpse in a paternoster. Meyn describes Bischop's reaction as he sees a paternoster for the first time. He observes the compartment disappear and reappear and once he spots the victim, jumps in to help, not knowing if he will have to climb the walls or stand on his head in order to come out the other side.
- In the Gunter Grass novel *Too Far Afield,* numerous scenes are set in an east German government archives building where one of the main characters, who is employed as a courier, rides a paternoster in connection with his duties and lobbies successfully for the paternoster's continued operation following German reunification.

- In the 1985 German film, "Männer", several scenes involve a paternoster. During the closing credits, some of those involved in the film ride the paternoster as their names scroll by.

Surviving Paternosters

Numerous working paternosters are known to survive in Europe (this is an incomplete list):

Austria

- City Hall of Vienna (at stairway 6 near the northern entrance)
- House of Industry, Schwarzenbergplatz 4, Vienna (oldest paternoster in Austria by Anton Freissler)
- Federal Ministry of Economics and Labour, Stubenring, Vienna
- Ministry of Defence, Rossauer Lände 1, Vienna
- Federal Computing Centre, Hintere Zollamtsstraße 4, Vienna
- Versicherungsanstalt für Eisenbahnen und Bergbau (Insurance institution of the railway and mining industries), Linke Wienzeile, Vienna
- The Ringturm (Wiener Städtische Versicherung/Vienna City Insurance Headquarters Building), Schottenring 30, Vienna
- KELAG Zentrale Klagenfurt, Arnulfplatz 2, 9020 Klagenfurt (Kärntner Elektrizitäts Aktiengesellschaft/ Carinthian electricity supplier).

Belgium

- A functioning paternoster can be found at the Flemish Parliament in Brussels, Belgium, where it is used as an art display.
- Another paternoster can be found in a building of the Belgian Railways (NMBS) at the station Brussels-Zuid/ Midi. It's still used daily.

Czech Republic

- The *Komerèní Banka* building on Václavské námìstí in

Prague. (This is a working office and not open to the general public, but it can be seen from the main lobby).

- The Municipality hall of Praha 1 (Vodièkova 18) has a working paternoster open to public combined with two classic lifts, one dedicated to baby trolleys and wheel chairs which are not allowed on the paternoster.
- Ministry of Foreign Affairs, Prague
- Faculty of Law, Charles University, Nám. Curieových 7, Prague
- Czech Technical University in Prague on Dejvice, Technická 2, Prague
- Within the *Lucerna* building in Prague, near the entrance from Štìpánská.
- Office building of KAUÈUK, a.s. in Kralupy nad Vltavou near Prague.
- Ministry of Finance in Prague
- Health center Building on Smíchov, Kartouzská 6, Prague
- Ministry of Agriculture, Prague Florenc
- CEZ (Czech Energy Corp) Jungmanova Street, Prague
- City Courthouse in 2 Prague on Slezska, open to the public (after passing through security)
- Trades Office (Živnostenský úøad), Malinovského Námìstí, Brno
- A working paternoster can be found at the Faculty Of Mechanical Engineering, Brno University of Technology where it is being used by students and faculty staff.
- Bývalý Krajský úøad Zlín (yellow building)
- Office building of Spolek pro chemickou a hutní výrobu (Spolchemie) in Ústí nad Labem
- *New Townhall* on Prokešovo námìstí in Ostrava, which are open to the public.
- SZIF, Hradec Králové, Ulrichovo námìstí 810/4
- Former Building of Rude Pravo Newspapers on Na Florenci street 19, Reception B, Prague 1 (about to be demolished, but occasionally working, for example

during Krétakör's performance, during 2011 Praque Quadriennial).

Denmark

- At the seat of the Danish parliament, Christiansborg, there is a working paternoster open to the public.
- Frederiksberg City Hall.
- At Danfoss Nordborg
- At the Axelborg building right across from the Tivoli main entrance
- At KVUC in Copenhagen
- At The Danish Dairy Board in Aarhus.
- At Horsens hospital, The hospital in the city Horsens, there is a working paternoster, but not open to the public.
- At Vejle hospital, The hospital in the city Vejle, there is a working paternoster, but not open to the public.

Finland

- The Finnish house of parliament, the Eduskuntatalo, Helsinki.
- Kansaneläkelaitos office building, Helsinki.(staff only)
- Stockmann department store, Helsinki (staff only)
- Office building in *Yliopistonkatu*, Turku (former headquarters of the Sampo insurance company).

Germany

- Trostbrücke 1, in the Altstadt district of Hamburg (accessible during office hours-no groups and guided tours). A paternoster still in operation and open to general public is in the Bezirksamt Eimsbüttel (Grindelberg 62/66). Qype's former office building at Deichstraße 29 also has a working Paternoster. Kaiser-Wilhelm-Straße 16 (Publisher Axel Springer) offers at least one paternoster. Ballindamm 25 (shipping company Hapag Lloyd) still has one in use (not open to the public). Stadthausbrücke 8 (authorities ›Stadt-Entwicklungs-Behörde‹) uses a paternoster. Another one being in service can be found in Rathausstraße 7, entrance via

Knochenhauertwiete, close to the town hall. Steinhöft 11 (office block ›Slomanhaus‹). There is also a paternoster in the St. Annen 2 building in the historic Speicherstadt, which is not in use at the moment.

- The IG Farben Building in Frankfurt-am-Main. The current occupants of the building, Johann Wolfgang Goethe University, have pledged to maintain and preserve the famous paternosters *"in perpetuity"*.
- Frankfurt, Fleming's Deluxe Hotel the paternoster provides service to six floors and the rooftop restaurant.
- Stuttgart, town hall, Literaturhaus, Universität Stuttgart, Allianz Lebensversicherungs-AG (only for employees), Kaufhof (near main station (only for employees)), Robert Bosch GmbH (Stuttgart-Feuerbach – only for employees), Arbeitsgericht
- Kiel Rathaus, or town hall. One of the best examples in Germany, it is 5 levels and it open to the public.
- Essen Deutsches Haus.
- Mannheim operations building of SCA (only for employees)
- Leverkusen, some at Bayer AG's plant.
- Dortmund, in the vestibule of the Signal-Versicherung building, situated by the junction between the Maerkische Strasse, and the Ostwall.
- Dresden, Alstom Grid/Schnieder Energy (Ex AREVA T&D) building. For staff and authorised visitors only.
- Duisburg, both in the city hall and the internal revenue offices.
- Düsseldorf, in the older of the three Vodafone Global buildings. Currently out of use following an incident; In the Polizeipräsidium (Jürgensplatz 40219).
- Cologne, in the IHK (Industrie-und Handelskammer/ Chamber of Industry and Trade) Building (Unter Sachsenhausen 10-26, D-50667 Cologne, Hansahochhaus (housing Saturn, Hansaring, Maybachstraße 115, D-50674 Cologne), WDR HQ (Wallrafplatz 1, D-50667 Cologne (only for employees); Kaufhof (Hohe Straße 41-53, D-

50667), Kaufhof Corporate HQ (Leonhard-Tietz-Str., D-50667 Cologne (not open to the public); Volkshochschule Building (near Neumarkt, D-50667 Cologne); Former Felten & Guilleaume Corporate HQ (Schanzenstr. 28, D-51069 Cologne-Mülheim, accessible public office building, 5 Stories); former downtown Bezirksamt „Dischhaus" (Brückenstr., D-50667 Cologne);Bezirksregierung Köln (Regional Government Center Cologne), Entrance: Zeughausstraße 8 (D-50667 Cologne)

- Berlin Foreign Office, Werderscher Markt 1; Finance Ministry, Wilhelmstrasse 97; Agriculture Ministry, Wilhelmstrasse 54; Axel Springer Building, Axel Springer Strasse 65; Bayer Schering Pharma, AG; ART+COM, Kleiststrasse 23-26, 10787 Berlin; (52°302 4.993 N 13°202 39.723 E), rbb (Radio Berlin Brandenburg) Masurenallee 8-14; Rathaus Schöneberg, John-F-Kennedy-Platz; Siemens AG, Siemens Damm (in several buildings).
- Bremen, Baumwollbörse, Wachtstraße 17-24 (near Town Hall); Haus des Reichs, Rudolf-Hilferding-Platz 1
- Wiesbaden, two still in operation in buildings in the industrial park "Infra-Serv Kalle-Albert", Kasteler Straße 45, not accessible to the general public
- Leipzig, new town hall
- Munich, Kaufhof am Marienplatz had a paternoster working for the staff. The building was erected in 1972, so it is one of the last ones ever in Germany. The Polizeipraesidium—the main police station—in the Ettstrasse behind the Frauenkirche has a paternoster, which is accessible to the public. One is in the Sueddeutsche Zeitung Verlagsgebaeude; another in the Hochhaus an der Blumenstrasse.
- Kassel, headquarters of the Wintershall Holding AG, a subsidiary of BASF, not accessible to the general public
- Wuppertal, in the town hall of Barmen and Elberfeld, in the headquarters of Vorwerk (not open to the public), and the fiscal office in Elberfeld
- Augsburg, Finanzamt Augsburg-Stadt, accessible to employees and visitors.

Hungary

- MOL Group's Headquarters in Budapest
- University of Miskolc
- Jahn Ferenc Hospital in Budapest
- MÁV Hospital in Budapest
- Hungarian Television's building in Budapest at Szabadság sqr (Soon to be renovated by new owner, the future of the paternoster is unknown)
- Ministry of Education and Culture in Budapest
- Ministry of Defence in Budapest
- Ministry of Justice in Budapest
- Hungarian Trade Licensing Office in Budapest
- Hospital of Kecskemét
- HQ of the Bkv Zrt. (Budapest public transport company) in Budapest, Akácfa street
- Building of the Hungarian Power Companies Ltd. at Vám u. 5-7., Budapest
- OTP Bank's Headquarters in Budapest, Nádor street
- Former HQ of the Hungarian Post Co. Ltd. at Krisztina krt. 6-8., Budapest
- Hospital of Szigetvár
- County hall (of Csongrád County) in Szeged
- Pesti Központi Kerületi Bíróság (Central District Court of Pest) at Marko u. 25. Budapest
- County Court of Pest County (Pest megyei Bíróság) at Thököly út 97-101. Budapest
- Central Bank of Hungary at Szabadság square 8-9. Budapest.

Italy

- Air Force Ministry, Rome.

Netherlands

- Paternosters are still in operation at the main office of the Corus Steelworks (formerly Hoogovens) in IJmuiden.

This remarkable building (by Dudok, 1951) was restored in 1999.

- The office building of Ziggo at Spaarneplein (formerly Main Post Office, architect D.E.C. Knuttel 1919) in The Hague also still is using a Paternoster.
- The Grand Hotel Amrath Amsterdam has a working Paternoster. The building, the Scheepvaarthuis, was originally built as the headquarters for the six leading Amsterdam shipping companies in 1913 forming the Netherland Line(architect J.M.van der Meij. This Paternoster although not open for use by residents appears to currently being used as a service lift.
- The Philips High Tech campus in Eindhoven had a paternoster in operation until 2006.
- The formerly Main Post Office at the Coolsingel in Rotterdam (architect G.C. Bremer, 1915).
- The formerly Raad van Arbeid/Sociale Verzekeringsbank at the Rhijnspoorplein 1 in Amsterdam (1919). In operation until 2006
- HaKa-building in Rotterdam (architects H.F. Mertens and J.Koeman, 1932). In operation.
- The formerly Belastingdienst at the Puntegaalstraat in Rotterdam (architect H.Hoekstra, 1938/1948). Working Paternoster; not in operation.

Norway

- Oslo: Landbrukets hus (House of Agriculture), Schweigaards gate 34 C. Not open to the public. This is the last remaining operating paternoster lift in Norway.
- Oslo (closed pasternoster lifts): There used to be paternoster lifts at Ullevål hospital (central block, sealed off), the old State Hospital building, the former Aftenposten building at Akersgata, Oslo Lysverker at Solli plass and a couple more.

Poland

- Katowice, the Silesian Parliament at Jagiellonska 25; 14 cabs, 7 floors; built by VEB Aufzugbau Leipzig

- Katowice, office building at Wita Stwosza 7; 12 cabs, 4 floors; built by Flohr (1951: Flohr-Otis, 1989: Otis)
- Wroc³aw, the head office of Bank Zachodni WBK at Rynek 9/11; 20 cabs, 10 floors; the paternoster is still in use, yet it is only available to the bank staff
- Gliwice, office building of "Bumar £abêdy" at Mechanikow 9; 14 cabs, 8 floors; build before 1945, only available to the company employees

Russia

- Building E of Moscow Power Engineering Institute, Moscow—non-working
- Ministry of Agriculture, Orlikov Pereulok, Moscow.

Slovakia

- Ministry of Finance, Štefanovièova street, Bratislava
- Ministry of Agriculture, Dobrovièova street, Bratislava
- Ministry of Transport, posts and telecommunications, Nám. slobody, Bratislava
- Ministry of Interior, Pribinova street, Bratislava
- Office building at Popradska @ Moskovska trieda, Košice
- Technical University of Košice
- Chirana Export-Import, Krajinska street, Piešany
- Slovakotex, Jilemnickeho street, Trenèín.

Removed and replaced in 2007 with a modern elevator:

- The Railways of the Slovak Republic HQ, Klemensova street, Bratislava.

Serbia

- One elevator still active, in HQ building of Serbian Railways.

Sri Lanka

- Head office, Ceylon Electricity Board, Colombo. Not open to the public.

Sweden

- Two elevators are still in active service at Norrland's University Hospital in Umeå.

- HSB head office, Kungsholmen, Stockholm. Not open to the public.

Switzerland

- Hôpitaux universitaires de Genève, hospital in Geneva (in use until 2009)
- Vaucher Sport, a sport shop in Bern

Ukraine

- Regional State Administration Building in Uzhhorod

United Kingdom

Some United Kingdom, multi-storey, university buildings were built in the early 1960s and 1970s with paternoster lifts: they included buildings at Aston University; Birmingham University's Gisbert Kapp building (the Department of Electrical and Electronic Engineering, completed in 1971), the Muirhead Tower, and the University Library); Birmingham City University's Baker Building; The Albert Sloman Library at the University of Essex; University of Leicester's Attenborough Building; Leeds University's Roger Stevens building, now closed, Salford University's tower block, now demolished; Sheffield University's Arts Tower, Imperial College's Chemistry Department (removed in the mid 1980s), De Montfort University's Fletcher Building (now replaced with high speed lifts) and James Went Building (now demolished), Oxford University's Biochemistry building and Thom Building (housing the Department of Engineering Science), and Newcastle University. Until the late 1980s, St. Thomas' Hospital, Westminster had a paternoster for staff use, whiles one administrative building at AEE Winfrith had one until the late 1990s.

- The Arts Tower at the University of Sheffield contains a 38-car paternoster. The building is a teaching block and not specifically open to the public, but the paternoster can be seen from the front door. It is the tallest in the UK. It is currently under renovation.
- Attenborough Tower at the University of Leicester.
- A seven floor Paternoster survives in *E block* at the Ericsson (formerly Marconi) site in Beeston, Nottinghamshire. Employees were banned from going

around the bottom or over the top following an incident a few years ago, when abuse caused by a group of visitors shaking the car had caused the car to get stuck at the bottom. The lift has been out of action since November 2007, and is unlikely to be put back into service.

- Rolls-Royce's seven storey tower block on Victory Road in Derby. The award-winning building housing this (designed by Rolls-Royce in-house architect Andrew Carr) has been demolished, and the paternoster scrapped.
- Staff in the main ward building of Northwick Park Hospital, Harrow, Middlesex, have access to a paternoster in the main ward block. This is regularly maintained and is frequently used by staff instead of the nearby conventional lifts due to its speed in transferring between adjacent floors.
- The Dental Hospital in Birmingham has one which used to be for staff use, until maintenance costs forced its closure in 2007.
- In Scotland, a working paternoster serves seven floors of the Pontecorvo Building (former Department of Genetics) at the University of Glasgow. The building is not open to the public. A paternoster was installed there on construction, in 1966–67 (by architects Basil Spence & Partners) because each floor has a small area and it was anticipated that staff and students would make many short journeys. This expectation has been fulfilled, and the paternoster is considered to have been a very valuable device. Occupants of the Pontecorvo Building are currently being relocated to allow its demolition.
- There is a paternoster at Technology House, the headquarters of Boxclever, in Bedford, which was switched off on February 11, 2008 for health and safety reasons
- There is a paternoster at Chadwick House, an office building at Birchwood Park near Warrington. Although covered over during re-refurbishments in 2005 due to maintenance costs, the paternoster is still operable if uncovered.

- There is a disused paternoster at Marks & Spencer in Liverpool. The lift was used until the late 1990s and was covered up due to health and safety concerns and rising maintenance costs. It is still fully in place behind access panels.
- There is a disused paternoster in Marks & Spencer Pantheon, London, which is covered up.
- There is a disused paternoster in the former Elliott Brothers research laboratories in Borehamwood, later renamed GEC, Marconi, and now the Elstree Business Centre. This paternoster was used in an episode of *The Unmutual Prisoner*, and taken out of service and covered up in 2001.

Hotel Energy Management

Hotel Energy Management is the practice of controlling procedures, operations and equipment that contribute to the energy use in a hotel operation. This can include electricity, gas, water or other natural resources. Because hotels can have complicated operations and extensive facilities they utilize many different types of energy resources. Hotel energy usages are tracked and classified by the U.S. Department of Energy and statistics are regularly published in the Energy Information Administration annual reports.

Modern practices to control energy usage includes contributions by the guests themselves which has been popularized by information cards requesting guests to save water by letting hotel housekeeping staff know if they would care to re-use towels and bed linens. Some celebrities endorse this practice and some for-profit companies such as Project Planet distribute or sell these kind of materials and or procedures to hotel operators. This reduces the amount of water and/or cleaning substances used by the hotel laundry department which also reduces the expense to the property owner or manager.

Recently consultants have developed entire organizations around advising hotels where they are operating inefficiently or using more energy than necessary. Some of them participate by providing the products to implement their advice for a share of the cost savings. These companies have proliferated over the previous years as public and business energy concerns grow and are known as ESCO's (Energy Saving COmpanies). Other practices include using infrared motion sensors and door contacts to control the heating and air conditioning systems (HVAC) when guests leave them on and leave the room or leave open balcony doors or windows. While energy saving practices are commonplace in Europe and Asia, American guests often do not understand these ideas or mistake the products to be cameras or an invasion of privacy. Because of this the use of these products are not widespread however they can be seen more and more.

Bibliography

Carl H. : *Internet Distribution of European Travel and Tourism Services*, Research Centre of Bornholm, Denmark, 1999.

Conlin, M. V. : *Proceedings of the Travel and Tourism Research Association twenty-second annual conference*, Hyatt Regency Hotel, Long Beach, California, 1991.

Conroy, B. : *Quality in Education and Training for Tourism*, London, Tourism Society, 1997.

Cukier, J. : *Tourism Employment in Bali: Trends and Implications*, London: Thompson, 1996.

David L: *International Tourism Policy, New York*, Van Nostrand and Reinhold, 1990.

Donald, M.: *Customer Service in the Hospitality and Tourism Industry*, Englewood Cliffs, Prentice Hall, 1994.

Douglas C: *Practical Tourism Forecasting*, Oxford, Butterworth Heinemann, 1996.

Eckel, Peter J.: *College & University Foodservice Management Standards*, Westport, AVI Pub. Company, 1985.

Fesenmaier D., Klein, S. : *Information & Communication Technologies in Tourism*, Springer-Verlag, Wien-New York, 2000.

Foster, Douglas: *Travel and Tourism Management*, London, Macmillan Educational, 1985.

Fowler, Peter: *Heritage and Tourism: In the Global Village*, London, Retailed, 1993.

Ghimire, Krishna: *The Native Tourist*: Mass Tourism within Developing Regions, London, Earthscan, 2001.

Harrison, Lyndon: *Tourism Means Jobs*, Chester, Lyndon Harrison, 1996.

Hoffman, Edward: *Project Management Success Stories: Lessons of Project Leaders*, New York, John Wiley & Son, 2000.

Holloway, J. C. : *Labour, Vocational Education and Training, in W. Pompl and P. Lavery,* Tourism in Europe - Structures and Developments, Oxford, CAB International, 1993.

Ireland, Lewis: *Quality Management for Projects and Programs,* Upper Darby, PMI, 1991.

Jakle, John: *Tourist, The: Travel in Twentieth Century North America,* University of North Nebraska, 1985.

Judi Radice: *Restaurant & Food Graphics,* Glen Cove, PBC International, 1994.

Judy A: *Tourism: Management of Facilities,* London, Pitman: M & E, 1993.

Karski, A: *Urban Tourism* - A Key to Urban Regeneration?, 1990.

Kotler, Philip: *Marketing for Hospitality and Tourism*: New Jersey, Prentice-Hall, 1998.

Larkham, P J: *Building a New Heritage*: *Tourism, Culture & Identity in the New Europe,* London, Routledge,1994.

Laws, Eric: *Tourist Destination Management: Issues, Analysis & Policies,* London, Routledge, 1995.

Lock, Dennis: *Project Management,* New York, Wiley, 1996.

Medlik, S: *Management of Tourism,* The, London, Heinemann, 1975.

Morrell, J. : *Employment in Tourism,* London: British Tourist Authority, 1985.

Nancy N.: *Choosing a Career in Hotels, Motels, and Resorts,* New York, Rosen Pub. Group, 1997.

Nightingale, M. : *Tourism Occupations, Career Profile and Knowledge,* Annals of Tourism Research, 1981.

Nijkamp, Peter: *Sustainable Tourism Development,* Aldershot, Avebury, 1995.

Index